Damion Luaiye Photography

About the Author

M. Chris Fabricant graduated with honors from the George Washington University Law School. After two years as a pro se law clerk in Manhattan's federal district court, he began his career as a criminal defense attorney.

BUSTED!

To Tonya
Ain't no companion like a blue-eyed girl

Contents

The Drug War Cheat Sheet

What Should I Do If

Disclaimer: This book is intended to amuse, inform, and outrage. It is no substitute for your own legal counsel (guidance in this matter can be found on page 262). Nor does this book condone drug use in *any* way. Drugs are illegal. They will get you busted. That's what we're talking about here.

Getting Wasted in the Drug War

A drug bust is one of life's defining moments. More expensive than your wedding. More painful than your divorce. More permanent than your tats, and harder to live down than a fat mullet and a piano tie. There's your mug shot floating around like a turd on the Internet as your first Google hit. Maybe there'll be a video of you on *Cops* shouting slurred obscenities and staggering through your DUI drills. And there will always be the haunting memories of your strip search and the cold sweat at the sight of latex gloves.

Don't believe that just because you don't get high and never DUI you won't get busted. The Drug War is all around you. Americans spend over *$65 billion* getting wasted on illegal drugs every year, *$75 billion* on booze, and *$3 billion* on good-time pills. Throw in another billion or so for some bongs and you have got yourself a party, my man. You could be at the wrong little get-wasted-together, in the wrong ride, in the wrong hood, living with the wrong roommate, or piss off the wrong cop, and find yourself peeing in a corner on Rikers Island for a long weekend before you've been charged with *anything*.

The good news is that you have wisely set yourself apart from the unsober masses by purchasing this book, putting a defense attorney in your corner to advise you before you throw (or go to) the "Hard-core House Party," before you "Pack for Your Drug Trip," before you "Hook a Brother Up," before you're nabbed in the "Dopemobile," before you take that "Drug Test?," and before you're "Face-to-Face with the Fuzz."

Expert counsel *before* you really need it.

Some of you, alas, will get nabbed anyway. During this dark period, *Busted!* will be your personal Jesus, shepherding you from the bust to the bang of the judge's gavel. From enduring your night(s) in jail to picking a drug-bust attorney to throwing yourself on the ground and groveling for mercy and/or fighting your bust like a stone-cold pro: Rush Limbaugh. A man whose pain and humiliation brought such joy to so many will serve as a guest guru, dropping the deep drug-bust knowledge of the rich and famous that any burnout can grasp between bong hits.

Sex and Drugs

The Busted! Philosophy

Sex and drugs have always gone hand in hand, and there have always been a lot of laws and (re)education aimed at getting the people to stop screwing willy-nilly and stop doing so many drugs. But, try and try, nothing seems to work. Everyone keeps fucking and everyone keeps doing dope.

Sex education has been forced to acknowledge this painfully obvious reality and has grudgingly turned the focus toward condoms. The time has come for drug-bust education, beginning with acknowledging the obvious: People are going to do drugs. Whatever the merits of the Drug War, there can be no debate about whether locking people up has been effective at quenching Americans' thirst for a good buzz. It hasn't. It never will. Mankind has been getting wasted since we crawled from the mud and realized that we are all in pain and going to die.

But *Busted!* isn't about the futility of the Drug War. It's about staying out of jail and out on bail. It's about the bare-knuckle reality of the criminal justice system fighting a dirty war. Like all dirty wars, anything goes. Perjury, racism, public humiliation, and medieval punishment are all fair game.

Knowledge is your only defense.

Sex education still begins with abstinence—no question, always the best way not to contract some gnarly disease. Similarly, in the Drug War, the best way not to get busted is not to possess drugs. So don't possess drugs. Drugs are bad. We all know that shit ain't broccoli. The difference, in my view, between marijuana and the host of other available inebriants is like the difference between casual sex with a condom and barebacking transvestites in truck stops. But that's your decision. A drug bust takes away all your decision-making authority, and wars are not about fighting fair. Bad things happen to people who get busted. Profoundly bad things. No matter what your dope of choice, the criminal justice system brings only pain and suffering. Consider the "Busted!" and "Now We Bring the Pain" chapters as warnings from God.

PART 1

HOW (NOT) TO POSSESS DRUGS

From Your Ass to Your Roommate's Stash

Everything You Need to Know About Drug and Drug-Paraphernalia Possession

There are almost as many ways to get nabbed for possession as there are drugs to possess, and all methods offer the same result in the same order: bust, strip search, jail, body-cavity search (*oh, yeah*), guilty plea, more jail, criminal record. Rinse. Repeat if necessary.

Drug-possession law ought to be simple enough: Have drugs, will get busted. And it's often that simple. But what if it's just some stems and seeds, or some flaky white stuff in a Baggie? What if some bastard sold you a bag of baby powder and called it cocaine?

What about that dope you stashed in your girl's panties? What if those are your panties? And who's on the hook for the fat lines on the drafting table at the "fashion show" that just got busted? How about the fatty in the ashtray of the Cooper-nowhere-to-hide-Mini that just got pulled over? Or the weed growing in your roommate's closet?

And how can you get busted on a paraphernalia charge when you bought that bong in a legit store and paid your damn sales tax? Maybe you just connected a friend to a source, or drove her to her dealer on your way to Sunday school. *What do you mean she OD'd? Manslaughter?! All I did was pass on a beeper number!* Maybe it's time you went to the emergency room yourself?

My God, the dope is everywhere. . . . I'm going to need a lawyer.

But Those Are Just Stems and Seeds, Man!

Drugs do not necessarily have to be of sufficient quantity or quality to get you high to get you busted for possession. Flakes of coke, *nine* pot seeds, a single crystal of meth, *baby* marijuana plants, bong *resin*, and needles with *traces* of smack have all been enough dope to make the bust stick, so long as the bustee was aware that it was dope. Awareness is usually inferred by where the drugs were found. It's assumed that you're aware of what you've got in your drawers.

A "very thin film of dust, comparable to one or two grains of salt": That, the take-no-shit jurists of the Texas Supreme Court decided, was a sufficient amount of coke to bust Dallas man Mark Scott for possession. Mr. Scott couldn't deny that he knew about that dust because the cops found it in a Baggie stuffed inside a larger Baggie, both of which were stuffed in his boxers. Since Mr. Scott could not offer an alternative explanation as to why he was keeping those Baggies there, the cocaine-possession charge stuck, and, since he had two priors, he got *thirty years* in prison for those salt grains.

As was the case with Mr. Scott, possession busts for not possessing drugs are most frequently visited upon those who are suspected of dealing and parolees caught with paraphernalia, or who flunk a drug test (see "Drug Test?" page 191); but such busts are also visited upon those caught eating the stash, or who successfully flushed the bulk of the dope down the drain enraging the police and making them determined to bring the pain, one way or another (see "Eating the Stash" page 87).

Some states require a "usable amount" of a narcotic, rather than a "detectable amount." In those states, an expert will testify that although she never does dope, has never done dope, and hates everyone that does dope, the dope that you had was sufficient to have had an "exciting effect" and was therefore "usable." The reality, though, is that any measurable amount is sufficient.

The lesson here is to lick your Baggies clean, throw them away, and break out the Dustbuster.

Fool's Dope

So you went down to Washington Square Park and scored yourself a dime bag of parsley from the droopy Jamaican cat. Nice. Perhaps you paid some jittery basehead a hundred bucks at the circuit party for a couple of aspirins with happy faces. Can you get busted for parsley possession? Of course! It's the Drug War! It's not supposed to be fair. In the drug-possession game, it's buyer beware. You may get fugazied, but the judge will not pity you. In most states, you will get busted for attempted possession. The dirty deed is done as soon as you pay for what you thought was dope.

A fool's dope bust will not usually befall you unless you score from a cop. (You can never trust those bastards.) If you're nabbed doing a big bong hit of tobacco that you thought was herb, for example, the chances are good you won't be prosecuted for giving yourself a migraine. But don't count on it. (See "Paraphernalia," page 41.)

Word to the Hustlers: Some states have *harsher* penalties for trying to rip someone off with bogus dope. This, as you may have guessed, is not an effort to clean up the dope-dealing business to ensure square dealing. The logic is that these guys are drug dealers *and* thieves.

Possessing the Good Shit

When is an eight ball not an eight ball? When you buy retail. Not when you get busted. Eight balls that are in reality two balls—mostly baking soda and enough speed to give you a headache—are still eight balls in the criminal justice system. You will be charged with possessing an eighth of an ounce of coke. In general, anything that you were planning to snort, smoke, suck, or jam in your vein counts toward the total weight of the drug.

But the Drug War can always get you coming and going. The lower down the food chain you are, the lower the quality of your dope should be. So if you have some very good shit, the uncut stuff your typical work-hard-play-hard Wall Street junkie doesn't come across, the DA will take that into account when he's deciding whether to charge you with simple possession (bad) or possession with intent to distribute (much worse). The difference is usually about five years. The better the dope, the more years. So if you like your shit good, you've been warned. (To avoid distribution charges, aside from simply buying down-market, see "If You're Keeping Dope Around . . . ," page 22.)

My Precious

Personal Dope Possession

Get busted with stems and seeds, or fool's dope, or the good shit, and the DA is going to have to prove that you had knowledge and control of the drugs. When you actually have the drugs in your hands, in your backpack, or in your drawers, this is of course very easy to prove. For this reason, most of this chapter is devoted to keeping you from being the one that's charged with possession at the party or out there on the Drug War highway to hell.

DOPE NOTE: *YOU'LL NOTICE THAT ALL ADVICE IN* BUSTED! *IS SOLELY AND PATHOLOGICALLY*

ABOUT WHAT IS BEST FOR YOU. AS YOUR IN-HOUSE COUNSEL I'LL SAY NOW THAT THERE IS NO ROOM FOR HEROES IN THE DRUG WAR (SEE "LIMBAUGH LESSON #6," PAGE 265). IN COURT, EVERYONE'S LOOKING OUT FOR NUMBER ONE.

But I Was Just Passing the Pipe, Officer!

One night in 1992, Wisconsin woman Denene McCuskey was passing the pipe around her car. A cop observed the warm glow, ran up to the car, grabbed the pipe, and busted her for possession, claiming that Denene had taken a hit. But the pipe was bone dry, Denene pointed out. So the DA took the pipe down to the lab and had it scraped for pot resin. When the lab techs found some, Denene was convicted and sentenced to a weekend in county jail and a $375 fine. (For what her *long* weekend was like, see "Jail/Holding Cell Hell," page 237.)

As Ms. McCuskey might tell you, even if you were just passing the pipe, didn't take a hit, didn't intend to take a hit, and never intended to take a hit, you *are* holding the pipe, and it looks mighty suspicious. And even if you're not actually caught pipe-handed, a determined DA will bust you on a stems-and-seeds charge for being in the vicinity of the pipe. Don't believe it? It happens. It happened to Leonard Hironaka.

Diddly Dope Ditty: Mr. Hironaka was sleeping in his van one morning at Dolphin Beach in Honolulu, Hawaii, during the summer of 2000. A cop came up to the passenger window and saw a glass pipe laying on the passenger seat. The cop woke Leonard up and busted him for possession. Leonard said that he had been camping with his brother and a friend, and that the pipe was theirs; he'd only smoked a *stinking little joint, man.* He explained that his prints were on the meth pipe because he tossed it on the front seat when he was packing up the campsite. The jury didn't buy it, and Leonard got *five years* for possessing the .044 grams of meth scraped out of the bowl. (*Yes, you'd need a magnifying glass to catch it, perhaps a microscope to be sure.*)

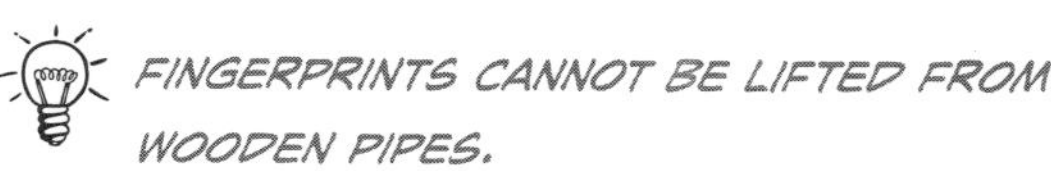

Yeah, but I Was Only Borrowing This Cocaine, Officer!

Like most defenses when you're caught red-handed, the momentary-innocent-possession defense is not very effective. And if you find your lawyer suggesting a just-borrowing-the-blow strategy like this you should seek new counsel pronto. Innocent, on-person possession of illegal drugs isn't going to fly unless you were on the way to the precinct to have it incinerated. Hard to prove. The law recognizes that most people don't abandon hard-earned drugs unless the cops are beating down the door, or when it's time for rehab (see "Limbaugh Lesson #4," page 259).

Found some meth in your ride after Junior borrowed it? Flush it immediately. Every second that passes with the dope on your watch makes your innocent-possession defense less and less likely to fly. It probably won't fly, though. Once you're caught holding the bag, you're in control of dem drugs. Your only hope is that you didn't know about the stash

Junior planted in your ride (see "This Isn't My Underwear!" below).

Come Mr. Tally Man, Tally Me Bananas . . . For those of you indulging in a variety of dope at once or over the course of a longish binge, keep in mind that each of your little buddies is its own separate crime. Say, for example, you're going to go get your freak on at your local underground. There in your junkie-on-the-go kit, you've got a stack of rollers for the beginning of the set, a fatty to smooth out the middle, and some Xanax for a soft landing. If you're in Texas, that's one year for the E, another six months for the spliff, and, unless you have a legal prescription for Zannies, another year for those babies. While this kind of time for this type of crime is not the norm, it's an effective threat to force you to plead guilty, and if you've got priors it's much more likely (see "Beg for Mercy, Punk," page 287).

This Isn't My Underwear! That's Not My Cocaine!

The Clueless Mule

Attempting to explain away drug possession by denying any knowledge of the drugs in your possession is a ballsy, usually doomed defense. But if you do get nabbed dope-handed, the more you can plausibly distance yourself from it, the better your chances. Maybe that junkie maid packed your bags. Or you're wearing your junkie roommate's clothes. Or you borrowed that junkie's car in which that junkie's drugs were very well hidden. Something like that. Desperate defendants call for desperate defense strategies, and the sun shines on every dog's ass once in a while; NBA Star Carmelo Anthony gave it shot last year.

That's My Houseboy's Dope! 'Melo got busted in October '04 at the Denver Airport with some bud in his backpack (see "Airport and Border Busts," page 167). But, as luck would have it, James Cunningham, who makes his living "catering" to NBA players, came forward and signed an affidavit claiming that he hid his dope in 'Melo's backpack without his knowledge. 'Melo's lawyer, Frank Moya, said that Cunningham stays in the Nuggets star's crib and arranges parties for him to make certain "all the right people" are there (and the dope presumably stays in his backpack). Moya conceded that "some people might be skeptical" about the houseboy's story, but . . . it worked! The DA dropped the charges and at press time was still deciding whether to charge the loyal houseboy with possession.

The true clueless mules are usually women set up by their boyfriends. (Snoop Dogg was accused of doing this to a concert promoter.) Men usually do this because there's no chivalry in the drug business, and because someone who doesn't know she's carrying isn't going to bust out in a mad sweat when she gets pulled over, or run screaming from the ticket counter when the agent asks her if she had any help packing her bags. Also, judges are more ready to believe a woman was unknowingly carrying for a man—sexism Drug War style, but you will not be complaining. The trouble with the "That's not my cocaine" defense, aside from the fact that no one really buys it, is that it will probably require the owner of the drugs to come down and take the weight for you—yes, the same hero who stashed his dope in your drawers.

Fleeing Dope Note: Any attempt to resist arrest or flee or act evasively in any manner will eliminate this defense. The thinking is, and it's hard to deny the logic, that if you didn't know about the dope in the trunk, you wouldn't have opted for the high-speed chase for your life when they tried to pull you over.

Finally, be aware that you can't willfully blind yourself to the dope. If you're offered \$10,000 to drive a rental car cross-country and leave it in the Hustler parking lot in West Hollywood no questions asked, you will get busted for possessing whatever was in the trunk, even if you never actually knew what was in there. And since no one gets a joint or two transported cross-county for ten G's, you will probably be carrying enough to be charged with distribution (see "Stepping Behind the Scale," page 19).

Whose Dope Is This in the Bushes?

Even if a cop hasn't actually witnessed you throw the dope away and refrains from using his "License to Lie" (page 273), you can still get busted in the great outdoors just being near dope if it appears that that's where you were keeping it or where you tried to ditch it. The judge is going to look at the circumstantial evidence when he's deciding whom to blame.

The Circumstantial Dope Ditty: One night on the banks of the Rio Grande in Texas, cops found Faustino Garza lying face-down in the dirt about fifty yards from the Mexican border. He had a pistol in one hand and half a pair of broken binoculars in the other. He also appeared to have been rolling in bud. He had dope in his hair, in his pockets, and under his armpits. About two hundred yards away from where Faustino had fallen lay eleven garbage bags stuffed full of weed. The cops suspected it was Faustino's. But Faustino said that he was as surprised as they were, and that he was just hanging around the Rio Grande to protect a buddy who'd gotten his ass kicked down there the night before. The judge didn't go for it.

Stepping Behind the Scale

Possession with Intent to Distribute

Like boxers finally carted out of the ring drooling on their nappies and slurring like winos, dealers usually retire the hard way: all the groupies gone and their defense attorney as their only friend, assuming they can keep the drug money coming. Sooner or later the dealers all need deeper legal advice and a lot more bread than the fourteen bucks that you plunked down for *Busted!* Breaking the First Commandment, "Thou Shall Not Deal" (page 327), changes everything.

That said, getting charged with distribution—stepping behind the scale, as the cocaine kids call dealing weight in the Bronx—is not as simple as not selling dope. Anytime you get nabbed possessing drugs, the cop who busted you is going to decide whether to charge you with possession for your "personal use," or with possession with intent to distribute; cops *always* err on the side of distribution because a felony bust looks a lot better on their résumés, and there are always court hearings for felony busts. Cops like going to these hearings because they're usually paid overtime for time spent on the witness stand (see "The Suppression Hearing," page 271).

The first thing the cop, and ultimately the DA, is going to consider is the amount of dope you were carrying. What's a "personal use" amount? The short answer is virtually any amount of drugs that you can convince a judge or jury that you were planning on smoking yourself or with select company. Reason, unfortunately, plays a role here. If you're apprehended with more dope than you and all your wasted friends could smoke in a lifetime, Johnnie Cochran reincarnated will have trouble making a convincing argument that you were planning on giving it a try all the same. As we have seen before, however, desperate defendants are always willing to give it shot. *What the hell?*

Devoted Dope Ditty: Fifteen deeply committed members of the Ethiopian Zion Coptic Church (*what, you never heard of them?*) were busted unloading about twenty tons of herb off the aptly named boat the *Jubilee* in the harbor off Stockton Springs, Maine. Since dope smoking is an integral part of their religion, the bustees gamely argued that they had acquired all that pot jointly for their own personal use in religious ceremonies. (See "Make It a Joint Venture," page 56.) But 2,600-plus pounds of weed—each devotee's share—is a lot for even the most deeply religious man to smoke on the long path to enlightenment (not to mention the challenge of keeping it fresh). So the sun did not shine on their asses that day; all were convicted of possession with intent to distribute.

But you don't need a thousand pounds of pot to get busted on distribution charges. It's all about the circumstantial evidence. Consider the scene at Catherine Berkland's crib when the cops dropped by: "Plastic bags lay all over the place on the floor of the bathroom; the toilet was still in the process of flushing; and there was a white powder in the sink and toilet bowl, later determined to be methamphetamine. There was a long trail of coin bags, used to package methamphetamine, leading from the place where [Catherine's roommate] had first been spotted into the bathroom. The officers found quantities of marijuana, psilocybin mushrooms, hashish oil, a trace of cocaine, methamphetamine, packaging materials, scales, $4,000 in cash, a scanner used for monitoring police radios, a set of brass knuckles, and a zip gun (a firearm not immediately recognizable as such) in the residence."

That was how Catherine's judge described it, anyway. (For more on the dope-flushing strategy she employed, see "The Race to the Toilet," page 113.) Catherine actually had very little drugs in the house—"quantities" and "traces" of drugs are criminal justice lingo for "none"—but once you throw in a set of brass knuckles, a zip gun, and a scanner, it's hard to argue that you were just going to party with some rambunctious girlfriends.

Catherine's and the Coptics' pain is retold herein to illustrate a couple of obvious distribution scenarios. You can and will get charged with distribution under far less blatant circumstances. The following tips are aimed at keeping you on the right side of the scale.

If You're Keeping Dope Around . . .
Since cops will always charge you with distribution if they can, and a distribution charge makes bail harder to get and will put more pressure on you to plead guilty (see "Defending Your Life," page 241), now is the time to take stock of your personal stash and think about the circumstantial evidence around your house. Any *one* of the following is probably not enough for a distribution rap, but start messing with combinations and . . .

1. Keep the Dope and Paraphernalia Together: Don't break your stash up into anything that could conceivably be viewed as packaging for sale. If you're a whole-pie kind of guy but your dealer sells it only by the slice, put it all together when you get home. Fifteen Baggies of weed looks a whole lot worse than one; and it will be difficult to offer up a plausible explanation for having so many, aside from dealing. Keep whatever device(s) you employ to do your dope with the dope, making it clear what your intent was.

2. No Bat Caves: Don't get too ambitious with your hiding places. Drugs for "personal use" are kept in wooden boxes on the shelf, in the freezer, under the mattress, in books, that kind of thing. Drugs for sale are kept under trapdoors in the floor, behind false walls, in hollowed-out televisions, that kind of thing. A determined cop will find the dope no matter where you keep it, so just keep it out of "plain view." (See "Hide That Shit," page 77.)

3. For the Drug *and* Gun Enthusiast: A weapon *anywhere* in the house will not only increase your sentence, but also be evidence that you were prepared to fight for your drugs. Rehab is in order if this is on your menu of reasonable options. Your average drug user is not prepared to kill for his stash, or bash you in the head with a set of brass knuckles for that matter. Drug dealers, however, have a higher stake in the merchandise, and they might just put a cap in ya ass.

4. Easy There, Moneybags: Wads of cash are always suspicious. A bunch of singles, and you're a low-level dealer. A stack of Franklins, and you're a player. Pay for a plane ticket in cash and you'll likely be searched (see "Airport and Border Busts," page 167). Walk around with a big wad or keep crazy dollars in the sock drawer and the dope is likely to be considered for sale no matter how little you actually have. (And it will likely be spent on some fancy new stun guns for the fuzz.)

5. Scales for the Bathroom, Baggies for Sandwiches: Only delis and drug dealers have digital scales. If you're not selling cold cuts out of your crib, don't keep a digital scale handy, and only stamp collectors have a legitimate use for those tiny plastic bags.

6. Consider Your Lifestyle: Fabulously wealthy? Trust fund got your back? Rejoice. You get to keep more drugs around for your personal use. Take Hall of Fame basketball player Robert "the Chief" Parish. A guy like the Chief is not likely to be dealing pot to supplement his paltry NBA income. So when he got busted with two Z's (about a bucket full) that he had sent to his house (see "Fed Ecstasy," page 118), the DA decided that the weed was for his personal use—he's seven feet tall, after all—and the Chief was fined $37. Nice.

7. Consider Your Past: If you're not playing in the NBA and you've been busted before, any one of the first five factors will likely lead to a distribution charge for much smaller amounts than the Chief's supply. (For all the bad news on your prior bust see "The Power of the Prior," page 31, and "Flying High Again," page 211.)

THE KIDDY CORNER

No one takes the whole DARE thing more seriously than the criminal justice system, so the Second Commandment (page 327) must be religiously observed if you like your freedom and have any regard for your karma. Like dealing, everything changes once the kids are involved. The Drug War will simply have no mercy on you. The sentences get longer, the Fourth Amendment (your right to be free of illegal searches and seizures) gets even flimsier, and you are less likely to get bail. Flip back to the "very thin film" Dope Ditty (page 8); the judge was careful to point out that Mr. Scott was busted as he was leaving a "teenage dance club." Nobody said it, but you can believe that the thirty years he got hooked up with had something to do with the clientele he was apparently servicing.

She Looked Eighteen to Me, Officer!

If you're a teen (or into teens), be aware that if you're caught supplying anyone underage with dope, be it for love, for friendship, or for show-and-tell, the DA will go crazy on you. In California, for example, possessing a fatty is punishable by a $100 fine. Passing that fatty to a minor is punishable by three to seven years in prison, even if she's seventeen and you're eighteen. And the first thing any smart little defendant who gets busted will do is turn you in. These statutes are the same as statutory-rape laws. It doesn't matter if the fourteen-year-old looked like Sandra Day O'Connor with a hangover and told you she was seventy-five, you are on the hook for furnishing a minor with illegal drugs. Period.

Don't even consider involving a minor in anything that could be construed as behind-the-scale work. In Colorado, for example, you can get up to life in jail for employing anyone under *twenty-five years old* in the drug trade, even if it's the family business.

Dad's Dope Ditty: Iowa man Charles Cartee was a pretty lenient dad. He let his boys bring their friends by the crib after school to smoke dope, drink beer, and huff petrol (*mmmmm*). But once in a while, the judge noted, "Cartee not only condoned the partying, he supplied the marijuana, joined in the smoking, and readily took money from the children in exchange for drugs." When school officials found out about the partying, that was about it for Cartee. He got busted for distributing dope to a minor, recruiting a minor in the drug trade (his son, since he brought his buddies over), promoting a gathering where drugs are used—see "The Hard-core House Party," page 34—and child endangerment. He got *thirty-seven years.*

Schoolhouse Rocks

Live in an urban area? Take a stroll around the hood to see how far you are from your local learning institution, or, put another way, how close you are to a mighty drug bust. Every state has "school-zone" statutes on the books to keep the kiddies away from drugs. (Not that they're working; it's easier for high school students to buy weed than smokes or booze, and most can score within a couple of hours.)

Effectiveness aside, school-zone statutes will drop you down a hole for dealing *or possessing* drugs near school grounds; anywhere from a thousand feet to a couple of miles away will do. In Alabama, for example, you get two to twenty years for selling coke, but no matter how much time you get, five years are *always* added for selling it within *three miles* of any school, or any school property, even if students never use it.

Nor does the school have to be a traditional institution for the extra pain: ITT Technical Institute counts, and virtually any other location where our nation's disaffected youth wile away their dull lives—video arcades, public pools, etc.—are usually thrown in. In most states it doesn't matter if the school was closed when the dirty deed went down, or whether you were even aware that there was a school anywhere nearby.

ZONKO

The Community Dope

Constructive Possession

Most people don't sit around doing lines or rolling on E by themselves. If you do, you can safely skip this section and perhaps consider a spot of counseling. The law recognizes that most people who party, party together, and it has come up with a typically simple solution: bust everyone. The cops aren't going to pull over a smoke-filled car with burning blunts in the ashtray and try to figure out whom they're going to bust. Nor will they burst into parties where the hookers are passing out cocaine and the guests are waving light sticks at each other and spend a lot of time sorting out suspects. The cops are going to bust 'em all and let the DA sort 'em out.

Whether it's in your own house, at a party, or in a car, your goal when caught hanging about Community Dope is not to be one of the bustees. Failing that, to be one of the little fish the DA throws out because you knew enough to put some distance between you and the drugs. All that it takes to get busted when there's dope on the premises is proof that you could have had some if you wanted some (known in the biz as exercising "dominion and control" over the drugs).

Dealers also frequently fall victim to this type of possession charge because they've usually been busted enough to learn to try to distance themselves from their dope (see "Limbaugh Lesson #3," page 258). Former dealer and current hip-hop superstar 50 Cent, for example, kept the merchandise in his girl's panties before he got busted in New York City. But since he had "dominion and control" over those panties, he was charged with dealing, even though he didn't actually have any crack on him. (*Busted!* readers will not profit from the kind of street cred 50 enjoys as the result of his bust.)

Busted for Your Roommate's Stash

Got a crack monkey living in the attic? Girlfriend a dope smoker? A dealer? People using your crib to get high? Maybe to stash their dope? Does your loft occasionally overflow with bimbos and cocaine? Are dope groupies spending a lot of nights passed out in puddles in your john? Trouble is brewing, my friend.

Living with a doper or a dealer, particularly a dealer, is always risky no matter who owns the drugs. If you happen to be screwing the doper (this assumes he or she isn't into pills) you must ask yourself these questions: Do I want this person to be the mother of my children? Is the sex really that good? Will it offset the pain and agony of a drug bust? If not, you should grab your toothbrush and hit the pavement. If so, then God bless, and good luck "Tipping the Scales of Bullshit." But see "Busted!" page 217 before you make up your mind.

Tipping the Scales of Bullshit . . .

This is important. This is your credibility. There will always come a moment in the Drug War when you'll be looking to tip the bullshit scales in your direction. And nowhere is this more important than when the DA's deciding whom to blame the drugs on. Righting the scales of bullshit will depend on the circumstantial evidence, which you have control over right now. Later is too late.

1. The Power of the Prior

Getting busted standing around the dope means that you will have to prove your innocence. Forget all that nonsense you've heard about the presumption of innocence. That's been tried, and that has failed miserably. Since your credibility has already taken a blow by getting busted with drugs in your house (or in your car), if you have an arrest record you can forget it. No judge or DA is going to buy whatever slop you throw in the trough if you've been down this road before. It may be that it was your roommate's (or child's or guest's), but it won't be the first time someone came into court and started pointing fingers. Skip ahead to "Beg for Mercy, Punk" (page 287).

2. The Dope Elephant in the Room

Special attention will be paid to where the drugs were discovered. Your roommate's dope should not be kept in an area that's accessible to everyone or where it would be hard to miss. So the fridge, the freezer, and the sin box on the bookshelf are all bad hiding places if everyone's not sharing the dope, because it will look like everyone was. And if your roommate is growing dope in the house or out back, you are on board all the way to the end of the line. (See "Growing the Felony Forest," page 45.)

But it's not just the drugs; it's everything drug-related as well. Every pipe, roach clip, puddle of bong water, Philly's Blunt, poster of Marley smoking a spliff, stanky ashtray, and copy of *Busted!*—that's right, *hide this book*—is added to the wrong side of the bullshit scale. On the other side of the scale sits your measly credibility. The more obvious it is that you are down with the drug scene, the harder it is to deny that you couldn't have had some of that dope if you wanted some.

NEVER SIGN FOR A ROOMMATE'S PACKAGE IF THERE IS THE SLIGHTEST POSSIBILITY THAT IT CONTAINS DRUGS. *(SEE "FED ECSTASY," PAGE 118.)*

3. This Land Is My Land, That Land Is Your Land

In order to prevent possession charges from being passed around like fatties, drugs and paraphernalia must be kept in the "exclusive space" of the person who owns the dope. Now is the time to designate each other's exclusive space. (Yes, it's silly, but it's the Drug War.) Essentially, this means that contraband remains in its owner's bedroom and no one ever goes in that room aside from the drug possessor, for any reason. No chance if you share bedrooms.

DOPE NOTE: MAINTAINING EXCLUSIVE POSSESSION OF YOUR BEDROOM IS THE ONLY WAY TO PREVENT YOUR ROOMMATES OR YOUR PARENTS FROM GIVING THE COPS CONSENT TO SEARCH YOUR ROOM OR YOUR COMPUTER (SEE "MY ROOMMATE DOESN'T HAVE ANYTHING TO HIDE," PAGE 114, AND "HELLO? WHERE ARE YOU TAKING MY COMPUTER?" PAGE 183).

4. Drug War Buddies

The court is going to look at how well you know the cat whom you're blaming the drugs on. This is where it helps not to be screwing, although sexism will sometimes work in a woman's favor. Assuming the man of the house is the chief junkie and his woman just nags him about it, judges are sometimes reluctant to blame the dope on the wife/girlfriend. Don't count on it though.

Just roommates? Does your roommate have a fat ride, a bitchin' stereo and HD flat screen? Is she on welfare? The judge is not going to buy that you didn't know she was supplementing her income and will assume you got your dope at a nice (free) discount.

5. Try Not to S . . . Sp . . . Spa . . . Spaz!

Breaking the Fifth Commandment, "Thou Shall Be Calm" (page 328), by running from the house, lying to the police, or other types of suspicious behavior when the cops come knocking will destroy any chance of tipping the scales.

The Hard-core House Party

While living amid the dope will not necessarily do you in if you can tip the Scales of Bullshit your way, host a party where drugs are among the substances of abuse and the shit starts to pile up. The Dope Elephant is passed out in a puddle on the living room floor, and the host(s) is/are always screwed if the party gets busted. At any party where drugs are being done more or less openly, everyone who lives there will be charged with possessing whatever was available. Your only hope lies in Part 2 (see "The Successful Drug War Party," page 130). Guests, however, still have a fighting chance (see "When the Party Gets Busted . . . ," page 37).

Hosting a party in the Drug War can get more painful than possession. You can get charged with distribution; if someone gets hurt you can expect to feel their pain; and if the party gets out of hand, you may be on the hook for "sponsoring or promoting" a gathering where "controlled substances are used unlawfully."

During the dawn of the dope (the sixties), many outraged city councils passed criminal statutes to prevent Woodstock-like debauchery from springing up in their backyards, attracting a bunch of wasted hippies to come roll in their mud. But these ancient laws are useful to bust the hippie's kids as well, both at large gatherings and to nail hosts of much more intimate gatherings.

Jeff Carter's Dope Ditty: Marshall County, Iowa's Jeff Carter decided to host a little get-wasted-together a couple of years ago. He rented a no-tell motel room and picked up a nice-sized ball of blow, and he and a couple of buddies proceeded to get whacked out. Other people rolled in and out, and of course the party was eventually busted. Because Mr. Carter had rented the hotel room, he was convicted not only of possession, but also of promoting an illegal party under a statute that was passed in 1970 after a bunch of hippies were spotted turning in circles and muttering, "It's the white rabbit, man," during the Wadena rock festival.

The Wadena-type laws have also been used to shut down raves and clubs where the patrons tend to consume nothing but water, yet still seem suspiciously happy (see "Evil Beats," page 134).

Nappy Time for the Kiddies

As we have seen in "The Kiddy Corner," dope is for grown-ups. Those of you who grew up in hippie households know that the kids are not naive; they stay up past their bedtimes, and when the dope gets passed around at parties they tend to have one of two reactions, depending on how effective the DARE program is at their school. Either they tell their teacher, who will tell the police, or they want a hit of that shit. Neither of these is a good option for the host (remember "Dad's Dope Ditty," page 26). So if you're over eighteen and you decide to roll the dice and host a hard-core house party, you should be carding guests like the most fascist club in your hometown. (You probably won't, but you've been warned, my friend.)

Someone at My Party Just Started Flopping Around and Foaming at the Mouth. Call 911? Go to the Emergency Room? Am I Going to Get Busted?

Yes. Yes. And yes again. If there are people at your party who can't handle their drugs it is not their fault. It's your fault. The law will lock you up long-term if someone gets hurt, and if someone clocks out, it's all over but the long, slow chase in the white Bronco. But you *must* bite the bullet and take him or her to the ER, not just for your karma, but because the DA will get nasty with you if you fail to call 911 or take your guest to the hospital.

If you had anything to do with supplying the dope—and even if it wasn't yours but you hosted the smoking/snorting/shooting—you are much more likely to end up with a distribution charge and, if things turn tragic, manslaughter. And rolling through the hospital's drive-through and pushing your fallen comrade out of the passenger door is not going to get the job done. You must go check him in and tell the doctor exactly what he's on and how much. Otherwise, time will be wasted diagnosing the symptoms, making death and hardcore criminal charges all the more likely (see "Distribution Resulting in Death," page 63). Time for a trip to the ER yourself? (See "I'm Really Not Enjoying My Buzz Anymore . . . ," page 65).

Busting the Party Guests

When the Bright Lights Shine, the Cockroaches Will Scatter

Scattering cockroaches are revolting and enraging. You want to smash those slimy bastards under your heel and grind them up in the garbage disposal. You might even want to see them suffer. To cops busting a party, scattering cockroaches are the guests running screaming through the house, jumping out the window, or flushing the stash. Cops will smash those roaches under the heels of their jackboots. Put another way, the roaches get charged with possession. Mere presence at a hard-core party is not usually enough for a possession charge to stick, unless you do something incriminating or piss off the police (they usually go hand in hand). Scattering-like behavior is both incriminating—people run because they have something to hide—and pisses off the police. Some additional tips on avoiding this grizzly fate:

When the Party Gets Busted . . .

1. Be Cooperative: Meekly leave the party and apologize for the inconvenience. Cops are not usually going to bust everyone, particularly if there's no hard stuff and no kids. If they bust you anyway, you've only been present at a Drug War party and you have a fighting chance of Tipping the Bullshit Scales, depending on how well you know the people and the size of the party. The more intimate the gathering and the more open the drug use, the harder it is not to have had the dreaded "dominion and control" over the drugs.

2. Leave the Dope Be: When the bright lights shine, it's too late to dump the stash. Your host is screwed. You can't help him. The fuzz is going to find the shit and they're taking scalps; whether it's yours or not depends on being *cool, brother.* Easy like Xanax and red wine. If you're so unfortunate as to be caught holding the bag, there's nothing to do but make things worse. (See "Ditching the Stash," page 84, for more on the variety of additional problems.)

3. **Prevent Consent:** Cops will sometimes order everyone at a party to empty their pockets. Do not empty your pockets just because the police say so. Often this is viewed as consenting to the search. While you should always be cooperative and leave the party without a lot of bitching, you have not given up your right to be free from an illegal search just because you happened to be at the party. (For more on dealing with suspicious cops and body searches see "Face-to-Face with the Fuzz," page 89.)

Driving the Dopemobile

Who Goes Down for a Joint in the Ashtray? What About the Trunk?

Like the host of the hard-core house party, the driver of the dopemobile has too much explaining to do; the car is thrown on the wrong side of the Bullshit Scales, making it very heavily weighted against you. Now you'll have to convince the judge that you were shocked and outraged when drugs were discovered in your car. Unless you're a chauffeur, as in Dogg's Ditty below, or the dope was in a passenger's luggage in the trunk, you have virtually no chance to avoid a possession bust, aside from a Hail Mary shot at a Fourth Amendment violation (see "Drug War Driving Lessons," page 141).

Snoop Dogg's Dope Ditty: Dogg's tour bus got pulled over for speeding a couple of years ago while he was on the appropriately named "Puff, Puff, Pass" tour. The cop said he could smell dope emanating from the bus as he approached, and a search revealed about two hundred grams of chronic in the cargo area. Since it was Dogg's tour bus, he was charged with constructive possession, not the driver.

Also similar to the house party situation, a scattering roach–like reaction to the bright light's shine—jamming down on the accelerator, slamming on the brakes, turning off the highway, ducking down in your seat, tossing shit out the window—will ensure that everyone is charged with possession. Just pull over and keep yourself together, man.

Once you've been pulled over, it is imperative that you tell no lies and that everyone on board agrees as to where the hell they were, what the hell they were doing there, and where the hell they were going. These are easy questions to answer unless you're transporting drugs from point A to point B or you're already really wasted. Lies and bizarre confusion about basic road trip agenda will be evidence that you had something to hide and therefore must have known about the drugs (see "Surviving the Traffic Stop: The Roadside Q & A," page 152).

The passengers will also be blamed for the drugs, particularly if the car smells like pot or there's any paraphernalia about. The more the dope and paraphernalia are spread around the car, between the cushions, in the glove compartment, etc., the more likely it is that there'll be plenty of possession charges for everyone. The more cleverly concealed the drugs, on the other hand, the more likely it will be that the driver will get busted for possession—probably with intent to distribute (in other words, "No Bat Caves," page 23)—because it will be obvious that *someone* knew about the drugs, but less obvious that everyone knew.

DOPE NOTE: *THE SUN MAY SHINE ON THE ASSES OF PASSENGERS ON SHORT TRIPS—NOT ONE OF THOSE GET HIGH, DRIVE CROSS-COUNTRY AND SEE AMERICA DEALS—WHERE THE DRIVER TAKES RESPONSIBILITY, AND A SMALL AMOUNT OF DRUGS IS DISCOVERED IN AN AREA AWAY FROM THE PASSENGERS' IMMEDIATE VICINITY, PARTICULARLY IF THE DOPE IS IN THE TRUNK AND NOTHING INCRIMINATING IS FOUND IN THE PASSENGERS' POSSESSION.*

PARAPHERNALIA

From Coke Cans to Crack Pipes

Paraphernalia law is similar to obscenity law. Just because you went down to the local smut shop, picked up *Jenna Takes Fifty Fists* and a new Anal Intruder, paid your sales tax, and took Jenna home for the evening doesn't make it all legal-like. If the fuzz stumbles upon your stash of unsettling porn or gnarly sex devices, you might be charged with possessing obscene material, particularly if you bought it in a porn palace like L.A. and got busted with it in a place like Dallas, where the authorities are not down with the backdoor, no matter what the Supreme Court says. (Texas had always banned butt-fucking for homosexuals, but the Supreme Court gave everyone the right to screw like they want to last year.)

The same is true with paraphernalia. Just because you walked into a head shop and picked up a new twelve-chambered Graffix bong, labeled "For tobacco use only," and paid your sales tax doesn't mean that you won't be charged with illegal possession of drug paraphernalia. Basically, the bong (or whatever) that you bought semilegally becomes illegal the first time you smoke out of it. After that, you'll never be able to get it clean enough (and you probably won't try) for it not to have some criminal residue. The resin will prove that the bong was used to do drugs, and that's all that's needed to bust you for possessing drug paraphernalia—a separate crime, punishable by jail time even if you're fresh out of dope.

What to Do with the Paraphernalia . . .
Paraphernalia can help you and it can hurt you. If you're fighting a possession-with-intent-to-distribute charge, you want paraphernalia around because it's an indication that your stash was for your personal use. But since paraphernalia is a separate crime, it can add time to your simple possession charge. Some tips:

On the Street: Keep your dope separate from your pipe (or whatever). Found together, it's an automatic paraphernalia charge on top of the possession charge. If you must carry paraphernalia, learn to roll a decent joint. People actually smoke tobacco out of rolling papers, and papers are sometimes excluded from paraphernalia statutes. It's also helpful to have some tobacco with you.

At Home: Keep the paraphernalia with the dope, making it obvious it's for personal use rather than for sale. Also note the tips in "If You're Keeping Dope Around" (page 22).

DOPE NOTE: *AS SEEN IN "BUT I WAS JUST PASSING THE PIPE, OFFICER" (PAGE 14), IN STATES WHERE A DETECTABLE AMOUNT OF A DRUG IS ENOUGH FOR A POSSESSION CHARGE, PARAPHERNALIA CHARGES ARE NOT AS COMMON, SINCE POSSESSING SOME STEMS AND SEEDS OR SCRAPING THE BOWL FOR RESIN WILL GET THE JOB DONE. (SEE "BUT THOSE ARE JUST STEMS AND SEEDS, MAN," PAGE 8.)*

Oh Yeah, Dude, That Would Make a Perfect Bong. Just Poke a Hole Right There, Put a Carb Right Here, and You're Golden.

Anything that can be used to do drugs, grow drugs, store drugs, weigh drugs, test drugs, or package drugs is illegal drug paraphernalia. Old-school favorites like carved apples, carefully mangled and poked Coke cans, toilet paper tubes, and gravity bongs (plastic bottles cut in half

Scales, balances, isomerization devices (fertilizer), testing equipment, diluents, adulterants, sifters, blenders, bowls, capsules, balloons, envelopes, syringes, pipes with screens, pipes without screens, metal pipes, wooden pipes, glass pipes, acrylic pipes, pipe screens, punctured metal bowls, water pipes, carburetion tubes, carburetion masks, roach clips, miniature cocaine spoons, vials, chamber pipes, carburetor pipes, electric pipes, air-driven pipes, chillums, bongs, ice pipes, or chillers.

—Just a few of the examples of paraphernalia included in Arizona's statute and immersed in water) turn everyday household items into crimes. In fact, the more MacGyver you get, the more likely it will be considered drug paraphernalia, because why the hell else would you carve a hole in mom's flower vase?

If there's no drug residue in whatever paraphernalia you were busted with and there were no drugs discovered during your arrest, the judge is going to look at the circumstances of your bust to decide whether or not to bring the pain. As usual, if you have any priors no one is going to buy that you like to smoke your tobacco in a one-hitter. If you have tracks on your arms, the syringes are always illegal. And if the police decide that's a crack pipe, not a pot pipe, paraphernalia charges are much more likely (see "Limbaugh Lesson #1," page 254).

Up in Smoke Ditty: "The illegal drug paraphernalia industry has invaded the homes of families across the country without their knowledge," fumed former attorney general John Ashcroft. In response to the covert bong invasions, Brother John took time out from hunting for terrorists to bust sixty-six-year-old Tommy Chong (of Cheech and Chong) for trafficking in drug paraphernalia through his company, Nice Dreams. More than a dozen DEA agents raided the Chong home before dawn, guns drawn, and took the famous old pothead away. Although his son was reportedly the brains behind the operation, Tommy eventually pled guilty and spent nine months in a federal pen for his wild crime spree.

GROWING THE FELONY FOREST

If weed is a gateway drug, hopelessly leading you down the dark alleys of smack shooting and crack smoking, then growing dope is a gateway bust, dragging you away in an orange prison jumper after a conviction for manufacturing and distributing drugs. And if you're growing dope on your property, the DA will take that shit, and your ride too (see "Gettin' Jacked by the Police," page 313).

But you just can't bring the good farmers of this country down. Pot is America's number one crash crop, raking in about $32 billion annually, more during droughts because the weed's kinder and more scarce. All this dope growing makes the feds very, very angry and frustrated. So when they find one of the felony farmers they treat them rough.

Growing Dope Ditty: R. P. Day sufficiently pissed off his wife one afternoon that she marched down to the precinct and told the cops he was an incorrigible dope smoker, growing his own supply. The cops came by for a look-see and found a few fatties, a couple of roaches, and a few plants. R.P. got *five years* of "imprisonment at *hard labor.*" The judge said that he "struggled" with having to drop the hammer, noting that "it was a small amount" of pot and "baby plants," or "whatever," but since it was the *minimum* sentence in Louisiana, that's what R.P. got, and he had to like it.

Flip back to "Busted for Your Roommate's Stash" (page 30). Growing dope is all in the family. A pot grow is hard to miss, so everyone's going down, probably on manufacturing and distribution charges, unless they turn your ass in like R.P.'s (presumably ex-) wife. Some states, including Washington, give rewards specifically for turning in pot growers. The pot tip programs are much more effective than those for your swinging Colombian cartel types because pot farmers tend to be fairly passive and no one's scared to dime them out. A priest in Ohio, for example, was turned in by an apparently repentant parishioner who used to share in the bounty of the harvest. *Now, who's going to hell?*

"You bet I did! And I enjoyed it!"

—NYC MAYOR MICHAEL BLOOMBERG ON WHETHER HE INHALED

Some more bad news. Dope growers need to hire some employees to make any significant bread. Once you start hiring people to help grow your dope, you enter the world of organized crime and the RICO Act (also known as the Racketeer Influenced and Corrupt Organizations Act). You will not like RICO. RICO will bash you good.

Plants also produce a hell of a lot of incriminating evidence and/or illegal drug paraphernalia. Miracle-Gro goes from Dr. Jekyll to Mr. Hydroponic; electric bills get out of hand and raise eyebrows; garbage, which can be searched willy-nilly, is stuffed with fertilizer, so better have a legit garden. Downwind neighbors better be down with the program because the smell can be mighty incriminating. (For more on the smell of dope as it relates to probable cause see "Oooh, That Smell," page 111.)

Lastly, growing dope or manufacturing chemical-based drugs has one additional drawback: there's no one to roll over on if you get busted. You are at the top of the distribution chain with no one else's scalp to offer up in lieu of your own. No bus jumping for you. ("Bus jumping" is what inmates call snitching; it refers to the Department of Corrections bus that takes a snitch from the joint to the stand to say whatever needs to be said to set him free.)

What's it all mean? Don't grow dope unless you aspire to the big time. It's a bad hobby. It's not "just a plant" to the authorities, particularly the feds. Your little herbs, even the babies who never had a chance, will not likely be considered for your "personal use," and in many states it just won't matter. It's a very stupid way to end up with a very long sentence.

Medical Marijuana

The New Civil War

Glaucoma, nausea, arthritis, symptoms of AIDS, and multiple sclerosis are a few of the medical conditions Americans smoke pot to help alleviate. A Harvard Medical School study found that 44 percent of oncologists had proposed marijuana use to their patients. Two congressionally funded, and circularly filed, studies have concluded that marijuana is an effective treatment for pain and the nausea associated with chemotherapy. Voters in California (twice), Alaska, Arizona (twice), Colorado, Maine, Montana, Nevada, Oregon, and Washington have given a 👍 to medical marijuana. Hawaii's state legislature passed a medical marijuana law in 1999. And some states, Maryland most recently, allow a "medical necessity" defense if you've been nabbed with pot and you have a doctor's recommendation.

But the feds do not want you smoking pot after your chemotherapy any more than they want you smoking it after the Dead show. So prescription, schurscription, they'll throw your sick ass in jail for smoking your medicine. This is because in 2001 the Supreme Court decided that since Congress decided that there is no valid medical purpose for pot, states are not free to legalize it for medical purposes. In other words, individual states can pass all the laws they want; pot is still illegal under federal law no matter why you smoke it.

Free Dope Ditty: In 1976 the federal government started supplying thirty-four people with marijuana for various ailments under an experimental drug program. This program somehow survived both Reagan administrations, but Papa Bush put a stop to that nonsense. However, seven of the original thirty-four are still alive and they still receive three hundred prerolled fatties in the mailbox every month.

The DEA also raided pot clubs that were distributing marijuana to people with doctor's recommendations in Santa Cruz, California, and fired other high-profile warning shots. But their efforts resulted in a lot of bad publicity and it's not practical to bust everyone who has continued smoking medical pot. So the Bush administration went after the doctors, threatening to revoke their licenses for "recommending" marijuana. Doctors argued that it was a violation of their free speech rights to prevent them from expressing their professional opinion to their patients. So far, most courts have agreed with the doctors, and the Supreme Court isn't touching this mess with a ten-foot bong.

Dope Ditty: Former *High Times* columnist "Ask Ed" Rosenthal was busted by the DEA in Oakland, California, for growing pot plants under the city's medical marijuana law. Rosenthal had been deputized by the city to grow the dope, but federal prosecutors got the judge to exclude any mention of this juicy tidbit during the trial. Not surprisingly, he was convicted. After the trial, the jury issued a statement regretting its decision and expressing outrage over not hearing evidence as to why Rosenthal was growing the pot. (The feds made it sound like he was a kingpin.)

If you have a medical condition for which a doctor will recommend marijuana in a state with a medical marijuana law, by all means get yourself a recommendation. The trouble is that acquiring the pot is almost always illegal. This is why Oakland deputized Ask Ed. But pot clubs are starting to spring up again in California. At press time, the Supreme Court was deciding whether the feds had the authority to bust people for possessing medical pot in states with a medical marijuana law. The smart money is on the feds, but no matter which way the Court goes, the chances of getting busted for possession by a DEA agent are relatively small. *But you are risking arrest.*

Hookin' a Brother Up

From Buying for the Bachelor Party to Recommending a Dealer

Aiding and Abetting Dope Possession

You probably know someone who could get you some weed, maybe a couple of rollers for New Year's or a little blow for the bachelor party. Maybe you're that guy. Maybe you're the guy who knows that guy. What we have here is a middle-class drug-distribution ring, and all the guys who know the guys can go to jail on distribution charges and/or conspiracy charges.

There are no buddy exceptions in drug-distribution law. No distinctions are made for friends scoring dope for friends out of the goodness of their hearts, or so everyone can party together. Nor are there exceptions for friends hooking friends up with a source. And once you put yourself into the drug stream everything that happens downstream is on you. The menu choices range from simple possession all the way to manslaughter if someone downstream gets hurt. The sentences range from a couple of days in the joint to life.

Dude, Why Don't You Go Score Some Dope for Us?

Raymond Washington of Virginia was the designated scorer for his party and lived to regret it. Silly Raymond believed that if he was just scoring some dope for his friends, he would not be convicted on distribution charges. Here he is at trial, withering under cross-examination by a federal prosecutor:

> ***Q.*** *This amount that you were caught with, the 12.1 grams [of blow], had you bought that for someone else?*
>
> **A.** I bought it for all of us.
>
> ***Q.*** *All of us. And you were going to give it to some of them; is that correct, the other people?*
>
> **A.** We were going to get high with it.
>
> ***Q.*** *You all were going to get high, so you were going to give it to them, you were going to distribute it to them. You physically gave the drugs to somebody else?*
>
> **A.** I weren't [sic] physically giving it to them. We just wanted, you know, to sit around and get high.
>
> ***Q.*** *Were they your drugs or somebody else's?*

A. Yes, they were mine, because I purchased them.

Q. *You intended to share them with somebody else?*

A. Right.

Q. *Now, sir, on this particular day you were planning to take those drugs and share them with your friends, is that a fair statement?*

A. Yes, sir.

Following Raymond's pitiful performance on cross-examination, during which he also admitted that he was going to get some free blow for scoring for the party, he got set up with seventeen years' imprisonment for distribution, including some extra pain because he had a gun and a prior bust.

Let's all keep Raymond's sorry dope ditty in mind as we consider hookin' a brother up.

> ***DOPE NOTE:*** *BEFORE WE GET ANY DEEPER IN SHIT, AS HAS BEEN SAID BEFORE HERE, THE SAFEST WAY NOT TO GET BUSTED IS NOT TO INVOLVE YOURSELF IN ANY TRANSACTION, PARTICULARLY FOR ANYONE BUT YOURSELF. BUT WE KNOW PEOPLE ARE GOING TO GET HIGH, PROBABLY WITH EACH OTHER, AND SOMEBODY'S GOING TO HAVE TO GET THE DOPE. THIS WOULD BE A VERY SHORT BOOK IF EVERYONE FOLLOWED THE BEST DRUG WAR ADVICE AVAILABLE. (DON'T DO DRUGS. DRUGS ARE BAD.) LIKE ALL THINGS*

DRUG WAR-RELATED, THE HARDER THE DRUG IS AND THE MORE OF IT, THE MORE LIKELY YOU ARE TO GET FLUSHED DOWN THE CRIMINAL JUSTICE SYSTEM.

The Designated Scorer . . .
If you're the man who knows The Man, the following is for you:

1. Make It a Joint Venture: By setting forth and foraging for drugs alone you become a middleman. Middlemen always get squeezed. Even if it's just to share with your people, making the buy alone adds a link in the distribution chain. You are now a deliverer of dope, rather than a plain old doper. If you're buying drugs for yourself and someone you love, go forth and gather together; join in what courts sometimes call a "joint venture" (ha-ha), which means that everyone is on the hook for possession no matter who's actually carrying the shit, but it's *less likely*—nobody's making any promises here—that you will be charged with distributing the drug to each other because you all made the buy together. (None of this makes sense of course; it's just the way that it is.)

2. Share the Weight: If your venture has landed more than the misdemeanor weight of your drug of choice (see "The Dope Law Index," page 331), you should divide it up and go your separate ways. Felonies are not to be trifled with. Don't be a hero and take the weight, and if you have any Drug War heroes with you, by all means allow them to carry that shit.

3. No Free Grass: Everyone who's doing the dope must contribute the same amount of money. No free rides, and no third parties can use the drugs that you all scored together; that's just more distribution, defeating the whole purpose of this bizarre exercise in Drug War resistance.

4. Observe the Ninth Commandment—*Know Thy Friends; Mistrust Thy Enemies* (page 329): Perhaps here is a good place to state the obvious. Should you decide to roll the dice and involve yourself in anyone else's efforts aimed at getting high, be very sure you know whom you're dealing with in an intimate, preferably carnal, way.

WORD TO THE HUSTLERS: *TAKING SOME POOR SCHMUCK'S MONEY AND PROMISING TO SCORE FOR HIM WILL NOT RESULT IN DEALING CHARGES IF YOU DON'T PRODUCE AT LEAST SOME BOGUS DOPE. IT'S THEFT BY DECEPTION AND BAD FOR YOUR KARMA, BUT IT'S NOT A DRUG CRIME.*

Dude, Give Me a Lift to My Dealer's Crib

Not doing the dope yourself? That's good, but even the most minimal participation in a transaction can lead to a drug bust. Think of scoring dope as a bank robbery. If you know that your buddy is going to hold up a bank and you drop him off, even if it was just on your way to work, you will be charged with conspiracy. The same is true with taking someone to the scene of a dope deal. You may not know the dealer, you may not care if your buddy scores, but if you know the deal is going down you can get busted for aiding and abetting possession. Bring the dealer to a customer and you can get busted for aiding and abetting distribution. Bring two dealers together and you have broken the First Commandment (page 327).

I Know, Let's Have a Dope Deal at Your House!

Hosting the transaction brings the pile of shit you've been trying not to step in right onto the living room floor. It's not automatic that you will be charged with any offense for hosting, but it's a very bad idea; your in-house counsel strongly urges you to check yourself. A down roommate is one thing, but in the Drug War only your attorney has to be on your side. If you own your house, hosting a dope deal or allowing your roommate to deal out of the house increases the likelihood that the Attorney General is going to own it after you get busted (see "Gettin' Jacked by the Police," page 313), and if you live in public housing hosting a deal—or even partying in the parking lot—will leave you homeless (see "Poor in the Drug War," page 316).

Your specific actions during the transaction will determine what type of crime and time you will be facing. But running from the house and calling the police is the only sure 👍 you'll get from your local magistrate at the bail hearing. Failing that, do not observe the transaction, and do not handle the money or the drugs, particularly if you'd like to practice law one day.

Dubious Dope Ditty: *"I was not involved in the transaction, but since I was in the house at the time, I was later taken into custody."* That's what "VMF" told the Florida bar when it discovered that he had an arrest record that he neglected to highlight in his bar application, which he thought had magically disappeared, since the bust had been "expunged." It seems that Mr. F's college girlfriend had arranged a dope deal in his house with an undercover cop. They both got busted on distribution charges, which Mr. F pled down to possession. Mr. F admitted to the bar that he had passed the pipe that night and, ah . . . oh, yeah . . . that he had brought some "foil packages" up from the basement for his girlfriend, but he had no idea those packages were bricks of hash and he never saw any money exchanging hands. Apparently a skilled advocate, Mr. F sold his story to the bar and they let him in with only a stern talking-to, although one of the judges wanted to have him disbarred.

As even Mr. F would probably concede, it was fairly stupid of him to host this transaction, but he was apparently not the ringleader and he was smart enough not to handle any of the money, which likely saved his ass, allowing him to plead down to possession and get a shot at expunging his record. But, as was the case with Mr. F, an expunged record does not necessarily make it go away (see "You Want to Pretend This Never Happened?!" page 323).

Say, Friend, Can You Recommend a Reliable Drug Dealer?

Recommending a dealer is a far safer alternative than going out and buying drugs for someone or affirmatively participating in bringing the criminals together, but aiding and abetting distribution of drugs, which is the fine line you walk when recommending a dealer, is a much more serious charge than aiding and abetting simple drug possession, assuming no one gets hurt.

Simply sending someone down to Venice Beach because he'll probably be able to score some schwag is not going to get you busted. Taking it to the next level by passing on a name, or a number, or a specific address, increases the chances, but it's relatively rare and you're not likely to get busted unless it's a cop you happen to be directing, usually at a club or a rave. (See "Evil Beats," page 134).

Should you go beyond merely passing on a name, your criminal liability depends on the role you played in bringing the two together. The judge is going to be looking at whether you had a profit motive when you made your recommendation. It begins with your instructions to the man in need.

Bring Four Fiddies and Tell 'Em the Dope Daddy Sent Ya for a Square Deal

This sounds bad. This line will be highlighted in the indictment filed against you. Directing someone to the dealer and instructing him on how to complete the transaction brings you much closer to stepping in shit. These are known as "delivery offenses"—generally not as harsh as a sales offense, but still bad news and worse than simple possession. The more detailed your instructions are, the more likely it will be inferred that you wanted that deal to go down because you were taking it further than simply passing on a name or a number.

DOPE NOTE: *DON'T LET A NICKNAME LIKE "DOPE DADDY" STICK. IT WILL BE USED AGAINST YOU. I'VE HEARD A NYC DA GET AWAY*

WITH CALLING A DEFENDANT BY HIS UNFORTUNATE NICKNAME "BLOODY BAD ASS" THROUGHOUT HIS MURDER TRIAL. THE JURY DELIBERATED FOR ABOUT FIFTEEN SECONDS.

I'm Telling You, Man, My Kid's Got the Chronic

A sales pitch like this? This sounds bad. It too will be highlighted by the DA throughout your trial as evidence that you had a stake in the transaction. Salespeople, or the people aiding the salespeople, tout their merchandise. You should have no interest in whether the dealer you're sending your boy to has nice stuff or is a solid guy. And say your dealer hooks you up with a free bag for each new customer you recommend—that also looks bad. Free drugs are a profit motive. Ask Raymond Washington of Virginia (page 54).

Bad Dope?! Why, I Oughta . . .

Recommending a dealer also means never having to say you're sorry. Salespeople say they're sorry. If your needy friend gets screwed, that is entirely her problem. Do not try to make things right or talk to the dealer. The more interest you show in a smooth transaction, the more likely you are to get busted for a sales offense. If your friend had other options, she wouldn't be asking. You merely know someone who might be able to hook her up. Preferably much less, but definitely no more.

The Death and Dismemberment Section

As noted at the beginning of *Busted!*, drugs ain't broccoli; sometimes people get hurt. When people OD, the drugs themselves are not blamed. Everyone left standing is blamed. The following is a heads-up on the criminal justice risks associated with bad trips.

Distribution Resulting in Death

When Irma Perez, a fourteen-year-old San Mateo, California, girl, died last year at a slumber party after she and two of her fellow eighth-graders took some bad E, the two girls who failed to tell an adult until early the next morning were arrested and charged in connection with her death. They were busted because they were doing the dope with her and rather than calling 911, the girls called their dealer, who told them Irma was having a "bad trip" and that she'd sleep it off. The investigation into Irma's death went right up the ladder, resulting in the bust of the seventeen-year-old who actually gave the drugs to the girls (and the "bad trip" advice). Lastly, eighteen-year-old Anthony Rivera—he got his name in the paper since he was eighteen—was charged with manslaughter, as the original source of the E. Rivera ultimately pled guilty and got five years on lesser charges. (Funny how they don't do that to gun sellers when kids accidentally blow each other's brains out.)

As with the tragedy in San Mateo, when bad things happen to people who do drugs, particularly children, bad things happen to everyone even remotely associated with the incident, be it procuring the drugs, or doing the drugs with the victim, or failing to take the victim to the ER. The designated scorer and the host of the party (the other eighth-graders in Irma's case) are always in charge of everyone's safety. Go off and score dope for someone you love and she OD's, the feds will charge you with distribution resulting in death, and you will be facing a life sentence.

Hey, Babe, Mind Shooting Me Up? I'm a Little Too Wasted to Poke Straight.

One need not actually have bought the drugs or had anything to do with the transaction to get hit with a manslaughter charge. Since no one has ever OD'd on pot, providing bong load lessons or holding a roach to someone's mouth is not going to lead to much more than aiding and abetting possession charges. But helping someone load up a fateful bowl of crack or shoot some smack is another matter. When people start getting into the hard stuff, they sometimes get a little sloppy, and the last one standing goes to jail.

Belushi's Deadly Dope Ditty: In the early eighties the late, great John Belushi was on an epic four-day jag with former Rolling Stones groupie and drug dealer Catherine Smith in West Hollywood's Chateau Marmont Hotel. After a night of shooting speedballs—a heroin and coke cocktail invented by our American GI's while stationed in Korea in the fifties—and doing lines with Robert De Niro and Robin Williams, Belushi had Smith shoot him up one last time, and on March 5, 1982, in bungalow 3, Belushi OD'd. Smith fled to Canada, but she was extradited and ultimately convicted of unintentional manslaughter and served three years. (Smith was charged with essentially the same crime that Jayson Williams, former New Jersey Net, managed to get a mistrial on after he blew away his limo driver with a shotgun he was playing with while he was wasted. But a mistrial, as Erik and Lyle Menendez would tell you, is not an acquittal, and Williams is being retried.)

I'm Really Not Enjoying My Buzz Anymore. In Fact, I'd Like to Come Down Right Now. If I Pop By the Emergency Room Can I Get Busted for Being Loaded Out of My Mind on Some Silly Drug?

Sometimes after a long, hard night of partying you don't wind up in jail or dead; you wind up in the emergency room. Or you sit naked in the dark, in the bathtub, ceiling tiles dripping down the walls, eyebrows shaved off, slowly losing more and more of your mind. Suddenly you're staring into the deep abyss of your subconscious, wondering if you'll ever know reality again, worried that you have expanded your mind a bit too far this time and it might not snap back the way that you'd like. There's a little speck of sober person floating through your mind, fretting about your safety, begging you to come home, nagging at you for a trip to the ER, but he's also in touch with the grim reality that dope is illegal. You could get busted.

Hmmmm . . . Death? . . . Bust? Bust . . . Death? Maybe I'll just lie back down in the bath here a little longer. I'm sure the ceiling isn't really doing that. My eyebrows will grow back.

Go to the emergency room. Tell them exactly what you had and how much, essential information for treatment; and if you don't tell them, tests will be done for everything imaginable, delaying treatment and sending a "You're insuring a junkie" message to your insurance company. A bill for testing you for anything you possibly could have inflicted upon yourself will make it obvious that you checked in after an outrageous, wandering-the-desert-type bender.

Generally, you will not get busted for possession when you check yourself into the ER to right the ship. Should you survive, you will get a lot of very stern tsk-tsks and your parents will be notified if you're at an age when that still matters, but you probably won't end up in jail, and you might just survive. It is very unusual to bust someone just because there is evidence that he did dope, and statements that you make in the course of seeking medical treatment usually cannot be used against you.

DOPE NOTE: IF YOU WERE WASTED AND KILLED SOMEONE, SAY IN AN AUTO ACCIDENT, THE MEDICAL RECORDS ARE MORE LIKELY TO BE USED AGAINST YOU, AS MANY STATES HAVE EXCEPTIONS FOR SERIOUS CRIMES AND THE POLICE WILL HAVE A GOOD REASON TO SEIZE THE RECORDS.

The ER does present some potholes, though. Pregnant women who haven't been able to put down the pipe can be turned in to the police and tried for child abuse if a blood test gives them away. (They can't be set up specifically to look for drugs to bust them, though.) And you should think about limiting what you say to what is necessary for your treatment, assuming you have some capacity for reason. That was the lesson Michael Harrison learned when he went to the ER in Sherburne County, Minnesota, in November 2002, complaining that the fumes from his meth lab had burned his face, and scorched out his nose hairs. The doctors fixed Michael up and then called the cops. When his buddies came to pick him up, they too got busted, and their lab (gasp) was discovered in a subsequent search of their house.

PART 2

SEARCH AND SEIZURE

On the Street, in the House, at the Party, in the Dorm, on the Road, at the Airport, in the Mail, Online, and on Your Hard Drive (Drunk Driving and Drug Testing Too)

The Incredible Shrinking Fourth Amendment

What should be clear from Part 1 is that if the police find you holding the bag at a hardcore house party or helming the dopemobile, you are in a Drug War battle. The only thing standing between you and a drug bust is the Fourth Amendment.

That should be of small comfort.

The trouble with the Fourth Amendment is that only people with something to hide, civil libertarians, and those on the darker side of white truly appreciate their right to be free of illegal searches and seizures. These people don't win many elections in this country, so the Fourth Amendment has been quietly eroding under your feet for the last thirty years. Now you can be tracked online, subjected to random drug tests, and arrested, jailed, and strip-searched for failing to wear your seat belt. And after September 11, all bets are off.

What you have going for you is this: there are many, many more citizens on drugs than there are cops to bust them. If you believe what the government tells you, Americans spent nearly $50 billion more on drugs last year than they spent trying to stop you from doing them. It's a war of attrition. The vast army of recreational drug users against the vast resources of the government. They are NATO, young and powerful. You are China, old and overwhelming.

As an individual, you're an Iraqi cop.

To avoid getting busted, you must not make yourself a target. *Say, by writing a book?* Consider mild-mannered Alabama housewife Loretta Nall, who wrote a letter to her local rag last year calling for an end to "cannabis prohibition." *Think she smokes pot?* The cops did. They included a clip from her letter to the editor in the application for a search warrant, and a week later the Tallapoosa County Narcotics Task Force raided her home, busting her for about a joint's worth of dope. She was convicted after a fifteen-month legal battle and now serves as the president of the U.S. Marijuana Party—no doubt destined to be a major player in Alabama politics.

While Mrs. Nall's bust was of the mess-with-the-bull, get-the-horns variety, seven hundred thousand people are busted every year on drug possession charges, and most of them didn't make themselves a target by publishing or otherwise getting political about their dope. Most of them stumbled into a bust by distinguishing themselves from the masses through a variety of risky, just-begging-for-it behavior, attracting the attention of the police, panicking when confronted by a suspicious cop, and pissing away the few rights they have remaining in a warm puddle of defeat.

You will not be among these lambs led to slaughter. You will understand our fragile friend the Fourth Amendment because the police know this stuff better than your average law professor, and they can usually count on your ignorance to bust you.

> **DOPE NOTE:** THIS CHAPTER DELIVERS THE FOURTH AMENDMENT AS THE SUPREME COURT SAYS IT IS AT PRESS TIME—BUT IT GETS WORSE EVERY TIME JUSTICE REHNQUIST, SCALIA, OR THOMAS PUTS PEN TO PAPER. YOUR STATE MAY (PROBABLY NOT) PROVIDE MORE PROTECTION THAN THE MINIMUM THE CONSTITUTION REQUIRES. IF SO, REJOICE. IF NOT, I'M SORRY. I LIVE HERE TOO.

Pissing Away Your Fourth Amendment Rights

Three Deadly Sins

Your Fourth Amendment rights are among the easiest of your rights to waive, and most of the time you won't even notice. The following Three Deadly Sins are the most common traps people fall into, giving up the game before it really begins. Commit any of these sins in the vicinity of a cop and skip ahead to "Busted!"

1. Petty Crime Leads to Big Time

Those who indulge in pharmaceutical diversion tend to commit a lot of minor crimes while they're staggering though life. They loiter, they litter, they piss in alleys, and they get inebriated in public. These people have no Fourth Amendment rights. In most states, the police can arrest and *jail* anyone they witness commit *any* crime, no matter how minor. Since the police can always search you and all your belongings if you're arrested, *never* commit *any* crime in front of a cop if you're carrying.

Nobody outside of New York knew who Rudy Giuliani was until he started busting people getting wasted in public, turnstile jumpers, and various other recreational scofflaws, and discovering that a lot of these people were jumping turnstiles because they were late for their drug deals. The crime rate went down, Giuliani was hailed as a mad crime-busting genius, and a cottage industry sprang up for NYPD brass to come to your town and bust all your low-level scumbags. Cities across the country now bust people for minor, "quality of life" crimes. So be warned, "zero tolerance" means what it sounds like. Fastidiously avoiding committing little crimes—sidewalk spitting, for example—should not be mocked as the paranoid delusions of a dope fiend; they *are* out to get you.

Act Normal, Dude, It's a Cop

Public intoxication is noted separately here because it's one of the more common petty crimes that can begin a slide down the black hole of the criminal justice system. Arrests for public intoxication and for pissing on buildings say one thing to the judge and anyone else reading your arrest record on the Internet: This dirt bag has a drug/alcohol problem. Whether that's true or not is between you and your conscience, but nothing like having a red flag tattooed on your forehead. If you must be inebriated in public, do not carry dope, because you can always be searched, and note the grooming tips in "Preparing for Battle . . . ," page 82).

2. Just Say No! (to the Search)

Cops are scary. Big guns. Clubs. Mace. Handcuffs. Jackboots. Mad Max rides. Usually some backup and always the ripe smell of authority. A cop tells you to turn out your pockets or open the door, and you won't feel like you have a choice and you will consent to the search. Perhaps you'll believe that by giving the cop permission to search he will assume that you have nothing to hide. Don't believe it. The police are already suspicious. They are never asking for consent to see how you'll react; they're asking so they can search you without worrying about whether they technically have the right to or not.

Sometimes, though, a determined cop will get old-school to get "consent."

Consensual Dope Ditty: On the morning of February 21, 1992, Mark Howe answered his front door and found himself face-to-face with three Nevada cops, informing him that they had "received complaints" that he had a quarter pound of bud in the crib. When Howe wouldn't let them in, Officer Mercado suddenly smelled burning marijuana: "We have probable cause to come into this house right now with the smell," Mercado announced (wrongly). "Let me tell you something else: Number one, if you want to cooperate, it makes it lots easier. (Not for Howe.) One way or another, we're going to search your house." (You can believe that.) Howe was not sure what to say, particularly because the cops were already inside his house, so he "consented" to the search. Once inside, Mercado "examined" Howe's mouth, and when he noticed some "green leafy matter" in his teeth, he took Howe to the hospital and gave him a choice: either provide a urine sample, or "accepted medical techniques" would be employed to get one. Concerned, Howe inquired as to the available "techniques." Mercado told him that a catheter would be stuck up his penis to "extract the urine sample" if he didn't pee in a cup. After duly considering his options, Howe "consented" once again. The trial judge gave a 👍 to Mercado's powers of persuasion. Four years later, though, the Nevada Supreme Court decided that Howe's consent wasn't voluntary and threw out the bust.

As the "Consensual Dope Ditty" demonstrates, when cops ask for consent it doesn't sound like a request; it sounds like an order. Refuse, and the police will tell you that they don't need your consent—and they may be right—but it does not matter what they say or how they say it, *never* consent to a search; it is *never* in your best interest. And anything short of NO! I DO NOT CONSENT! is consent once you're inside a courtroom. Judges have found that people *voluntarily* consented to a search, even though they "consented" while they were handcuffed with guns pointed at them, and by suspects who couldn't even speak English. (For you Spanish speakers: "NO DOY MI CONSENTIMIENTO PARA LA BÚSQUEDA!")

3. Hide That Shit

Drugs and drug paraphernalia are illegal, right? I mean, that's what we're talking about here, so don't leave anything incriminating in "plain view." Don't grow dope on your windowsill. Don't leave roaches in the ashtray of your car. Don't leave your backpack open. Don't host outrageous dope parties. And don't keep accidentally pulling dope out of your pocket when you're digging for change, dumb ass!

You must hide your shit from your fellow citizens as well. Anyone accusing another citizen of a crime—"*That dude over there hasn't blinked in three hours, Officer*"—gives a cop the authority to make a bust, even if the cop didn't see anything incriminating himself. The same is true with a warrant to search your house; and on the road, an accusation by a fellow motorist is enough for a stop.

If you haven't pissed away your Fourth Amendment rights through one of these Three Deadly Sins, the police can of course still bust you, but now you're not such easy prey, not a straggler from the herd to be mauled by the cheetah. Now the police will at least need a reason to search you. If they search you anyway, the cops will have to tell some outrageous lies at your suppression hearing, making the bullshit harder for your judge to digest (see "Trial? You Don't Get No Stinking Trial!" page 269).

Close Encounters with the Police

From a Friendly Question to a Cavity Search

All drug busts begin with a suspicious cop and end with him finding your stash. The following Three Levels of Doom are what the courts have come up with to discourage the police from simply ripping off your clothes in the street and searching you like a barnyard animal. Each level of suspicion brings the cop closer to your dope.

***DOPE NOTE:** THE THREE LEVELS OF DOOM APPLY TO ALL SEARCHES, WHETHER ON THE STREET, IN YOUR CAR, OR IN YOUR HOUSE. MARK THE PAGE.*

The Three Levels of Doom
There are three types of encounters that you can have with a cop (all bad):

The First Level of Doom—Q & A Time: The police are trained to ask suspicious people like you questions for no good reason, but they can't detain you or search you without offering some reason that doesn't make you laugh like hell or isn't illegal. *Yeah, I stopped the defendant because he was black and bustin' a lot of bling, so I figured he was a crack dealer, a* *pimp, a rapper, or all three.* Try not to get visibly upset because a cop has decided you look suspicious, even if you suspect it's because you're black or because you're a dark-skinned man standing near a tall building with a camera. A suspicious cop is asking you questions to see if you'll lose it and provide him a reason to search you. (See "Face-to-Face with the Fuzz," page 89, for some Q & A tips.)

The Second Level of Doom—Reasonable Suspicion: If the cop actually has some specific reason to suspect you of possessing dope, but hasn't witnessed you commit a crime or found you hanging around the Community Dope, she can detain you and frisk you—and just last year the Supreme Court decided that she can demand identification as well—but at Level Two, she can't go into your pockets or your bag unless she feels something suspicious during "The Frisk" (page 92). Something like, oh, a crack pipe. Crack pipes will get ya every time.

Aw, Maaaan, Groove Is in the Heart, Officer—A Level Two Situation: Say you're sucking on a lolly at a circuit party, the DJ's set is over, but you're still getting your groove on—the cops can detain you, pat you down, and, if they find any of your little buddies, bust you.

The Third Level of Doom—Probable Cause: Time to get a lawyer and keep thy mouth shut. Probable cause means that the police can arrest you, either because you have committed a crime in their presence, someone told them you did, or they found the dope. And once they're at the Third Level of Doom, they can search down your throat and "Into Your Ass" (page 95).

Oooh That Smell: Weed has one great disadvantage compared to virtually all other drugs. It reeks like hell, and even your mamma knows the smell of burning bud. That smell is the Third Level of Doom. It automatically gives the police the right to search you on the street or in your car. (Your house is a little different, see "Oooh, That Smell," page 111.)

How far the police can take the quest for the dope—be it on or into your body or elsewhere—depends first on the Level of Doom, but the rules change when you're driving your dope around; they change when you take your dope to the airport, keep it in the crib, put it in the mail, buy it online, or pimp roll with it down the street. We'll start with street busts, typically outside a club, a bar, a noisy house party, or any other place where the people tend to really grab the weekend by the horns.

Street Busts

The "Street Busts" section is preventive defense, designed to bend to police authority without breaking. It's not about standing up to the police. They will squash you and some of your rights too; there's nothing you can do about that but whine and make things harder on yourself. The police have all the power and usually all the knowledge. This is the knowledge you'll need to make exercising all that power more difficult from the moment you walk out the door and onto the Drug War battlefield. . . .

Preparing for Battle . . .

A few tips to avoid being one of the obvious search candidates and/or bustees any time you're in public:

1. **Check Your Look in the Mirror:** Looking as though you're on drugs is suspicious. Some grooming tips: Comb your head. Tuck in your shirt. Pick the toilet paper off your heel. Eyedrops if you've got 'em. Tic Tacs all around. (Peanut butter if you're paranoid.) Don't wear sunglasses at night, stud. Ladies, try to keep the lipstick between the lines. (The Tenth Commandment, page 329, makes clear how essential this battlefield tip is.)

2. **Clean Your Hands:** Your hands can give you away. Don't trust them. Obviously if there are flakes of coke or particles of bud under your nails, you're screwed. But hands also retain the smell of whatever you've been ingesting. Cops know this. Hands that smell like pot smell like the Third Level of Doom to them. Nails bitten to the blood are suspicious. (Meth heads loathe their fingernails.) Also, wash off any stamps applied at the front door of a club, and cut off any plastic "Over 21" or "I got drunk for free" bracelets. Got track marks? Long sleeves and rehab are in order.

3. **Avoid Amateur Hour:** Consider the time of day, day of the week, and time of the year while you're out there on the battlefield. Cops do. Closing hour is suspicious. Weekends are suspicious, Thursdays too; obviously New Year's Eve; SuperBowl Sunday; and God bless drunk driving on the Fourth of July. More American than the PATRIOT Act. Avoid the temptation this year (see "Driving While Wasted," page 157). Amateur hour is also when you will spend the most time in jail waiting for arraignment with everyone else who took the party to the bitter end (page 237).

4. Beware of the Battlefield: Aside from open-air drug markets, which you should avoid, the parking lots and sidewalks in front of clubs and outside concerts are among the easiest places to draw police attention. It's suspicious simply to be in the vicinity and easy to get charged with possessing the Community Dope when it gets passed around. Clubs that get noise complaints, and/or an OD or two, get an undercover cop or two. Neighborhoods known for a lot of ridiculous partying, and concerts involving any jam band (the Dead and whoever's going to take over for Phish), reggae shows, or any venue with a couple of decks and spendy water, attract undercover cops, who go round up the lawbreakers once in a while to make their point. Put a couple of fingers in the dam, so to speak.

5. Chill: Don't make a memorable exit, needlessly attracting attention in places and/or on occasions where people are likely to be getting wasted. The cops, you'll remember, tend to go for the scattering roaches when they start taking scalps.

6. Be Prepared: You should not be walking city streets with dope in your possession. If you insist, you're going to have to get nasty with it. That's right, you've got to stick it where the cop really doesn't want to go and won't find with a casual pat-down. Too funky for you? Keep your stash in something like a Tic Tac box, which doesn't feel like anything particularly suspicious. *Caveat*: If you lose your little Drug War battle and get busted, offer up the dope. If the cops don't find it, it will be discovered during your jailhouse strip-search and you may get charged with an additional crime for smuggling drugs into jail. (I know, it doesn't sound fair. Always remember it's not supposed to be fair.)

Your fight-or-flight instincts on the Drug War battlefield are as useful as flapping your arms after jumping off a building. What follows is an effort to retrain your instincts when a suspicious cop is hot on your funky scent.

Ditching the Stash—Smooooth, Right?

Those whacked-out on drugs tend to be paranoid and panic-prone. (Not without good reason.) Instinct screams to dump the stash when the bright lights shine. Sometimes they throw it out the window, sometimes down the drain, sometimes down the hatch, but usually they just get busted and/or much too wasted (see "Eating the Stash," page 87). Frankly, the only time abandoning the stash is helpful is if you can get away with it, but once you have attracted police attention you probably can't. And if a cop witnesses you toss *anything* that *might* be drugs or paraphernalia, he has the authority to search you, which he may not otherwise have had. In any case, just being in the vicinity of dope is usually sufficient for a good bust.

Ditching the dope will take a couple of other guns off your defense attorney's rack. Try selling it to the judge that you were not aware of the drugs, or didn't have control over them, after you tried ditching those babies (see "This Isn't My Underwear!" page 16). The DA will knock that weak shit out of there before you can say "Not guilty." Worse, if the DA's feeling nasty—and DAs usually are—you could be on the hook for some bonus crimes. Destruction of evidence and obstruction of justice are always favorite throw-ins, as Martha Stewart might tell you.

But abandonment is not always of the frantic ditch-the-stash-in-the-trash variety. It can sneak up on you. Say you're sprawled out on your blanket at a Dead show and a funky old hippie sidles up and suddenly pulls out a shiny badge, suspicious that you're the source of that nefarious smell mingling with the patchouli. You glance at your backpack. He looks at you. You look at him.

Q. *Is this your bag, son?*

A. I've never seen that bag before in my life, Officer.

You have now successfully abandoned your backpack and the faux hippie is free to search it. Sadly, you have not abandoned your drugs, so when he finds your Hacky Sack, the keys to the VW, and your dope, it's off to Part 3 of this book, and you won't be able to complain that the cop didn't have the right to search the bag in Part 5.

DISCLAIMING OWNERSHIP OF A BACKPACK, OR LUGGAGE AT THE AIRPORT OR IN A HOTEL ROOM, ALWAYS GIVES THE POLICE THE AUTHORITY TO SEARCH.

Sometimes an abandonment case isn't really an abandonment case. It's a "dropsy case." A cop who illegally searched you will solemnly swear that you ditched your stash when the bright lights shone. Like any good lie, it's profoundly simple and impossible to disprove. Compare the story NYPD officer Charles Frisina told the judge with dope smoker James McMurty's version:

Officer Frisina: "I was on duty driving a patrol car. While stopped for a light at West Third Street and Broadway, I observed two men in a doorway of the building at 677 Broadway. One of these men—James McMurty, as I later learned—saw the patrol car and stepped out of the doorway. From his right hand he let drop a small plastic container . . . its contents were marijuana. I approached McMurty, who had begun to walk away, and asked him if the container was his. He said no. I said I had seen him drop it and placed him under arrest."

Sounds simple enough, right? But let's hear what the junkie has to say anyway:

Mr. McMurty: "I was walking on Broadway near West Third Street when I saw Patrolman Frisina coming toward me. I knew I had a container of marijuana in my pocket. I also knew, after twelve years of involvement with drugs and four or five prior convictions, that illegal search and seizure was my only defense. The last thing I would do is drop marijuana to the ground. I simply left it in my pocket. Frisina told me to get into a doorway. I obeyed, hoping that he would search me. He did just that, found the marijuana, and arrested me."

Although the judge commented that it was "extraordinary . . . that every year in our criminal courts policemen give such [dropsy] testimony in hundreds, perhaps thousands of cases," and that it was "apparent that policemen are committing perjury in some of them, and perhaps nearly all of them," she nevertheless sided with the cop. (See "The License to Lie," page 273.)

McMurty's was an old-school bust. The dropsy cases are not as common as they used to be. This is not because the cops have gotten religion. It's because the police now have the right to stop you for picking your nose. If lying is necessary nowadays, it's usually more subtle, something Bill Clinton might come up with to describe a blow job.

Eating the Stash

Don't eat your stash. You're not that desperate. First, if the cops see you put anything into your mouth as they approach, they will attack. And you don't want that. Some of the most hard-core beat-downs that judges have given a 👍 occurred when suspects attempted to eat their dope.

The "One Hell of a Fight" Dope Ditty: Alarmed when he opened the front door of his house one afternoon to discover three cops searching the joint, Raymond Tapp decided that he'd better eat the dope he was possessing. But the cops noticed and decided to beat the piss out of him. Tapp was a tough old bastard, though, and wouldn't spit it out. The three cops "pummeled [him] in the face and head" and threw him out the front door, down the front steps, and into the front yard, where two more cops jumped in the action. For *twenty minutes* the five Drug Warriors whaled away on Tapp. One cop described it as "one hell of a fight." While it wasn't clear how Tapp would describe it, he wouldn't give up the dope. Finally, though, the cops got him on the ground, choked him while plugging his nose, and forced the dope out at last. The judge found this a perfectly reasonable method of extracting contraband and slapped Tapp with ten years. The appellate court told Tapp to *talk to the hand, lawbreaker!* Years later, however, the Louisiana State Supreme Court decided that the cops had gotten a little carried away in their quest for the dope.

Should the beating be unsuccessful, the police have the authority to take you down to the ER for a forced enema or a stomach pump to extract the stash. Perhaps worse, though, is that no matter what your drug of choice is, eating your stash will likely get you extremely wasted. Aside from the danger of overdosing and dying an ignoble death loaded out of your mind, dribbling in the corner of a holding cell, it is never a good idea to be wasted in police custody. You will not only be wasted, you'll be getting more and more wasted, and way beyond denying it. But unless you are to the point of what courts refer to as "mania"—not the fun mania, more the emergency room variety—whatever you manage to slur will be used against you in court, or for a reason to search more than just your body. Start muttering that Junior's going to get grounded if he forgets to water the pot plants, and a warrant to search your house will follow.

Run, Junkie, Run!

Good ol'-fashioned running like hell at the first sign of the fuzz. Always a favorite. Fleeing is just like abandoning dope; it's never a good idea unless you can get away with it. You probably won't get away with it, and if you don't, the police have the right to search you, and most will give in to the temptation to administer a couple of whacks with the nightstick.

> **"[T]he worst that happened is that the officers grabbed defendant by the throat, slammed him to the ground, possibly rendering him unconscious, searched his pockets . . . and found two packets of cocaine. Such force is not so unreasonable [that it's unconstitutional]."**
>
> —A FEDERAL JUDGE, GIVING A TO THE KNOCKOUT BLOW DELIVERED BY A COUPLE OF COPS WHO CAUGHT LLOYD DESMOND EATING HIS DOPE

> **Poor in the Drug War:** The Supreme Court says that bad neighborhoods are suspicious. People standing around in bad neighborhoods are suspicious. Running from the cops in a bad neighborhood is suspicious enough for a search.

Face-to-Face with the Fuzz

If you haven't panicked, a suspicious cop will likely ask you to produce identification in order to prolong your chat. You have the red-blooded American right to keep walking and refuse to answer his damn questions, and you do not have to produce identification. But your typical beat cop is not going to let it go at that. Walking away from the police and/or standing on your rights is suspicious, making a search inevitable.

What to do?

Your goal is always to minimize fuzz face time, ending your little get-together as quickly as possible without being suspiciously quick about it. If that sounds difficult, it is. The following is not so much a strategy to avoid being searched as a strategy to force a determined cop to search you illegally, giving yourself a shot at the suppression hearing (see "Trial?" page 269).

1. Give Respect

Antagonizing a cop or challenging his authority is absolutely pointless and unsatisfying, unless your goal is to get arrested. But this ain't no civil rights march, man. It's the Drug War. And there's no nobility in a drug bust. Pissing off the police will undoubtedly get you arrested for disorderly conduct and probably an "Oops, sorry about your head" as he's throwing you in the back of the cruiser. Respect the authority. If you don't feel it, you better act like you do. Answer the questions. Produce identification. No matter how painful, "Yes ma'ams," "No sirs," and "I'm sorry, you're rights" are excellent.

Less obvious but equally important is not sounding as though you've been reading this book, announcing that you "know your rights." This says two things to a cop: (1) Asshole. Must bust. And (2) this asshole knows his rights because he's been busted before, which makes a search inevitable. (See "Flying High Again," page 211, for more on how a prior bust does away with your Fourth Amendment rights altogether.)

2. Be Cool

Always maintain eye contact if you are confronted by a cop, be it on the street or on the road. Keep your hands away from your pockets, don't flee, and never let them see you sweat. Pitting out your T-shirt with sweat, stammering, throbbing neck veins, shaky hands, and the like are all suspicious. Nervousness alone is not a sufficient reason to search you, but it's a damn good start. Nervous types are screwed. Sorry.

Keep in mind that everything you manage to slur, the rank smell emanating from the depths of your esophagus, the debauched woman in a G-string and fur coat that you were "escorting," will all be ammo for the cop when he's justifying the search to the judge. It's not only your words that can be used against you, in other words. *So let's look alive out there!*

3. Be Late

Ask if you are free to leave. This is essentially asking the cop what Level of Doom you're at, and it will be a crucial fact if you do end up getting busted, because the cop needs some reason to detain you. You, on the other hand, need a reason not to be detained, and it's always legitimate to be in a hurry. Planes to catch are good, wives giving birth, Mom receiving last rites—that sort of thing. Being late is of course harder to pull off if you were sitting on your ass when the cop approached you. But it's never a good idea to be sitting around in public possessing dope anyway. Loitering is not only a crime for which, like all crimes, you can be arrested; it's suspicious.

4. Be Real

Lying to the cops about who you are and where you live is always tempting. If you end up getting arrested, however, it's a crime. Worse, this amounts to scattering-cockroach behavior, making it hard to deny that you didn't know about the dope your debauched "date" was carrying when you started lying to the police. Also, if you're evasive during your bust, it will make it harder to get released on bail. (see "Defending Your Life," page 241).

Body Searches

In Your Pockets and Up Your Ass

Predictably, you haven't been able to explain away the cop's suspicions. Your pupils look like manhole covers. Your T-shirt is soggy. Your "date" has started mumbling something about getting this party started. Your hands shake as you struggle to extract your ID from your wallet. You're a little confused about where you live and where you've been. All of this is perfectly legal behavior, but it's pretty suspicious.

Welcome to the Second Level of Doom. The cop doesn't have the right to do anything other than frisk you and ask you questions here at Level Two, but it's starting to look bad; you are approaching the point of no return. If you have failed to heed Tip 4 on "Preparing for Battle" (page 82), you will need an attorney shortly.

The Frisk

The Dark Doorstep of the Criminal Justice System

The frisk will be the first time the criminal justice system reaches out and grabs you. If the cop likes what he feels, it won't be the last. A frisk ranges from a mild patting down of your clothes to an ungentle massaging of your genitals—you too, ladies. What the cop feels (or says he felt) will determine if you're about to take that fork in the road that is a drug bust, or if you're going to have a Drug War story with a happy ending.

What the cop will be feeling for is anything that feels like a weapon or drugs. If she doesn't, she does not have the right to go into your pockets or your bag. Needless to say, everything feels like dope to the cops.

Hmmm . . . That Must Be, Wait, Wait, It's Coming to Me . . . Acid, Yeah, That's It: One afternoon in Michigan, Billy Holder and Michael Custer were getting soused in Billy's parked car. (Bad idea. See "Keep It Out of the Ride," page 141.) Officer Michael Greenleaf (ha-ha) sidled up next to the boys and noticed that Billy was much too wasted to drive and busted him. On his way to the squad car, Billy yelled back at Michael, *"Don't tell him a fucking thing!"* This made Officer Greenleaf suspicious. He went back to the car, frisked Michael, and he felt a two-by-three-inch card in his pocket. Officer Greenleaf's years of experience led him to conclude that the card had to be a blotter of LSD. Out it came. Reeling in astonishment, Officer Greenleaf discovered that the card wasn't acid after all. It was, however, a couple of Polaroids of Michael sporting a big grin, and holding a sack of pot large enough to need both hands, and another shot of him posing by a suitcase packed with more bud. *Oh, yeah,* thought Officer Greenleaf. He got a warrant to search Billy's house, where he found the subjects of the Polaroids and the boys got busted for possession with intent to distribute. Pulling the Polaroids out of Michael's pockets could be legal only if the judge believed Officer Greenleaf when he testified that he thought the Polaroids felt like acid. He did, and the bust stuck.

Rocks Is Rocks: One of the many ways powder cocaine is superior to crack is that powder blow doesn't obviously feel like drugs. Crack rocks, on the other hand, feel like crack rocks, at least according to the justices of the Supreme Court in their experience in this area. *Caveat:* If the cop feels a Baggie of powder where your penis should be (or shouldn't be), that's suspicious. Expect the search to get a 👍.

Fraidy Cops

In some states, including New York, a cop can go into your pockets only if he feels something that feels like a weapon or something that might contain a weapon, not just to get your drugs. It's probably unnecessary to say that in these states, everything feels like a weapon. Judges have given the ole wink and nod (see page 281) to cops testifying that a pack of smokes felt like a knife, a wad of cash felt like a knife, and a couple of crack rocks felt like the butt of a gun.

Nor is the judge going to be picky about whether it was reasonable for the cop to be worried that you might have a weapon; as the quote by Judge Luttig indicates, it's always reasonable in the eyes of the law. And since pat-downs are always fair game, cops will frisk you out of concern for their safety or simply because they want to see what's in your pockets.

"Where there are drugs, there are almost always guns."

—The Honorable Michael J. Luttig of the Fourth Circuit Court of Appeals, on why we must frisk the dopers early and often

Into Your Backpack

Your backpack is a safer place to keep your dope than your pockets because it's a little harder to justify searching. The bare-knuckle reality is that a cop giving you a frisking is probably going to look in your bag as well, and if the bag is open (or the cop says it was open) and he sees something suspicious in there—35mm film canisters, prescription pills, blowtorch lighters, eyedrops, club flyers, a copy of *Busted!*—basically the standard junkie-on-the-go satchel—the bag can be searched completely. If the bag is closed and the frisk hasn't incriminated you, the officer can't go in there without a reason. That's what the Constitution says, anyway.

HARD-SIDED BACKPACKS AND SUITCASES CANNOT BE SQUEEZED AND EMIT LESS ODOR.

Into Your Ass

The Third Level of Doom

The Third Level of Doom is like dropping that pill that you scored from the fidgety guy with the scabby arms at the circuit party. There's no going back once the pill goes down; you just have to go with it in whatever direction it takes you and hope for the best. The dope owns your mind once it's down the hatch; the police own your ass once they have probable cause. They will go searching for the drugs *wherever* they think you've hidden them.

WARNING: ENTERING THE THIRD LEVEL OF DOOM IS NOT FOR THE SQUEAMISH. RETRIEVING DRUGS FROM INSIDE YOUR BODY IS UP-TO-YOUR-ELBOWS DIRTY BUSINESS. CONTINUE READING WITH THE UNDERSTANDING THAT I'M NOT MAKING THIS SHIT UP. IT HAPPENS. PRAY LIKE HELL IT NEVER HAPPENS TO YOU.

You Can't Take My Pants Off Right Here!

Most cops don't really want to look up your ass, even back at the precinct, which is why experienced bustees let go of their squeamishness and get nasty with their dope if they have to. In an "emergency situation," however, a cop can force you to strip, bend over, and spread your butt cheeks for a visual inspection. Right here. Right now.

What's an emergency? you should be asking yourself. Say, for example, the police suspect that you have indeed gotten your dope dirty and fear it will be absorbed into your bloodstream if they don't go in there and get it. Under these unfortunate but not uncommon circumstances, a judge will usually give the search a , although your chief concern is not likely to be whether the search you are enduring is going to be held up in court. Not for now, anyway.

Dope Ditty: On a bright September afternoon in the early nineties, twelve-year-old Maria Gonzalez was taking a taxi to New Bedford, Massachusetts, with her guardian. Acting on a bogus tip that the two might be smuggling drugs, local police followed the taxi in an unmarked car. When little Maria started looking back at the crime busters "suspiciously," they pulled the cab over. The frisks revealed no dope, so the cops decided to strip-search the girl, right there by the side of the road. A New Bedford cop couldn't understand what the big deal was when little Maria sued, testifying that the city police had conducted *more than one hundred* roadside strip searches during the previous three years.

Maria's search is an example of a simple strip search. Degrading. Humiliating. Sometimes painful. An aggravated ass search is when you have hit rock bottom.

So Your Ass Is Clean. It's Still Suspicious . . .

Aggravated Ass Searches

If your ass is shiny like Vasoline, or you're wearing rubber underwear, or you're having a little trouble sitting down, or you're taking suspiciously short little steps, the cops are going where the drugs are. The same is true if the cop observes you reach into your drawers, but didn't find the dope when she had a look-see. Because there is a "clear indication" under these circumstances that the stash is in there, an anal/vaginal probe is acceptable, provided it's done in a "reasonable manner." Which basically means that the cop didn't put you over her knee, yank down your pants, and go fishing without a good reason, a clean pair of gloves, and some lube.

To the Drug Warriors your body is just another container to hide contraband, and the warriors can go anywhere the drugs can go in your body, and they can keep going and going until a judge decides that the search was "repulsive," "shocked the conscience," or was "too close to the rack and screw." What "shocks the conscience" will depend on the sensibilities of your particular judge. Your average magistrate is not going to be outraged very easily. He's seen it all, heard it all, and your ass ain't special to him. Even the most brutal searches, forced enemas, and the like are almost always given a 👍 by the trial court. If the search is ever found "repulsive" it will be years later by an appellate court, whose judges don't hear about this kind of thing every day.

Generally, a deep probe will be done at the hospital after the cops have phoned in for a warrant, but it can be performed "in the field" too.

Repulsive Dope Ditty: Betty Jean Guy was seven months pregnant and wearing only a pair of panties and nightgown when the cops came by her house one afternoon for some drug bust action. The house was clean, but the cops thought Ms. Guy had stashed the dope in her holiest. They took her in the bathroom and ordered her to take off her panties, bend over, and spread her butt cheeks. Since she was so pregnant it was difficult and painful for Ms. Guy to bend over, but she managed. The cops looked in her "privates" and discovered no dope. Undeterred, they took Ms. Guy down to the precinct to have another go at her. There, the cops had her strip again, bent her over a chair, and "assisted her" in spreading her butt cheeks, while another cop held a flashlight to get a better look. Finally, they saw a plastic bag poking out and, at last, busted her. The judge thought this search was a perfectly reasonable method of fighting the Drug War and so did all of the appellate courts in Wisconsin. By the time a federal court decided that its conscience was shocked and overturned the conviction, Ms. Guy's unborn baby was preschool-aged.

If you got nasty with your stash and the cops suspect what you've done with it, give it up. You're obviously dealing with a determined cop and better that you go in there and get it than someone else.

Stomach Pumping, Enemas, and Laxatives

If the drugs are lodged too far up your nooky for a probe to dislodge it or you've swallowed your dope, a harrowing trip to the ER awaits. Under their "community caretaker" function, the police have the authority to force the contents of your stomach out if they have reason to believe that the dope you swallowed may be dangerous to your health. Under their "bust the junkie scumbags" function, the police can arrest you if drugs are discovered in your bowels.

These types of searches are known in the biz as "below the skin" searches. The further "below the skin" the police go, the more positive they have to be that there's dope down there, and since pumping your stomach—judges prefer "gastric leverage"—and forced enemas always smack of "rack and screw" treatment, the cops usually have to have a warrant, and precinct house enemas are frowned upon.

That does not mean that it isn't done.

Rough Texas Dope Ditty: At about 5:30 a.m. on a lonely stretch of Texas highway, Officer Jason Lowry pulled Jody Lewis over because he "had a dealer's tag improperly positioned in the rear window" (see "Bullshit, Er, Pretext Stops," page 143). When Officer Lowry noticed Lewis chewing something when he got out of the car, he pulled his pistol and ordered Lewis to "show his hands." Lewis kept chewing, and Lowry attacked, tackling him, cuffing him, and ordering him to spit it out. Lewis kept chewing. Then another cop happened by and joined the fun. Lewis spit out some weed. Convinced there were more drugs where that came from, Lowry and the other cop grabbed Lewis's jaw and choked . . . er, applied "pressure to certain points on his neck." But choking Lewis didn't work, so they broke out the Mace and gave him a blow to the face. That didn't work either. Tweezers were next deployed, bloodying Lewis's mouth. Still no dope. Finally, they took him to the ER and had a tube inserted down his throat and his stomach pumped dry—all without a warrant and against the instincts of the strangely reluctant doctor. Among other things, about a gram of blow was discovered in the contents of Lewis's stomach, and he was busted for possessing that coke. The Texas Court of Appeals decided this was excellent police work and ordered Lewis to stop all that whining.

Laxatives, enemas, and monitored bowel movements are much more likely to occur when you're crossing a border (see "Airport and Border Busts," page 167). But, as we have seen, it can also happen if you're driving around with your stickers out of whack.

Now you've been warned.

Home Searches

Keep It in the Crib

By far the best place to keep your dope is in your home. The Supreme Court has stashed the few Fourth Amendment rights you have remaining under your bed, with the lights out and the shades drawn. You and your contraband stay down there and keep quiet, you're probably safe from a drug bust, making the Eighth Commandment (page 329)—Thou Shall Leave Thy Dope at Home—among the most essential of our commandments, if you like your freedom.

The cops, however, have license to be the ultimate Peeping Toms. They can climb trees and peer into your windows with high-powered binoculars, hover over your house in a helicopter, put a microphone outside your door, lie down on the floor and sniff for dope under the crack, peep through the keyhole, dig through your garbage, follow your neighbors into your apartment building and hang out in the hallway, or bang on your door, all without a warrant or any particular reason. Essentially, the only limit, aside from simply busting down the door, is when the fuzz uses X-ray vision to see inside or employs some other piece of technology that is so tricked-out that the judge has never heard of it.

Think of your house as a balloon. You and your dope are safe in there so long as it remains airtight and opaque. Once the police suspect that there are drugs in there, that thin layer of rubber is the Fourth Amendment. But anything the police can see is fair game. Any air you let out, they're free to smell. Any noise you make, they're free to listen to. They can squish their faces against your balloon or hold it up to the light to get a better look, and if they see, hear, or smell anything suspicious, they can get a warrant and pop your balloon. And all too often they won't need a warrant at all.

Consider actor/Stetson man Matthew McConaughey's bust as a cautionary tale on the hazards of getting too happy in a leaky balloon. One evening a few years back, Mr. McConaughey was at home doing bong hits, playing the bongos, and dancing naked to loud music (with another man, by the way, *not that it matters*). Unwisely, he left his front door open. The cops walked in without a warrant and busted him for pot plus bong possession, and Mr. McConaughey had to like it because he had made no effort to keep his session private.

The more effort you make to keep private what's happening in your house or in your backyard, the more likely the search will be illegal. Got land? Post No Trespassing signs. The judge will consider the signs when deciding if the search was legal. Good signage is a clear indication that you have made an effort to protect your privacy.

Warrant? We Don't Need No Stinking Warrant!

Warrants are required to search your home, but this constitutional right, as Mr. McConaughey would probably complain to you about, is about as effective at keeping a suspicious cop out of your house as an R rating is at keeping the kiddies out of *Raping and Pillaging XII* playing at the cineplex. In fact, the police are free to break into your house illegally, observe your dope, go get a warrant, and then "rediscover" the dope. All that they need is an "independent source" for their knowledge of the drugs, which is as simple as the smell of pot or the good word from the mysterious "known informant." (*Yes, the cops go looking for some clues after they've solved the crime.*)

Applications for warrants are usually fill-in-the-blank forms, based on what the officer says he, his snitch, or your neighbor saw/smelled/heard. One of the blanks will state that there is a "fair probability" that evidence of [*junkie scumbag lifestyle*] will be found in [*junkie scumbag's apartment*]. Judges sometimes deny warrant applications, but she won't—and even if it turns out that the information used to get the warrant was all rumor and lies, the search will still get a because cops are entitled to rely on any warrant that has been rubber-stamped, unless they're caught flagrantly lying to the judge to get the warrant, which I have never seen. (Not that I haven't seen flagrant lies.)

One nice thing about warrants, however, is that they don't lie. A vague or overly broad warrant, or a search that exceeded the bounds of the warrant, can be attacked *after* you're arrested. Beating the rap on a bad warrant is profoundly lucky, usually the result of the magistrate getting so handy with the rubber stamp that she doesn't even bother to read the application before stamping it.

That was how Kansas woman Rebecca Cardenas won the liberty lottery. Sheriff Overbeck came by Rebecca's house one evening in response to a domestic-dispute call and noticed a pot pipe in her bedroom. He left and came back with a search warrant, discovered a couple of bongs and some baby pot plants, and busted Rebecca. But because the sheriff hadn't bothered to fill in the "items to be seized" blank, and the judge didn't bother to read the application, Rebecca hit the jackpot, as warrants cannot be issued to search for any old evidence of any old crime. All that Sheriff Overbeck needed to do was to write "pot pipe" and Rebecca's Drug War story would not have had a happy ending.

Having said all that, unless you're raising a felony forest on your property or you're selling drugs out of your house, your house/dorm room/bedroom will likely be searched without a warrant because someone—maybe you without meaning to—will let the cops in, or you will have a party.

It all starts with the fateful knock at the door.

Police! Open Up, Dirtball! We Know You're in There!

Consider the fear that grips your chest when a police cruiser suddenly lights up your rearview. A spike of adrenaline. A mental search of the interior of your car. If your mind stumbles upon something incriminating, the knuckles go white and the panic sets in. That bottom-of-the-belly cold sweat is perhaps more pronounced when you open your front door to a couple of suspicious cops who've been chatting with their "known informant" again.

The police are of course aware of the terror they strike in guilty hearts, and they, of course, use it to their advantage, usually to get your consent to come in for a little chat about your drug habit. These are known in the business as "knock and talks," and they are remarkably effective at getting people to piss away their Fourth Amendment rights. You won't feel like you have the right to refuse. You will feel like refusing will make your problem worse. You will believe that you're such a smooth talker that the police will cast aside their suspicion and apologize for troubling you. But as a *Busted!* disciple, you will know better.

> ***DOPE NOTE:*** *KNOCK AND TALKS ARE SO INHERENTLY COERCIVE THAT SOME STATES, INCLUDING NEW JERSEY, WASHINGTON (THE BEST STATE TO PARTY IN IN THE COUNTRY), INDIANA, ARKANSAS, AND MISSISSIPPI, REQUIRE THE POLICE TO INFORM YOU OF YOUR RIGHT NOT TO CONSENT.*

Come On In, Officer! We're Getting Wasted!

The criminal justice system has little patience for the wasted. No one gets to blame anything on the dope. You can confess while you're wasted, you can sit through trial whacked out of your mind and so can your attorney as long as she can handle her booze, and you can consent to a search of your house when the cops come knocking, pretty much no matter how out of your mind you happen to be.

Dangling Dope Ditties: Raymond Ruiz snorted enough blow and smoked enough pot one night in Florida that he decided streaking through his hotel would be an excellent way to get the most out of his buzz. Raymond was observed bare-assed and "running about" the Ramada Inn, which the judge said was "upsetting the guests." The fuzz were summoned, knocked on Raymond's door, and identified themselves as police officers. Raymond was still extravagantly naked, as was his inebriated woman friend, and they had a pile of pot and a Baggie of blow sitting out on the dresser. Nonetheless, Raymond hollered at the cops to come on in. And so they did, asking Raymond for his identification, as they're wont to do, even the naked and inebriated. Raymond ambled over to the dresser to search for his ID and began slyly snacking on the mound of dope. But he wasn't clever enough for Deputy Sisk, who busted him for possession. Still Raymond had no pants. But when he was finally allowed to put some shorts on, Deputy Sisk searched his pockets and found some more dope. *Curses!* At trial, Raymond complained that he was much too wasted to voluntarily consent to the cops coming in, evidenced by his nude behavior and the fact that his woman was similarly bare-assed. But the judge was having none of it and busted him anyway.

Answering the Bell . . .

Assuming you haven't collapsed in despair at the bad news on the doorstep, or are not so deeply inebriated that you aren't scared of the police anymore, the following are some tips on handling a knock and talk:

1. Never Let the Police Inside Without a Warrant

Do not answer the door if you wouldn't feel completely at ease talking to the police in your present state of mind, or if you have *anything* incriminating lying about *anywhere.* Once the police are inside, they're harder to get rid of than Jehovah's Witnesses. They will find the stash if they look for it. If they claim they have a warrant for your arrest or a summons, go outside to speak with them. If you do get busted, *do not go back inside the house* to feed the dog or to put on clean drawers or to call a lawyer because the cop will follow you inside and anything he sees/smells is fair game.

The Supreme Court came up with this little rule after a cop saw Carl Overdahl, an inebriated Washington State University student, wandering the campus one night with a bottle of Jack. *Smart, right?* Carl didn't have his ID on him. Unwisely, he took the officer back to his dorm to get it and left his door open. The cop followed Carl into his room and busted him for possession when he saw the pot seeds and the pipe that was sitting on his desk. (See "The Dorm Room Free-for-All," page 122, for dorm searches.)

2. Don't Open the Door Wide If You've Got Something to Hide

If you haven't been smoking pot, your crib isn't a wild kingdom of smelly bud, and all drug-related matter is out of sight, it makes sense to open the door because hiding from the police is suspicious. Remain at the door with it open wide enough for the officer to see that you are not armed. The wider and longer the door is open, the flimsier your balloon (Fourth Amendment rights) becomes. To a judge interested in seeing your bust stick, a wide-open door is an invitation, your consent for the cop to have a look around.

> **Poor in the Drug War:** Food stamp recipients must allow welfare inspectors into their homes, no warrant required. If the inspector sees evidence of dope in the house he can have their food stamps cut off.

3. Don't Slam the Door

Like most people, cops hate to have doors slammed in their faces. It's suspicious to be too hostile to or scared of the police. Undoubtedly, you will be asked for identification while you're at the door. When asked, you should politely *shut the door*, go get your ID if you don't have it, and come back to the door as quickly as possible. *Stand outside your house* while you endure the Q & A. You will not like this. It will feel intrusive, and of course it is, but it's better than letting the cops inside.

4. Do Not Abandon the Homeland

The only place you have any real Fourth Amendment rights is in your home. Once you bolt out the back door you're just another scattering cockroach running from the cops, and the cop waiting out back has free rein to give you a smackdown as a fleeing suspect. Don't make his day. Similarly, don't go running through your house. Behavior that demonstrates the panic the cop's presence has triggered will provoke him to bust down your door to prevent you from destroying evidence and/or to smack you around. (See "The Race to the Toilet," page 113.)

Fleeing *into* your home will do you no good either. You cannot take refuge from the police in your home without also taking up arms. A standoff will ensue, likely resulting in your death and, at last, your fifteen minutes of fame on your local news (national if your death is truly spectacular). The same is true if you're being followed in your car, but make it home before you actually get pulled over. Flying into the garage and slamming the door is like toppling over old ladies to slow your pursuers. Not very effective, and it looks bad.

5. Get Naked

Remember that desperate defendants call for desperate defense strategies—and you are desperate when you've got cops knocking on your door. Since being late is not going to work very well when you're home, you want to be engaged in an intensely private, preferably legal activity. The more intimate, the better. Screwing is excellent. Consider tearing off your clothes at the sound of cops at the door. Counterintuitive, yes, but this is the Drug War—you've got to think outside the box. The histrionics serve a purpose in this alternate universe: they provide you with a reasonable explanation for why you'd like the cops to leave, and the more humiliated you were when the police barged in, the more likely the search will be unreasonable, i.e., illegal.

DOPE NOTE: *ALWAYS ALSO REMEMBER THAT IF YOUR CRIMINAL ATTORNEY STARTS MAKING YOU ANY GUARANTEES, START SHOPPING FOR A NEW ONE. (SOME TIPS CAN BE FOUND FROM "LIMBAUGH LESSON # 5," PAGE 260.)*

Hotel*-Motel-*Holiday Inn* . . . Saaaay *What? Don't get too comfortable in a rent-a-crib. You have fewer privacy rights in a hotel room than in your home, particularly if your name is not on the credit card bill and you hid in the trunk during check-in—something spring breakers should keep in their "minds."

Deadly Sin #3 is particularly deadly (page 77). Anytime someone else has the keys to the joint, you gotta keep it discreet. Also be aware that once you have checked out, or it's significantly past checkout time, you lose all right to privacy in the room, meaning that anything incriminating left behind is on you. Double-check under the bed for that bag of blow you keep forgetting about—you have constructive possession of it because it's very strong circumstantial evidence that it's yours. You'll have to blame it on the maid, and your karma will have trouble withstanding the blow.

Oooh, That Smell

Flip back to the "Consensual Dope Ditty" (page 76). Notice how Officer Mercado used the alleged smell of pot to pressure Howe to let him in, telling him that it was the Third Level of Doom (probable cause). While Officer Mercado was right, the smell did not give him the right to enter the house without a warrant, because he was in Nevada, where cops can't bust down the door solely because they say they smell weed. But in Arizona, Wisconsin, and probably Kentucky, the smell of MJ wafting from the crib is reason enough to bust down the door (only hotel room doors in Colorado). These states have decided that smoking pot is destroying evidence of a crime, which creates an emergency situation that the police must respond to without waiting around for a stinking warrant. In other words, you get busted for possession as soon as you score. As soon as you start smoking it, you get busted for destruction of evidence as well, unless you manage to smoke it all down before you get nabbed (as the Arizona Supreme

Court is worried about). If so, you'll only get a destruction-of-evidence charge, and maybe they'll throw in a paraphernalia rap. Get it?

This odor indicated that evidence of a crime, that is, possession of marijuana, was in the process of being burned and thereby destroyed. As such, we conclude that there was a very real and substantial likelihood that contraband would continue to be destroyed before a warrant could be obtained.

—THE ARIZONA SUPREME COURT, ON SMOKING THE MJ RIGHT DOWN TO THE BITTER END

In the other forty-seven states at press time—neither Scalia, Thomas, nor Rehnquist has weighed in on the matter . . . yet—the smell of weed *by itself* doesn't give the police the right to bust in. But if there is any indication that the weed may be for sale (say, a neighbor has noticed people coming and going at odd hours) or that there are children present, the smell of dope will probably be enough for the cops to bust in because if the police believe that a third party is in danger inside your house they don't need a warrant. Yet another reason not to mix kids with dope. Children are *always* in danger when there's dope in the house in the eyes of the law.

Tepees, Tents, and Lean-tos: Park rangers cannot search your tent without a warrant, but they can if they smell dope or see incriminating evidence. Much like your house, you've got to keep your tent flaps zipped. Your campsite, on the other hand, is fair game if you're on public land, which includes any national park, where park rangers do in fact bust campers, who are tried in federal court.

The Race to the Toilet

The High-Stakes, High-Reward Strategy of Flushing the Stash

The sound of a toilet flushing is the Third Level of Doom. Cops standing outside your house will break down the door if they hear that sound or anything else that could conceivably be the sound of destruction of evidence. On the other hand, if there's no dope, there's no possession charge, unless you fail to get it all down the drain, leaving enough residue for a stems and seeds bust (page 8). Like fleeing and abandoning the drugs, flushing the stash is never a good idea unless you're sure you can get away with it. Otherwise, you have a smashed door, pissed-off police, and a couple of additional charges.

Word to the Neighborly: Shouting a warning that the cops are coming is an easy way to share some criminal liability with your neighbors; either you'll be charged with constructive possession of the dope inside the apartment or with obstruction, or you'll wind up with an aiding-and-abetting distribution charge, depending on what's going on inside the apartment.

Third-Party Consent to Search

A third party can give the police consent to search your house unlike your car or your body, and it's one of the more effective end-runs around the warrant requirement. Vindictive ex-boyfriends can give their consent, so can the kids, so can Mom and Dad, and the babysitter too, unless you prevent it from happening.

My Roommate Doesn't Have Anything to Hide, Officer

The Ninth Commandment (page 329)—is particularly important if you have roommates. Your roommate can ruin you because anyone who answers the door when the cops come knocking can consent to a search of the house, so long as it appears to the police that she has the authority to do so. Answering the door is a sufficient demonstration of authority for your typical beat cop; he won't be asking your roommate if she actually has the authority to consent, or even if she actually lives there.

Your fate is therefore in your roommate's hands. Now is the time for the "This Land Is My Land, That Land Is Your Land" chat (page 32). Similar to when we're deciding whom to blame for the community dope, the Drug War requires that roommates declare areas of access with clear boundaries; otherwise everyone gets busted for possession and everyone can consent to a search of everyone else's room.

Establishing borders right now saves the innocent roommate from a possession charge, and it prevents her from consenting to a search of the guilty roommate's room. If you do not have "exclusive control" over your room, it's fair game. This means locking your doors and not getting drunk and sneaking into each other's room to beg for sex. Drug War roomies must keep their distance.

Poor in the Drug War: The poor are much more likely to be sharing space and therefore do not have "exclusive control" over any space in the house.

So I'm Twenty-nine and I've Pretty Much Been Getting High in My Parents' Basement for the Last Decade or So. They Stopped Coming Down Here a Couple Years Back. Can They Still Let the Cops Search My Room?

Still eating out of the folks' fridge, eh? The first thing you should do is start kicking up some of the extra money you've been making selling tube socks down at the swap meet. Paying rent isn't just the least you can do; it's the first step toward establishing your bedroom as your exclusive space. You'll also have to start locking your door from the outside, which your parents might not go for, particularly if you're not paying rent. And you must keep everyone and all their belongings out of your room. Lastly, you have to have a sit-down with the folks:

"Mom, Dad, should cops ever drop by, and, oh, I don't know, say they're looking for drugs, Busted! *says it's better for all of us if you tell them that my bedroom is under my exclusive control. Sound good? Let's not get into the whys, please. Here's some tube sock money."*

Only under the above circumstances will a judge even consider a parent's consent to a search of his or her child's room invalid. If you're under eighteen, forget about it, unless you've got a sitcom or you're fronting a boy band.

Come On In, Officer, Mommy's Dope Is in the Freezer

Kids do the stupidest things. They dig through Daddy's "special drawer," snort Mommy's "special pills"; they stay up past their bedtimes watching the hypocrites get high, they take your dope to school for show-and-tell, and sometimes they consent to the police searching the house. While kids have virtually no authority over their own rooms, they have the authority to invite the cops over for a little drug-bust action, and they usually know where the bodies are buried.

Whitey Pig Dope Ditty: Dope dealer Clara Penn taught all her children "to hate whitey" and never to talk to whitey "pigs." Not surprisingly, when the cops came by to search the house one afternoon, Clara's kids were not very cooperative, one of them telling an officer "that he was too smart for the pigs to catch them." *Yes, he does sound like a bright lad.* After a half hour of abuse and searching the house for smack, the exasperated cops had still not found it. But then Clara's five-year-old son Reggie needed to go wee wee. A cop took him to the john, where he offered the boy five bucks to tell him where Mommy's heroin was. Little Reggie, who apparently hadn't quite got with the program yet, waddled out to the backyard and dug up a bottle of brown stuff and got Mommy sent to prison.

Clara's bust is an admittedly unusual example because cops actually had a warrant to search the house and could have kept digging, but they decided to get the five-year-old to roll over on Mom instead. The point is that the judge will have no problem allowing the police to use your kids against you. Here is one of the few opportunities you will have to get some mileage out of your slow children, since the smarter and more independent your kid is, the more likely the court will find his consent to search valid.

Word to the Newly Minted Exes: Get the dope out of the crib immediately. A vindictive ex—*is there any other kind?*—can do you in and will likely have a better reason than your roommate for doing so (see the "Growing Dope Ditty," page 46, for a particularly pitiful example). If your ex still has keys or any possessions remaining in the house, the chances are good that the judge will not care that he or she didn't have the authority to allow the cops in.

Okay. Got all that covered? Keeping the balloon airtight? What about that suspicious package the "postman" is delivering to your door?

Fed Ecstasy

When they're not toting M-16s to work and smearing everyone all over the Publishers Clearing House sweepstakes, postal workers are looking for suspicious packages. (It's very, very monotonous work.) What's a suspicious package? Anything shipped from overseas, particularly "source countries"; the usual suspects include just about every part of the world for one reason or another, terrorism here, drugs there. Domestically, anything from California, a "source state," is automatically under suspicion.

A package mailed miles from the return address will always raise eyebrows, particularly if the return address happens to be a vacant lot or a "source neighborhood"; the usual suspects include virtually every urban environment. Anything mailed express mail must contain drugs because nobody likes to wait fifteen weeks to do his dope, and since drugs are packaged with much more love and care than Mom's Mother's Day present, heavily taped boxes are suspicious. Handwritten return addresses are not good, particularly if the box was allegedly shipped by a business. (It's assumed that all businesses have typewriters.) Cash payments are bad. Phony phone numbers: bad. *Any* type of smell: bad.

It's all bad.

Accepting a Suspicious Package and Controlled Dope Deliveries

Signing for a package of dope is the ultimate roll of the dice. Mail privacy went the way of the 2001 anthrax attacks in D.C. (remember those?), and once you've picked up the dope, the game is pretty much up. A typical arrest begins with a postal worker awaking with a start and stumbling upon your suspicious package and alerting the feds. A drug dog will come down for a sniff and bark. The box will be opened *very carefully,* and the dope will be photographed, put back into the package *very carefully,* and sent on its way. If you've summoned the courage to get the criminal liability delivered right to your doorstep, it will be delivered by an undercover cop in what is known as "controlled delivery"—easily the most efficient mail system the feds run, tracking you straight from IGrowDope.com to a small room and an hour of rec a day.

Accept a controlled delivery and the only Hail Mary shot you have at beating the rap depends totally on "Tipping the Scales of Bullshit" (page 31). This time, you will have to make a convincing argument that you received something that you had no idea contained drugs. This is why drug dealers send each other of lot of big pieces of hollow furniture from ACME, Inc. A desperate defendant will go to jail still arguing that she thought she was just getting a dinette set. No matter how cleverly concealed, as soon as you fetch the dope, it's off to Part 3 of our book. And if you sign for a package using a phony name, the explaining gets into the realm of the inexplicable.

Going with a PO box? Plainclothes detectives will be lingering over the junk mail down at Mail Boxes Etc., waiting for your jones to overcome your paranoia, sending you down to pick up the drugs. If your paranoia keeps you in check, they will go looking for you because it's suspicious to be afraid of your mail. (Registering incognito, by the way, is an additional crime.)

DOPE NOTE: *NEITHER FEDEX NOR UPS IS RUN BY THE GOVERNMENT, AND BOTH ARE THEREFORE FREE TO OPEN YOUR PACKAGE ANY OLD TIME. IF THEY DON'T LIKE THE LOOKS OF YOUR MAIL, THEY GET THE FEDS ON THE HORN, AND THEY BRING THE DRUG DOGS. USE A U.S. POSTAL SERVICE MAILBOX AND THE PACKAGE CAN BE SEARCHED WILLY-NILLY. IF YOU HAVE THE FORTITUDE TO ACTUALLY GO DOWN TO THE POST OFFICE, A WARRANT IS SOMETIMES REQUIRED BEFORE OPENING A SUSPICIOUS PACKAGE, DELAYING THE SEARCH BY ABOUT THIRTY-FIVE SECONDS.*

Poor in the Drug War: The cheaper the method of shipping a package, the less right to privacy the sender has in the package. You always gotta pay for that privacy.

THE STUDENT HANDBOOK

STUDENTS' SO-CALLED RIGHTS

College students, particularly freshmen, have been, are now, and always will be among our nation's most enthusiastic drug experimenters, committed to field-testing the outer limits of livers, brain cells, and serotonin. Later in life you will be able to say, "Yeah, I did some dope, but I was in college." That flies. It worked for Dubya, who reportedly liked his blow before the Lord showed him that drugs are bad. Even Newt Gingrich blamed it on college, and nobody even bothered asking John Kerry if he likes dope. (And since he was in Vietnam the chances are very, very good that he does, or at least did. Who knows? He might have had a couple of bong hits after the election.)

But it's one thing to wax nostalgic about your wasted youth before you dutifully donned some Dockers and joined the rat race—an entirely different matter to get busted. The criminal justice system doesn't have a college kid exception the way that you might like it to, and no one is nostalgic for his drug bust, which might make strapping on the khakis and assuming your rat race position problematic, or even getting into college if you need a loan (see "Now We Bring the Pain," page 311).

The Dorm Room Free-for-All

Your dorm room rights are your Fourth Amendment training wheels. They amount to pretty much whatever your university says they amount to.

"The notion of participatory democracy may be inviting and challenging but it is not advanced by smoking marijuana in dormitories or shooting heroin in obscure corners of the campus. . . . [But w]e cannot stamp out drug addiction, marijuana smoking, glue sniffing and assorted illegal practices at a campus by breaking into dormitories. Abandonment of constitutional protections and reliance upon illegal methods can lead only to the destruction of democratic processes."

—The Honorable Beatrice S. Burstein in an old-school '68 opinion (not bloody likely to be cited by your hometown judge)

Although private institutions have usually adopted some guidelines that they are required to follow, campus security can search your room for no reason and with no warrant. (This is because only the government can violate your stinking rights. Everyone else more or less has free reign, which a lot of Second Amendment types like to point out.)

If you're enrolled at a state school, you're free to get as wasted as you like in your dorm room. (Just kidding.) Check the residence hall contract that you probably signed without reading, and the university's student handbook that you probably threw away during orientation. The handbook is a legally binding document, and somewhere in there you have consented to a search under certain circumstances: turning off the stereo, the lights, checking the heater, removing strange pets, or good old-fashioned "inspections," which means what it sounds like: a search. This will be your first lesson in what the law terms as "notice," even though you didn't notice. (Notice that sign that says Drug-Free Workspace—that's notice that you can be drug tested.)

Nowhere is it more urgent to hide that shit than in a dorm, where you have already consented to a search. While you generally have the same rights in your dorm that you would have in an apartment, you can leave a stereo on at home without consenting to the police coming in to turn it off, and your neighbors are not allowed to take you out of bed when a fire alarm goes off. And, unlike a house, you already have someone inside your balloon—the RA, who is there to prevent you from losing your mind your freshman year.

Dorm searches without warrants are illegal only when the administration is cooperating with a police investigation aimed at busting students. Under these circumstances, the administration will apply for a search warrant, usually after one of your fellow dorm residents has had enough of the dope smoking and complains. Here's a taste of how the administration will write up an affidavit to apply for the warrant. (Notice the trouble one can get into for rolling good joints.)

Search Warrant Application for a McNeese State Dorm Room
This Department has received information from two (2) sources, both who state that Boudreaux is a frequent user of Marijuana. This first source is a responsible citizen of the utmost character and integrity, and has a great interest in the youth of Lake Charles, Louisiana. This informant reported to this Department in the interest of keeping the youth of Lake Charles from abusing drugs, that Boudreaux frequently uses Marijuana in Sallier Dorm [now Alpha Hall]. . . . On several different occasions, this source has seen [Boudreaux] rolling and smoking Marijuana in his room at McNeese, room 113 of Sallier Dormitory. This same person stated that Boudreaux frequently goes to the room of Jack Blacketter, room 124, and they have Marijuana in the rooms, and often hold parties. . . . This second source further stated that on several different occasions he has observed Boudreaux . . . hold Marijuana parties on the second floor of the dormitory and also in his room, room 113. This second source also reported that Boudreaux rolls Marijuana in Jack Blacketter's room, due to his rolling expertise.

This affidavit got the job done—all students were busted—but one wonders what a "responsible citizen of the utmost character and integrity" with such an interest in the youth of Lake Charles was doing at all those "marijuana parties" watching young Mr. Boudreaux roll nice fatties.

Hmmm . . . Would I Rather Get Busted by the Administration or the Fuzz?

While training wheels are annoying and make it hard to chat-up the ladies, they can prevent you from hurting yourself. An RA knocking on the door is fundamentally different from a cop. Now you'll have to decide whose authority you'd prefer to submit to, the school's, or the police's, assuming the knock is not one for a routine inspection, but because of the nefarious smell seeping from under the door and the howls of irrational exuberance.

As much discussed above, consenting to a search is never a good idea. But if you refuse an RA's request for a search, he will likely call the police, and then you can refuse their request to search the room. The problem here is that the police will simply wait in the hall while a warrant is being processed and then search your joint.

On the other hand, if you allow the RA to deal with the dope you *may* avoid dealing with the police altogether. The school's disciplinary policy for small-time possession *may* be less damaging than a full-blown drug bust. Dig that handbook out of the trash and bone up on your school's drug policy. Then study *Busted!*, comparing that policy with the dope laws in your hometown (see "The Dope Law Index," page 331). Pick your poison now. A public school might simply refer the matter to the police, but since campus police are not government officials, a private school is more likely to have a lenient policy about a small quantity of drugs. As of 2002, Dartmouth, for example, simply confiscated a small quantity of drugs if campus security determined that you weren't operating Behind the Scale (page 19).

DOPE NOTE: THE DOPE ELEPHANT (PAGE 31) IN THE DORM IS IMPOSSIBLE TO IGNORE. SINCE DORM ROOMS ARE TYPICALLY LUNCH BOX-SIZED,

ODDS ARE THAT ALL ROOMMATES WILL BE BUSTED AND CHARGED WITH POSSESSION, NO MATTER WHOSE DOPE IT ACTUALLY IS.

Also keep in mind that most schools have a disciplinary policy concerning off-campus drug busts. Get busted by the police, go through everything that entails, and you could still get booted from the dorms or expelled from school. Finally, the university will undoubtedly inform your parents after the disciplinary process is complete.

High School Heads

Note the Second Commandment, shorty (page 327)—you people are not supposed to be having sex, let alone doing dope. But of course many of you are having lots of sex and doing lots of drugs, and no one can stop you if you're determined to get knocked up and locked up. The feds have tried with a lot of memorable brain-frying ads, routinely mocked on T-shirts and by the users, usually while they're doing drugs. The law has responded with random drug tests for any student involved in extracurricular activities and searches for even flimsier reasons than the ones paid lip service to for Joe Junkie on the street.

Are you a nineteen-year-old sophomore? A regular at detention? Do you need lots of time-outs to get through the school day? If you answered yes to any or all of these questions, searching your delinquent ass will be very easy to justify. "Reasonable grounds"—somewhere in between the First and Second Levels of Doom—to believe you have broken a school rule is all that is needed for a search. If a teacher or administrator sees you nodding off in class a lot, notices you smell like *any* kind of smoke, or overhears an incriminating conversation—"Yo son, we got, like, crazy wasted last night"—or if you're fingered by a fellow student, then the school authorities can search you, your bags, and your locker.

In a high school setting, only abject humiliation involving a strip search and/or cavity search is frowned upon, usually after outraged parents contact the local chapter of the ACLU and sue because Junior had to squat and cough during homeroom. But school officials can conduct strip searches if there are reasonable grounds to believe that a student is concealing contraband, usually weapons or drugs (getting naked for stolen money is a little harder to justify). Strip searches must be done in a "reasonable manner." What's reasonable will depend on how uppity the parents are in your local school district. But if the smarmy male principal hikes up the cheerleaders' miniskirts to dig for dope, a loud lawsuit is sure to follow.

The only other significant limit placed on school searches is when all students are searched for no reason at all. The solution is drug dogs, used to sniff everyone's lockers and the cars in the parking lot for no particular reason. If the dog "alerts" on your locker (or drives its head into your groin area as you happen by), the administrator can search, usually with a cop at her elbow to bust you if anything is found.

DOPE NOTE: *LIKE DORM RESIDENTS, PRIVATE SCHOOL BRATS HAVE NO FOURTH AMENDMENT RIGHTS.*

Word to the Class of '05: Check "Jail/Holding Cell Hell," page 237. Juvie is all that and more violent, and even a misdemeanor drug bust can cost you financial aid for college.

The Party Section

From the House to the Fraternity to the Club to the Rave

The Hard-core House Party and the Fourth Amendment

The trouble with hosting a Drug War party is that these parties are leaky balloons; they tend to get big and sloppy and smelly. Big smelly parties are body blows to your Fourth Amendment rights. At a more intimate gathering the greatest dangers are having children present (see "Nappy Time for the Kiddies," page 35) or if someone starts flopping around (page 36). At larger parties, guests get tired of waiting for the john and go outside to piss and/or vomit in your neighbor's bushes and go wobbling around the hood with open containers. Police are called and often can search because you have committed the First

Deadly Sin (page 74), typically by violating a noise statute or a city ordinance that outlaws parties over a certain size.

The Successful Drug War Party

A hard-core party is always risky no matter what, but you already knew that. The unprepared host, however, is easy prey. The following are some planning and in-case-of-emergency tips:

1. Invite Only

Throw-downs that are announced via mass e-mail (see "Doooope . . . in . . . Spaaaace," page 177), at clubs, or by flyer will attract more people than you can handle, more people than you can trust, and will make it that much more likely to be on police radar, particularly if you're doing a loft party and the DJ has a following. If at around 4:00 a.m. you find yourself looking about your party and noticing that you really don't know anyone anymore, it's time to shut it down.

2. No Cover Charges

A cover charge will ensure that you will be charged with the maximum available penalties if anyone hurts himself. You will get a distribution charge if dope is being done, and you could be on the hook for running an illegal bar. Worse, if someone drives home wasted and takes out a minivan full of shrieking nuns, it's much more likely that you will get busted and sued all the way to hell.

3. Alert the Neighbors

Unless your party is a dismal failure—which hardly ever get busted, if that's any solace—the neighbors are going to find out about it one way or another; it's best to hear it from you first. Give the neighbor your number; slide it under the door if you have to. If your neighbor's got a problem it will be you she calls before the cops. It's fine to invite your neighbor if it's a booze thing, but heed the Ninth Amendment (page 329) if you suspect things may take a turn toward the dope.

4. The Dope Situation Room

Big lines in the living room are always a good way to celebrate your outlaw lifestyle, but it's so much better to be a poseur in that regard, and if the police come knocking they won't be able to ignore the drugs; possession charges will go all around. While it's pointless to suggest keeping the noise down, the drugs/paraphernalia must be kept indoors, away from the windows, and confined to locked bedrooms during a party. (Yes, it's lame, but that shit's illegal, and that's what we're talking about here.) Police responding to a loud party complaint will often walk around the property, look in the windows, and have a smell of the backyard before knocking on the door.

5. Prevent Consent

Keep the front door closed and *locked*. Cops banging on the door of a noisy party are not likely to bust down the door, but they are going to check the knob if no one answers. A locked door just means louder pounding. Nobody should be answering the door aside from the hosts, who have all read *Busted!* and know better than to consent to a cop entering without a warrant. If the cops do come to the door, follow the directions in "Answering the Bell," page 107, and find that attorney's number.

Here's Texan Nick Waugh, an unprepared host; Nick demonstrates an all-too-typical walked-right-into-that-one house party bust.

A Don't-Do-This-at-Home Dope Ditty: Nick had some guests over for bong hits around the bonfire one night a couple of years ago in Abilene, Texas. The music got too loud for his neighbors, and they called the cops, not Nick. Officer Brent Irby stopped by; he couldn't tell if the music was coming from outside or inside, but he was sure that was a fat bong he could see sitting on the living room table, a gross violation of House Party Rule 4. Suspicions aroused, Officer Irby went to the backyard, where Nick and his buddies were sitting around the fire. He asked the boys if they wouldn't mind talking "up at the residence." They agreed, in utter disregard of House Party Rule 5, as this was considered consent for the cop to enter. On the way to the house one of Nick's party guests, James Lockwood, began scattering like a cockroach under bright lights, sprinting ahead of Officer Irby and slamming the door behind him. But the cop stuck his foot in the door in time to see Lockwood running through the house with the bong. Lockwood of course ensured that he would be busted along with Nick, and his behavior inspired the cop to search the entire house. Although no more weed was discovered, Nick's judge noted with great distaste that he had "dope writings" lying about, evidence he was down with the drug scene, making Nick's constructive-possession bust stick. (See "The Dope Elephant in the Room," page 31, and notice the point about hiding this book.)

Take a lesson from Nick. A simple low-key soft-drug party with no kids and not much dope went horribly wrong and everyone got busted because they stepped onto the Drug War battlefield without a game plan.

Fraternity Parties

Most of the same rules apply to fraternity parties as to any other house parties, and there is probably already a Dope Situation Room in the house, closely guarded by the more subversive brothers. But it's not the owner-residents of the house that are typically arrested when parties get out of hand. The president of the fraternity and/or the social chairmen are usually held responsible, both criminally and by the parents who sue the house after Junior swan-dives off the roof on pledge night, his blood running at about 10 percent Wild Turkey. (Sorority girls like dope too, but their parties are not held at sorority houses, since beer bongs are not very ladylike.) Some additional insight . . .

Ritual Will Set You Free

If someone stops by your house during a party claiming that he's from another chapter or says he's an alum, you better put him through ritual before you let him in. Undercover cops have been known to pass themselves off this way, assuming that no one will go through ritual in public. When they observe the inevitable underage drinking, the party's over, the house is on probation, and there will be some busts. (For the uninitiated, "ritual" is generally a secret handshake, an odd exchange of words, and perhaps a hand gesture, not unlike traditional gang members.)

Selling Booze Will Not

No matter how bad your house's financial situation is, don't sell booze, particularly shots. And no big buckets of mystery juice, designed for the ladies to guzzle like Nestlé Quik. One clearly labeled drink at a time. Disguising alcohol like this leads to nothing but liability.

What About the Freshmen?

Everyone knows that there has been underage drinking at every fraternity party that has ever been held in the history of undergraduate education. Nevertheless, the hosts are still on the hook for preventing it (or at least giving it the old college try).

Evil Beats

The Rave Scene vs. the Drug War

Hard as it is to believe, a scene that was about dancing and drugs and going off with a few thousand of your *best* friends to music that rolls like waves of electric happiness across the floor and through your body went without police response for over ten years. But it happened. And it happened in Dallas fucking Texas in the eighties. Now it's happening anywhere you can get a couple of decks, a friendly police force, and ass-loads of E, Ice, GHB, and any other part of the alphabet of club drugs you're into. From Ibiza, Spain, to Goa, India, to the islands off the coast of Thailand, to Rio, to the beaches of Cambodia, to clubs in Reykjavík, Iceland, they do it inside, outside, aboveground, underground, and all around. All day. All night. All the time. Sometimes for years. Those who make the scene a way of life tend to spend a few good years cashing out the brains cells they weren't using anyway, cycle out, and tell the new kids how much better it was back in the day.

> **"No event more illustrates the failure of the 'Just Say No' campaign than a rave."**
>
> —Peter Jennings

Although it's taken a few generations of scenesters, the authorities here in the States have caught on to the dance/rave scene, and they do not like it. The feds are fighting the madness on many fronts, including a lot of laughably unscientific studies about horrible brain damage as the result of a single hit of E, but the bottom line is that the feds are not going to let thousands of people get that happy together, even if they're having trouble proving that E will seriously fuck you up. (Bad E, all too typical, is another matter altogether, however; see "Death and Dismemberment," page 63.)

Since everyone's wasted at the rave, you really need to distinguish yourself to get busted. Which means doing your drug transactions on the dance floor. Never buy dope, sell dope, or help someone else get dope at a rave or rave-esque event. Period. The feds are more interested in ending the scene. The promoters and the dealers are the ones making the money, and they're the ones that are going to jail for the long stretches.

That said, a well-publicized/mainstream rave will be crawling with undercover cops dressed like stark-raving candy kids (pigtails, Betty Boop backpacks, barber pole stockings, Raggedy Ann makeup, etc.). So if you're on the floor at a club and someone asks you if you're rolling, just smile. This will be hard if you actually are. You'll be tempted to shout

out, *"Hell yes! The DJ is God, my man! God!"* But you must check yourself. If that same person asks you if you can get him some E or Ice or whatever, say you're sorry and dance away to liberty.

Old-School Antidance Laws

A few years ago a mainstream rave came to Racine, Wisconsin. In a quandary about how to declare the whole idea illegal, the authorities got old-school and issued criminal citations to over four hundred of the boys and girls in attendance for violating the city's "inmates of a disorderly house" ordinance. When the ACLU pointed out to Racine officials that the bustees had a First Amendment right to freely assemble, the city dropped the charges, although they reserved the right to think of another way to stop the madness.

Dusting off an ancient city statute to squash a new dance/music scene is a common city strategy to force the people to stop dancing. This is because for as long as there has been music, the people have liked to get a buzz on to get their freak on, and dope *always* makes the scene. Not too long ago New York City got old-school to stop the dancing by dusting off the now infamous cabaret laws.

Aimed at keeping black and white people from "mixing" in Harlem jazz clubs in the twenties, New York's cabaret laws are almost a hundred years old and went largely ignored for decades. But Mayor Giuliani dusted them off and busted everyone for dancing without a license, forcing the best of the Manhattan dance scene to Brooklyn and then to Queens, and now it's going to Berlin. Nobody can go dancing in NYC these days unless the bar/club/lounge or whatever has a cabaret license. There are actual signs insisting that no matter how good the music is, no dancing will be tolerated under pain of law. People are ordered to stop dancing by management should they get looser than swaying on their barstools and nodding their heads in orderly fashion.

I'm not making this shit up. And you know what they say: if they can do it there, they can do it anywhere.

New Jack Laws

The RAVE Act

Not since the heyday of the Haight-Ashbury scene during the late sixties has one drug been so associated with one type of music. The hippies liked their acid, rock, and trippy light shows at places like the Avalon Ballroom and at festivals like Woodstock. The party kids like Ecstasy, House, and trippy light shows at places like the Sound Factory (see below), raves, and West Coast massives for the underage set. The shrill "scientific" studies that were once aimed at demonstrating the brain rot caused by dropping acid are now aimed at dropping E, and the laws passed to stop Woodstock-like, drug-fueled togetherness are now being passed to stop ravelike, drug-fueled togetherness.

> **"To erase the grim legacy of Woodstock, we need a total war against drugs."**
>
> —Richard Nixon

The Reducing American's Vulnerability to Ecstasy Act, better known as the RAVE Act, is the feds' latest effort to make it all go away. Similar to the hosts of "The Hard-core House Party" (page 34), the promoters are treated like drug dealers because they are supplying the space, the decks, and the plain old water at Cristal prices. The law is an extension of "stash house" laws, designed to bust slumlords in the eighties for allowing their property to be used to sling crack. Now it's being used to stop promoters from hosting raves, or venue owners from allowing their property to be used "primarily for drug offenses." (Remember poor old Mr. Carter, page 34? He didn't even get to screw a model.)

> **"Sounds wholly or predominantly defined by the emission of repetitive beats."**
>
> —UK'S ANTIRAVE STATUTE ON THE SOUND OF EVIL BEATS

Basically, rave/dance promoters get busted if they were aware that drugs were being consumed. If they act responsibly by having paramedics on hand, or chill rooms to prevent overheating from dancing for the kids who were inevitably going to off, it's hard for them to deny that they didn't know what was going on. On the other hand, if they're cavalier about safety and don't have paramedics on hand or call them to the scene when someone launches himself into orbit, they are held responsible.

The Sound Factory Goes Boom: Manhattan's Sound Factory had been on the NYPD's radar for a few years before its owner, sixty-one-year-old Richard Grant, was busted on "stash house" and aiding and abetting drug distribution charges. The massive club—big clubs are essentially the only venues with cabaret licenses in NYC—was raided in the late nineties and closed, but a New York judge refused to close it permanently because the owners could not be blamed for the behavior of thousands of people. As a condition of reopening, the judge ordered a drug dog to be put on patrol at the front door. When the Sound Factory reopened, the NYPD and the DEA set up an undercover operation, and the cops bought mountains of E, K, GHB, etc., paid nine bucks for bottles of water, and observed patrons "vomiting, convulsing or passing out from drug use"; they also said that an unnamed DJ kept a "personal" bag of meth next to the decks. There were some OD's, and the patrons who weren't enjoying their buzz anymore were laid out in what the staff referred to as "crack alley" to sleep it off. Soon the fun had to end. At press time, Grant and his partners were facing twenty years. (Fanta, the much-maligned drug dog, was asleep when the cops raided the joint the second time.) Eight promoters, most of whom were college students, were also busted for selling E to undercover cops. The feds have accused Grant of organizing the promoters, er, dealers, and encouraging them to bring their customers to the club.

Glow Sticks, Dust Masks, Minifans, VapoRub, and Pacifiers

No, it's not the stuff of neurotic coal miners; it's the stuff of raves, and the feds don't like it either. The ACLU says it's a violation of free speech to ban inherently legal objects used in "expressive communication." *Wicked tracers, man.* But the feds say that's right off the stable floor; we know the kids are using this crap to get even more wasted or enjoy being wasted even more. So rave gear has been used as evidence that the promoters were aware that clubgoers were doing E, but it's very hard to prove, and it's what lawyers call a slippery slope. *Could they have banned tie-dyes in the Sixties?*

Merely possessing rave gear is of course legal, but it's mighty suspicious, a great temptation for the police to search you and/or your bags. Also, if you're busted in a Community Dope situation, having a glow stick will guarantee that you will be one of the poor bastards charged with possession. Pacifiers, by the way, are wrongly thought to be used by evil-doers high on speedy club drugs to give their teeth something upon which to grind. Pacifiers are employed simply to be outrageous. (Candy is preferred to keep mouths happy, something from the Sweetheart or lollipop family.)

The RAVE Act has taken shots at your stinking First Amendment rights in other ways. The very first time the DEA took its new toy out for a test drive, it used the law to shut down a NORML benefit concert in support of medical marijuana. When the feds got wind of the show, a DEA agent presented a copy of the RAVE Act to the venue's owner and noted that he could be busted if/when someone smoked dope at the show. The owner folded and canceled the show.

Drug War Driving Lessons

Keep It Out of the Ride

Your car is a bad place to party. Putting aside the whole fiery-death thing, nowhere are you more likely to be stopped and searched than in your ride, and nowhere are your Fourth Amendment rights less respected. There used to be a lot of little rules about when the police could pull you

over and why. And there were some more little rules about what parts of the car they could search, what containers inside the car they could search, and whom they could search. It was all very picky. Recently the Supreme Court has said fuck it, no more little annoying rules; we're drawing a "bright line": the police can pull over anyone they want, for any reason they want, search anything they want and all the passengers too. Even if you get busted *near* your car *after* you parked it, they can still search the car.

"Under today's holding, when a police officer has probable cause to believe that a fine-only misdemeanor offense has occurred, that officer may stop the suspect . . . arrest the driver, search the driver, search the entire passenger compartment of the car including any purse or package inside, and impound the car and inventory all of its contents."

—Supreme Court justice Sandra Day O'Connor in 2001, marveling at the fuzz's new H-bomb

The police are given carte blanche on the road because cars are movable objects, and, unlike with your underwear or your apartment, the police are in charge of keeping the roads safe and drug-free. This rationale and "officer safety" basically eliminate any right to privacy in your ride. The last little rule left standing is that police can open only these containers that are capable of holding whatever they're looking for. If a cop is looking for a gun, for example, she can't open the envelope she found on the backseat. She's going to be looking for drugs in your case, and since even big-time drugs come in small packages, nothing will be spared. In any event, as Sandra D. points out, if the cop decides to arrest you for *any offense,* there are no rules. (In the Supreme Court case that gave the police this authority, Texas soccer mom Gail

Atwater was arrested and *jailed* for failing to wear her seat belt.)

I'll say it again. Your car is a bad place to party. This is no less true just sitting in your Benz. It's always suspicious to sit in parked cars, and it will *always* attract police attention, particularly windowless vans, or if you have rainbow-colored dreadlocks like Funkadelic's legendary front man George Clinton, who was busted in December '03 for possessing some blow he was enjoying in his parked car. (Dr. Funkenstein's lawyer said he was "just minding his own business" and was "singled out" because of his hair, which is not hard to imagine.)

> **Word to the RV Crowd:** If your crib is on wheels, it's not a crib; it's a car, and it more or less can be searched as easily as any other car, even though you live in it. Same is true with boats, trailers, and anything else you can think of that can go from point A to point B.

The following provides fair warning on how easy it is to get nabbed behind the wheel, and some survival skills from your in-house counsel for the outrageous risk takers among you.

First, of course, they've got to pull you over.

Bullshit, Er, Pretext Stops

Stopped for exceeding the speed limit by two miles per hour? Failing to wear your seat belt? Are those fuzzy dice obstructing your view of the road? Getting pulled over for piddly offenses like one of these is known in the business as a "pretext stop," used by police to investigate you when there isn't a good reason to pull you over.

Funky piercings, wacky hair, Dead stickers, white people in black neighborhoods, and black people everywhere else will all attract the attention of the police. They just can't say so because none of these observations are legal justifications to pull you over. What's a suspicious cop to do?

Wait and follow.

In most states, if the police suspect you of carrying drugs or committing any other offense, they can pull you over for *any* minor traffic infraction or equipment violation as an excuse to smell your car, ask you questions, and develop enough information to search you. The police can follow you for no reason, for as long as they want, waiting for you to commit a traffic offense. And you *will* commit an offense. Many, many a drug bust began with a broken taillight or an unsignaled lane change.

The Long and Winding Dope Ditty: M. Rubio was driving around with forty pounds of weed in his trunk one afternoon in southern Florida. Officer Michael Wilbur began following him because he looked just like the kind of dude who might have forty pounds of bud. Rubio kept his cool. *Drive straight, man,* he told himself, *drive straight.* Twenty miles he drove, hands wet on the wheel, eye in the rearview, knot in the belly, but he finally swerved just over the yellow line. *Curses!* Officer Wilbur hit the rollers with grim satisfaction. Now he had a (bullshit) reason to pull Rubio over. Officer Wilbur detected a "very moderately strong" odor of weed coming from the car when he pulled Rubio over. When he found the dope, Rubio knew the game was up, telling the cop he'd done a "nice job," and commenting, "I guess that'll be about 10 years." That sounded about right to the judge, and that's exactly what Rubio got.

Total Bullshit Stops and Racial Profiling

So you managed to sweat out the trailing cop without committing a single traffic infraction and you have no equipment violations. Now is not the time to pass around the victory smokes. You can be pulled over for trying too hard not to get pulled over. Complete stop at a stop sign? That's downright suspicious, and cops can always pull over anyone driving around in the Second Level of Doom (page 79).

Here is where a menacing cruiser rides up into the rearview to watch you squirm. Constantly checking your rearview, failing to make eye contact when he sidles up next to your ride, white-knuckled grip on the wheel, fidgeting in your seat, sitting too rigidly, out-of-state rental plates, trunk riding a little too low (indicating a couple bales of Mexico's schwagiest), pulling off the road at the sight of the fuzz or at a sign reading Narcotics Checkpoint 1 Mile Ahead (page 155)—this is all suspicious behavior, particularly if you happen to be of Middle Eastern persuasion, and cops tend not to be too picky about what qualifies as Middle Eastern. Dark skin? Dark eyes? Confusing headdress? Last name kind of a mouthful? That'll do.

Whether it's understood police policy, part of a quasi-legit drug courier/terrorist profile, or an individual cop's racism, racial profiling is a simple fact. It happens on the street. It happens at the airport. It happens on the road. It's not going the way of separate drinking fountains.

"I seriously doubt that the Clark W. Griswold family, on their way from Illinois to Wally World in the borrowed family truckster . . . would face such an array of police interest and interdiction, including 'Gunnar' the drug dog."

—A JUDGE IN IDAHO, DISSENTING IN A RACIAL-PROFILING CASE INVOLVING AN HISPANIC FAMILY TRAVELING FROM ILLINOIS. *(ALTHOUGH THE LITTLE GRISWOLD SISTER DID HAVE SOME POT, DIDN'T SHE?)*

The bare-knuckle reality is that if you're poor and/or of color, you're subject to more police scrutiny. More scrutiny leads to more searches. More searches lead to more drug busts. Before the Supreme Court legalized bullshit stops, a cop's motivation for why he pulled you over was something that you could attack. Now it's virtually impossible to litigate without evidence that the same cop has been pulling over nothing but black people, and you'll have to cite hundreds of incidents of his doing so. Very, very hard to prove. Consider the fairly obvious racial profiling a cop in Oklahoma got away with, only made obvious by a dissenting judge.

Racial Profiling Dope Ditty: On the afternoon of October 1, 1999, Michael Brumfield and Gilbert Houston drove past Officer Mark Black's cruiser on Interstate 15 in Oklahoma. Brumfield and Houston were young and black, were wearing tracksuits, and had braided hair. Officer Black swore that the reason he started following them was because they didn't have a front license plate and they were driving two miles per hour over the speed limit. Officer Black ran the plates and learned that the car's registration was not in order. He pulled the boys over, got them out of the car, frisked them, and asked them if they were into "gang banging." *Why would he ask them that? Had he been using a racial profile? asked Brumfield's defense attorney.* "I'm not certain what you mean by profiles. Could you explain that to me?" Officer Black responded. *Not heard of them, eh?* The defense attorney explained what a racial profile was to the veteran cop, but Officer Black said that he still couldn't "understand the question." The defense attorney had to let it go, and since the car's registration was out of whack, the stop and subsequent search, during which a whole lot of marijuana was found in the trunk, was given a 👍.

That's racial profiling. It's basically legal, and after September 11 more and more people find it acceptable, although the law doesn't make distinctions between potential terrorists and potential "gang bangers." In this case, the cop happened to score. Impossible to know how many black people Officer Black pulled over before Houston and Brumfield, but all those people can do is file a futile lawsuit to complain about the violation of their stinking rights.

Packing for Your Drug Trip

Packing for your drug trip is not as simple as sticking your blow up your yin-yang and hitting the road. (That's a good start, though.) First, you must be prepared to go to jail, because the odds of getting busted jump as soon as you're at the helm of the dopemobile. Second, you must be prepared to be jailed and stand trial wherever you're taking your dope or anywhere along the way. Stay close to home and your bust will be like any other, painful and humiliating. Leave the city or state and you will have to return to this place again and again for court appearances, assuming you make bail. This will be breathtakingly expensive and hard to explain to your employer, should you still have a job. Leaving the country? Things could get very ugly indeed (see "Crossing the U.S. Border," page 172). Finally, get busted carrying drugs in your car and it will get Jacked by the Police (page 313).

With all the dire warnings and advice duly considered and apparently unheeded, the following survival skills are offered up like spitballs for knife fights, but they should save you from yourself and from making matters any worse. They are not likely to prevent a cop from searching you if you're pulled over because he suspects you're carrying dope or might be a little wasted.

1. Legalize It

Bullshit stops are not always pure bullshit. There are equipment violations that will attract police attention no matter what. Nothing should be hanging from the rearview, and your windshield should not have spiderweb cracks. Expired tags and emission stickers will always get you pulled over. Always have *clean* license plates on the front and rear bumpers, even if your state requires only rear license plates. License plate bulbs must be fully operational. Headlights and taillights? Check. Correctly lined? Check. The police must be able to see clearly into tinted windows. And wear your seat belt. If not to save your dull life, then to save you from a drug bust. Ride around with any of these equipment violations, and you ride in the Third Level of Doom (page 79).

> **Poor in the Drug War:** Because poor people are more likely to be riding around in just the type of piece of crap with an assortment of equipment violations, pretext stops are still another reason it's easier to survive the Drug War with some loot.

2. Keep It Clean and Odor-Free

Clean people have clean cars. Nervous junkie freaks ride around with butts overflowing in the ashtrays, Happy Meal boxes strewn all over the car, porn mags (a must for any meth head on the go), and soggy parking tickets wadded up on the floorboards. A ride littered with debris is a sure sign of debauchery behind the wheel. Flip forward to "Live by the Tats, Die by the Tats" (page 169) for recommended driving attire; flip back to "Preparing for Battle" (page 82) for some grooming tips.

Obviously, if your car smells like booze or drugs you are screwed. At the same time, air freshener is always suspicious. Cops call those air fresheners that look like pine trees "felony forests" because they're so often used to mask the smell of weed. Although anything is preferable to that new dope smell, only rides with something to hide smell like fields of daisies.

3. Keep It Anonymous

America's so-called love affair with the car has criminal justice consequences because your loved ones reflect who you are, and they're suspicious, too. Don't let your car give the police a window into your corrupted soul. No matter how committed you are to the legalize-it movement, or the Dead, or Marley (Brother Bob is always suspicious), or Peace, or Justice, or your stinking First Amendment rights, do not put stickers on your ride that scream liberal dope-smoking commie faggot to the cop as he's walking up to your ride (see our unfortunate hippie's ride on page 172, for example): Something like a Support Our Troops, or a Mothers Against Drunk Driving sticker is a nice touch, unless it's obvious just by looking at you that you've taken a stab at irony.

Similarly, hip-hop whips are suspicious, as is anything else associated with young, urban culture, and even the wannabe white kids are suspicious. If your ride would be at home in the pages of *Dub* magazine (if you have to ask, your ride's probably safe), better not have any dope in there. The NYPD and the Miami Police Department deny it, but there have been allegations of hip-hop profiling by both police departments, and those are the cats with their rides in *Dub,* and too many have violated the Ninth Amendment (page 329) by talking or singing about their love of dope.

Cars That Go Boom: Like to roll through the hood rattling your neighbors' windows with six thousand watts of deep bass? Better not have any dope in the car. Most cities have noise ordinances, and you can be pulled over for a violation.

4. Keep It in the Trunk

Anything incriminating in the interior of your car—a couple of Philly's Blunts, for example—gives the cop the right to search the interior, but probably not the trunk (just yet . . .). Once the bright lights shine it's too late to be hiding the stash. The police will see you moving around in your seat and that is usually enough of a reason for a search. Your luggage—better yet, someone else's luggage—in a locked trunk is the only area of your ride that the police need even a mild excuse to search. But if a cop reasonably suspects that you have dope in the trunk (usually by blowing the Q & A session discussed below), he can detain you by the side of the road, sometimes for hours, waiting for a drug dog. If the dog "alerts," and it usually will, you have entered the Third Level of Doom, and the cops can bust open the trunk.

Surviving the Traffic Stop

The Roadside Q & A

The worst-case scenario has come to pass. If you haven't packed well for your drug trip, the following will not save you. If you have, the sun may shine, but keep the defense attorney's number handy.

1. Wait in Your Car and Keep Yourself Together

Cops don't like it when you jump out of the car to meet them halfway. This is aggressive and suggests that you have something to hide in the interior of your car. Calmly wait until the officer comes to the window and asks to see your license and registration. Keep your insurance and registration in the glove compartment and leave the glove compartment open wide, demonstrating that there is nothing incriminating or illegal stored in there.

Keeping yourself together also means having your license, insurance, and registration up-to-date and legit. If your papers are not all legal-like and straightforward, you are screwed. This is particularly true if you're driving a rental car. Drug dealers are always renting cars through one person, then paying someone else to drive the car. The more tangled the web is between who actually owns the car and who's doing the driving, the more suspicious it is.

2. It's Your World, Act Like You're Living in It

As noted in "Personal Dope Possession" (page 13), everyone on board should agree on (A) where you've been, (B) where you're going, (C) why you're going there, (D) how long you're staying there, and (E) whom you're staying with, including addresses and phone numbers. If you blow these questions, skip to "Busted!" (page 217).

The police are trained to ask you these types of questions to confirm their suspicions. It will not sound like an interrogation, but that's what it is. You are being observed very closely. You should not need questions repeated, you shouldn't be too helpful or too talkative, and it would be good if that vein in your forehead doesn't start throbbing. Again, no help for you nervous types. Deep breaths, maybe.

A few skills that you should carry over from the "Street Busts" section (page 81): Do not sound as though you've read this book and start announcing that you know your rights, always be in a hurry, and tell no lies; traffic cops can usually check anything you would want to lie about from the computer in their cruiser.

3. Get Ticket. Get Going.

Should you happen to clear the initial round of Q & A's and have your license and registration back in your sweaty palms, *it is time to leave,* credibly, because you're in a hurry. Any more conversation by you is considered a consensual chat, known in the biz as a "fishing expedition," which is technically illegal if it drags on too long.

Here's how your roadside drug bust will play out:

> **The Officer** [handing you back your license]: *We've been having godawful trouble with motorists transporting drugs and firearms right along this very stretch of highway.*
>
> **You** [developing knot in belly]: Good God, Officer! That's disgusting!
>
> **The Officer** [not buying your outrage]: *By the way, you wouldn't happen to have any dope or weapons in the car?*
>
> **You** [beginning to panic]: Of course not, Officer!
>
> **The Officer** [moving in for the kill]: *Then you wouldn't mind if I take a look, would you?*
>
> **You:** Ummmm . . .

If you refuse to consent, the cop will assume you have drugs, likely in the trunk, and call a drug dog. (The Supreme Court recently decided the police do not need any reason at all to have a dog sniff for drugs during a roadside stop.) If you do consent, the cop will tear apart your ride looking for the drugs. Cops have been known to keep electric drills in their cruisers to take apart cars right by the side of the road.

If all this sounds unfair and hard to beat, it is. Your attention is directed to the first sentence of your "Drug War Driving Lessons" (Your car is a bad place to party).

Narcotics Checkpoint 1 Mile Ahead. Drug Dogs in Use.

Say you're tooling along on the open road with some dope in your ride. A flashing yellow sign announcing a roadblock aimed at detecting drugs appears, causing you to panic, bail off the side of the road, and ditch your stash. This is what the police hiding in the bushes are waiting for. If you see a sign like this, *do not pull over* and *do not ditch your stash*. Keep driving, right into the belly of the beast. The chances are excellent that there is no roadblock at all, and even if there is, you are better off taking your chances than exiting the road or throwing dope out the window.

Warning signs like these are often a ruse, designed to send already paranoid drivers into a cold panic. Police are hiding in the bushes to observe the motorists' reactions, and, as you may have guessed, motorists usually start throwing dope out the window and pulling off the highway, right into the Third Level of Doom. A phony roadblock in Connecticut a couple of years ago yielded sixty-one arrests; the officer in charge commented with some satisfaction that "quite a bit of dope" was also discovered along the highway.

Ironically, the Supreme Court recently decided that a roadblock aimed specifically at detecting drugs is a violation of your stinking rights, since it's a search with no particular reason to suspect you of committing a crime. A sign announcing a violation of your stinking rights one mile ahead, however, does not violate your stinking rights. The police, moreover, are still free to set up sobriety checkpoints to keep the roads safe, or a roadblock to make sure everyone has their insurance, and if they happen to catch a few dopers, so be it.

Driving While Wasted

I think we can all agree that driving wasted is stupid and crazy dangerous and thousands of people die every year as a result of drunk driving. You already knew that, but the chances are excellent that you've done it anyway, probably more than once. (Maybe you didn't feel so inebriated, but that won't matter; there's no high-tolerance defense.) DUI's are the second most common crime in this country, right behind drugs, checking in with about a million and a half busts a year. Your in-house counsel, as always, recommends getting wasted at home and staying at home when you're wasted. But drunks tend to be the stubborn belligerent types. . . .

If You're Pulled Over . . .

The following is a modified version of the Roadside Q & A because stops for drivers actually on drugs or drunk are different from stops for motorists carrying dope. Your hopes and dreams are different.

1. **Remain Calm:** Repetitive advice that's worth repeating.

2. **Adjust for Lighting Conditions:** Turn on your dome light if it's nighttime. This eliminates the need to shine a flashlight in your eyes, and it's the law in some states. Take off your shades no matter what.

3. **Roll Down Your Window:** This will shorten the encounter and will prevent a waft of boozy air from blasting the cop in the face.

4. **Have Your License, Insurance, and Registration Ready:** Digging through the glove compartment prolongs the encounter.

5. **Keep Your Hands Where the Cop Can See Them:** This keeps the cop calm, which is as important as remaining calm yourself. Relax your grip on the wheel. White knuckles are suspicious.

6. **Maintain Eye Contact:** It's suspicious not to look the cop in the eye. For you meth heads, try to remember to blink.

7. **Be Observant:** Note the weather conditions. Did those high winds blow your Cooper Mini over the yellow line? Are those yellow lines faded? Do you have a mad hornet buzzing around your ride, affecting your driving?

Okay, I Had Two Beers Six Hours Ago

To get your bust rolling, the officer will ask you how much you had to drink that night. Don't tell a little lie; put some mustard on that dog. *"Nothing to drink tonight, Officer. As you can see, I'm the designated driver."* Never answer questions about how much you have had to drink that night. It's not okay to have had "a couple of beers," or a couple of bong hits, let alone anything hard-core. No cop is going to be understanding. He's going to be psyched you made his job so easy.

> ***DOPE NOTE:*** *HERE IS WHERE* PREPARING FOR BATTLE *IS VITAL. WHEN YOUR LIPSTICK IS SMEARED OVER THE SIDE OF YOUR FACE AS YOU HAND OVER YOUR ID WITH HANDS SMELLING OF DOPE, WEARING AN I-GOT-LOADED-FOR-FREE BRACELET, THE GAME IS UP.*

Should I Refuse to Do the Field Test or Take a Breathalyzer Test?

If you've never been busted driving drunk before and you're not deeply inebriated, you are probably better off rolling the dice and performing the roadside dexterity drills and taking the Breathalyzer. All fifty states have "implied consent" laws, meaning that as a condition of driving you have consented to the police checking your blood-alcohol level if they suspect you've been drinking. The penalties for refusing a test are usually harsher than actually getting busted for your first DUI. And if you're staggering about and reek like Wild Turkey when you get pulled over, you'll be convicted without any test. Worse, there's an excellent chance you'll get more time for refusing the tests.

"But I can't do that when I'm sober, man!" You're soggy-brained and more loquacious than usual; nevertheless, if you're doing the drills, try to not walk into a DUI bust by complaining that you couldn't recite the alphabet backward even during those few moments of the day during which you're not inebriated. Obviously, you're drunk if that's the case. Field sobriety tests are designed to be hard for drunks to pass, and they're not easy for straight people to get all A's on either. Thus, you shall not pass yours if you've been belly up to the bar for a while.

That said, be aware of conditions that might affect your performance. Soft shoulders, high-heeled shoes, tight shoes, tight jeans, crazy saggy jeans, slick surfaces, a physical handicap, and windy, cold, or rainy weather are all better than having no reason at all why you couldn't walk a straight line. A little something for your attorney to gnaw upon.

IF A POLICE OFFICER ASKS YOU TELL HIM WHEN YOU THINK A MINUTE HAS PASSED, DON'T STAND AROUND SLOBBERING ON YOUR SNEAKERS, IMAGINING A SECOND HAND GOING AROUND A DIAL. COUNT IN YOUR HEAD, ONE-ONE-THOUSAND, TWO-ONE-THOUSAND, THREE . . . NOW YOU'RE GETTING IT.

If you have been busted before, you may be better off refusing to consent to any sobriety tests and accept the penalty for failing to do so, which is sometimes less severe than a second or third DUI bust. *You are not required to perform the roadside sobriety test,* and it's best to refuse to do one if you're intoxicated, because all it does is strengthen the case against you. This is particularly true if you were *really* soused, because aggravated drunk-driving laws bring more pain for being more wasted.

As for the Breathalyzer, blowing tiny breaths of air or exhaling through your nose is not clever; it's a refusal to take the test, resulting in the same penalty as a DUI and probably pissing off the police, breaking the Sixth Commandment (page 328), and experiencing the consequences.

Lastly, if you happen to be wasted on drugs rather than booze, take the Breathalyzer; it only works for booze. If you're given the option between a urine and a blood test, take the urine test. Urine tests are much less reliable.

Can They Force Me to Give a Blood Sample?

It's "rack and screw" time again, boys and girls. If the cops want your blood, they are going to get it, one way or another, particularly after an accident. State legislatures have gotten wise to defense attorneys advising their clients to refuse sobriety tests. Most states have authorized "reasonable force" to be used to get blood from belligerent drunks. Like when the cops suspect you of eating your stash, "reasonable force" means the police can pretty much go off on you if you resist their attempt to draw blood—to the extent that it would be preferable to be simply bashed in the face and have a sample cup placed under your nose. Here's a San Diego judge describing a beating administered by six cops after a drunk "resisted":

I guess [the cops] could have talked to him for a long time and tried to talk him into [giving blood] or calm him down or change his attitude, but I am satisfied that the facts here were that when confronted with that prospect, the defendant, and he doesn't deny it, initially resisted with his left arm, tensing it, drawing it back. The police interpreted that, and not unreasonably, as not only resistance, but perhaps a threat to their own security. . . . [W]hen the police officer came and put a carotid restraint [choke hold] on him, there was a temporary, perhaps a couple of seconds . . . maybe four or five seconds, where he was limp, but that is the only evidence the court has before it as to the defendant's body essentially going in a limp fashion and otherwise cooperating.

The choke hold is "very common." "It is a very humane hold. It doesn't leave any marks. . . . This stops the person from swallowing, or eventually it stops the blood flow to the head, and he then passes out."

—A CALIFORNIA COP, TESTIFYING ABOUT HIS PREFERRED METHOD OF EXTRACTING BLOOD FROM AN UNCOOPERATIVE DRUNK. THE DA DESCRIBED IT AS A "LEGITIMATE JUDO COMPETITION HOLD." AND THE JUDGE? 👍

The judge went on to note with approval that "in the struggle, the police officers did cause substantial bruises both to [the drunk's] arms, perhaps wrenching his shoulder, caused in part by his own resistance. Also, caused marks in and about his neck by virtue of the [choke]holds they had on him, and that during all the scuffling more than likely his head, face, cheek and eye areas came into contact with police officers' arms, bodies, shoulders, floor and so forth." In the end, the judge—and the California Court of Appeals—

decided that the amount of force the cops used to get the blood was reasonable enough for government work.

Since we have seen how easy it is to find yourself in a "limp fashion" and have your face come "in contact" with a cop's "arms, body, shoulders, floor and so forth" during the "scuffle," give up the blood if they want it. A verbal objection is in order, but do not put up *any* physical resistance; they will bring the pain, and the judge will not have pity on you. If you have never been convicted of a DUI offense before and you don't resist, you may be able to work out a deal to plead guilty to a lesser offense, something like reckless driving.

At the Precinct . . .

1. **Call a Friend:** This excellent fellow will be able to testify as to how lucid and sober you sounded, and can get you an attorney, preferably one who specializes in DUI busts.

2. **No Talking and No Walking:** You are always being watched and listened to, and most likely videotaped, in a DUI bust, both by the side of the road and down at the precinct. A video of you shouting slurred obscenities and stumbling around your holding cell will not look good at trial (or on *Cops*).

3. **No Sobbing and No Sleeping:** Drunks tend to get weepy when they get busted, and then they pass out in a puddle on the floor. Sit upright in your cell looking as dignified as possible; if you must sleep, try not to sprawl limbs akimbo, as though you passed out.

4. Request an Independent Blood Test: If forced to give blood, ask to have it tested independently; most states allow for an independent blood test, which may produce different results and give your attorney a little something to work with.

I'm Not Drunk but I've Been Doing Crystal Meth All Night. Will the Police Be Able to Tell?

Driving high on drugs is also illegal and unwise and the police will be able to tell if they get a blood sample, or it will be assumed if there is evidence of drugs in the car. Sometimes a blood sample won't be necessary for the police to be fairly certain you're unfit to drive, as in actor Nick Nolte's drugged-driving bust. Anyone who saw Nolte's infamous mug shot, snapped after he was pulled over foaming at the mouth, driving down the Pacific Coast Highway whacked out of his mind on GHB, did not have to wait for the blood test results to be convinced he was having one of those out-of-body experiences GHB fans enjoy.

Nolte-esque episodes aside, drugged driving can be more difficult for the police to detect because many are not trained to do so, and driving on some drugs, particularly weed, is not as hard as driving when you're smashed.

That doesn't make it a good fucking idea.

Another problem with drugged driving that states are grappling with is that there is no standard for what it means to be high on drugs. Unlike booze, it's always illegal be on dope, but whether you were actually high at the time you were driving can be a little dicey to prove, since blood tests can't say exactly when you did drugs, unlike Breathalyzers. Some states rely on field tests. What has frustrated the authorities is that drivers high on drugs, particularly pot, are a lot better at passing field sobriety tests than drunks. It's hard to say that you were incapable of driving, or even impaired. You're just stoned.

> **"The drunk driver blows through a stop sign, the stoned driver waits for it to turn green."**
>
> —Anonymous

Nine states (Arizona, Georgia, Indiana, Illinois, Indiana, Iowa, Minnesota, Rhode Island, and Utah) have solved this problem in the usual manner these problems are solved: bust everyone. These states have "per se" laws, meaning that if evidence of illegal drugs is found in your car or in your blood, it is evidence that you were intoxicated. So if you smoke dope all the time, you will test positive for drugs, and it's possible to get busted for drugged driving, even if you happened not to have been high at the time. Usually, however, the cop, an "expert" on drug users, will testify at trial that in his expert opinion you were high, as evidenced by your smell, wild-eyed look, and slurred speech, and by the fact that you sat through three cycles of stoplight changes before easing through the intersection, giggling like a crazy person.

DOPE NOTE: DON'T PASS OUT IN YOUR DRIVEWAY; THERE ARE NO BONUS POINTS FOR BEATING THE ODDS AND MAKING IT HOME. YOU CAN GET BUSTED FOR DUI JUST FOR BEING BEHIND THE WHEEL OF A CAR. AND IF YOU ONLY MAKE IT

TO, SAY, SOME BUSHES OFF TO THE SIDE OF THE ROAD, GET OUT AND WALK HOME.

Aiding and Abetting the Wasted Driver

Like Hookin' a Brother Up, encouraging the driver to do some shots or have some dope to smooth out the ride is not only unwise and unsafe, it can result in a drug bust of your own.

Dumb Ass Dope Ditty: During the Fourth of July weekend in 1995 ("Avoid Amateur Hour," page 82), Lisa Ryun was a passenger in a car driven by Erin Ciccio. Lisa decided to share the weed the two were smoking with her brother, who was driving the car in front of the ladies' on Interstate 5 in Oregon. Erin pulled the car parallel to the brother's, and Lisa passed the pipe to him as they were rolling down the highway. About five minutes later, Lisa's brother drifted off the road, flipped over an embankment, and hit another car, seriously injuring everyone. Lisa thought it was her brother's fault, since he'd decided to smoke the dope. The judge saw it differently, deciding that Lisa was just as responsible for the motorists' injuries as her brother because she was the dumb ass who handed him the loaded pipe.

Airport and Border Busts

The Airport

Abandon All Rights Ye Who Enter Here

Criminal defense attorneys tend to keep in touch with a lot more of their old friends than your typical corporate cat. This isn't because we're a particularly sentimental lot. No, it's because old friends always call when they get busted. When your in-house counsel gets a call from an old, sometimes obscure, friend, he or she has usually been busted at the airport carrying drugs. This is for two reasons. One, people like to get wasted on vacation, more wasted than the typical night on the razz. While packing, they do a quick risk-versus-reward analysis and decide that they just can't be without their dope and hide it in the

The Airport All-Star Team

Bill Murray, Carlos Santana, Paul McCartney, Writer Aaron Sorkin, Whitney "And AyeeeeAyeeee will always love dope" Houston, Montel Williams, Dionne Warwick of *Solid Gold* and *Psychic Friend* infamy, Johnny Cash, NBA players Carmelo Anthony, Mookie Blaylock, Damon Stoudamire, Kareem Abdul-Jabbar, and Chris Webber, skateboard legend Christian Hosoi, and Olympic Gold Medallist John Drummond

—ALL BUSTED AT THE AIRPORT FOR DOPE POSSESSION

toiletry bag, maybe inside a shampoo bottle if they're feeling really sneaky.

But while the old friends (usually) know what being without their dope is like, they don't truly appreciate what the risks are, bringing us to the second reason people are always getting busted at the airport: you have no Fourth Amendment rights there. You can always be searched. It does not matter if you check your bags or carry them on; you are consenting to a search ahead of time. The toiletry bag is the first place they're looking, only stoners bring baked goods on airplane rides.

And the detection technology is getting tricked out. In 2002, for example, the Orlando International Airport employed some new-jack X-ray machines that could see through clothing to display everyone's naked body as they walked through security, essentially a strip search for all kiddies off to Disneyland. (There were a few objections, and they apparently stopped the high-tech go-go show.) General Electric's "ion track" machine, for another ominous example, can detect particles of dope (and explosives) emitted from vapors on the outside of luggage and clothes as small as a billionth of a gram (sufficient for about thirty years in Texas, page 8). New York City's JFK Airport should have one of the ion tracks this year.

Even with old-school technology, walking into an airport terminal is like walking nude through a police station with your belongings in a grocery cart, so you know where the only place to hide the dope is. That's right, you're going to have to get nasty with it, which is why it's so easy to wind up bent over a desk (see "Behind the Gray Door," page 171). If you cannot vacation without your dope, at the very least, keep it on your body and heed the fashion tips below.

DOPE NOTE: THE FEDS HAVE JURISDICTION OVER ALL AIRPORT BUSTS. ACTUALLY THEY HAVE JURISDICTION OVER ALL DRUG CASES, SINCE DOPE POSSESSION IS A FEDERAL OFFENSE. (FUNNY THAT THEY PASSED A CONSTITUTIONAL AMENDMENT TO OUTLAW BOOZE; THEY JUST KIND OF TOOK A SHOW OF HANDS ON DOPE.) SHOULD YOU GET BUSTED AT THE AIRPORT, IT'S POSSIBLE TO END UP IN FEDERAL COURT, BUT THE DEA'S POLICY—NOTICE THIS IS NOT A RULE OR A LAW OR A PROMISE—IS NOT TO PROSECUTE SIMPLE POSSESSION CASES, INSTEAD TURNING THEM OVER TO STATE PROSECUTORS.

Live by the Tats, Die by the Tats

Airport Fashion Tips

Though cured by a trip behind the gray door, there is a perverse sense of pride some people, usually dope smokers, have at being just the type of dude that is likely to get searched. We know you're a radical, not some corporate pig-in-a-suit, but wait until you arrive at your destination before distinguishing yourself from the bourgeois masses. Don't be so attached to your personal style that it ends up costing you your dignity. Take a shave. Take off your sunglasses, stud. Cover up the tats. Platform shoes are suspicious, since they can be hollowed out. Ridiculously saggy jeans are suspicious because they're easy to hide drugs in and because they're associated with young, urban, black culture. Tight Republican is, as always, the look you're going for. If you can't, or refuse on principle, to pull this look off, you should not be carrying dope, which you

Woody's Dodgy Dope Ditty: Itinerant traveler, surfer, dive instructor, and dope smoker, Woody, an Englishman from the Isle of Wight, looks just like the kind of guy you'd be sure to search if that was your job—shaved head, sleeves of tattoos, always looks a little wasted. Woody was at the airport in Athens, Greece, last year and happened not to have any dope on him. Confidently he strode up to the security area, tossed his carry-on into the X-ray machine, and proceeded through the metal detector, which immediately went off. A burly Greek security officer nodded at him to remove everything in his pockets and sent Woody back through. When the metal detector sounded again, the Greek got the wand out and passed it over his body. It went crazy for Woody's nipples. The Greek nodded at him to lift up his shirt. When he observed with great disgust the steal barbell studs protruding like pinky rings from each of Woody's nipples, he nodded toward the dreaded gray door. There, he pointed at the desk, snapped on a pair of latex gloves, and nodded at Woody one last time.

shouldn't be doing anyway. And for God's sake, take out the piercings.

Take a final fashion tip from Woody, who gets a faraway look in his eye when he tells that little ditty: Never wear any metal through the airport, and check for metal buttons, tinfoil in gum wrappers, Altoids, etc. You don't need to be carrying drugs at the airport for a grim Drug War tale to tell.

A more obvious but related lesson can be gleaned from NBA player Damon Stoudamire, recently busted by airport security in Tucson, Arizona. Damon cleverly concealed the ounce of bud he was carrying in tinfoil, which of course set off the metal detector and led to his third drug bust. Ironically, he was in Tucson attempting to finish his college degree.

Behind the Gray Door

Profile of a Jet Set Doper

Although there are never any guarantees at any airport, body searches on domestic flights are less common than on international flights. Fitting a drug courier profile and/or setting off the metal detectors is the easiest path behind the gray door, where there's always a lot of protesting and plenty of Vasoline. Candidates for rough treatment now, of course, include anyone who looks as though he might pray five times a day and/or any combination of the following standard fare stuff: Frequent round-trips to the same city and long flights with quick turnarounds are suspicious. Peeling off a few Franklins from a fat wad to buy your ticket will raise eyebrows. Not remembering how you paid for your ticket is hard to buy. Not having luggage is suspicious. Not having any particular idea why you're going where you're going is odd, particularly if you go there a lot. Needle marks on your arms are not good. As always, criminal records, which are at their fingertips, are suspicious. And good ol'-fashioned nervousness will screw you every time (although one judge in Florida found "excessive calmness" suspicious).

Get enough check marks on this list, ignore the fashion tips above, and you're in for a body search, and if your ass is clean, but still suspicious (page 97), the search will leave a scar. The factors cops consider in deciding to perform a cavity search are the same used by airport security, except airport security has lots more practice.

Crossing the U.S. Border

The rest of the world is divided into two halves. You're either going to a country with better, cheaper, easier-to-acquire drugs, or you're going someplace with the death penalty for importing drugs. Either way, it makes little sense to pack your little buddies and roll the dice. Anytime you cross the U.S. border, coming or going, you abandon your Fourth Amendment rights completely, and your passport can be revoked if you get busted coming into the States with dope, even for a misdemeanor drug bust.

International flights or drives across the border get the dogs out and the dour customs officials, who have the power to seize you longer and search you deeper than any other authority in the criminal justice system, save prison guards. And unlike with the ticket agent or airport security guard, lying to a customs agent is illegal. So when you're asked if you have any medication or contraband to declare, you are screwed because your only options are silence, lying, or admitting that you're carrying. Staring dumbly at the customs agent will not work, making a false statement is a separate crime, and confessing defeats the purpose of hiding that shit in the first place.

The border treatment is the search you endure to set foot on American soil and enjoy all the benefits of our criminal justice system. It can be a very rough initiation. Since more and more couriers are using their digestive system to smuggle drugs (something to think about the next time you're bent over a big line), the Supreme Court has set the bar very low

Eighty-eight Red Balloons: Arriving at LAX shortly after midnight on a flight from Bogota, Colombia (you know where this is going), Rosa de Hernandez presented her passport to customs officials, who were immediately suspicious. Not only was

Rosa coming from Bogota, but she had $5,000 in cash, no hotel reservations, and only a small piece of luggage. She was taken behind the gray door and given three choices: consent to an X-ray of her belly, take a crap for customs, or return to Bogota. Not surprisingly, Rosa chose the latter, but somehow they couldn't get her on a flight. For sixteen hours, Rosa refused food and water, and made "heroic efforts to resist the usual calls of nature," as one judge put it. Finally, after nearly twenty-four hours, Rosa was taken to a hospital for a cavity search, and a balloon full of cocaine was discovered; over the next four days Rosa passed eighty-eight more balloons. The federal judges of California's highest court thought the twenty-four-hour seizure, strip search, and cavity exam were unreasonable, but the Supreme Court gave it a 👍.

for what amounts to a "reasonable," "below the skin" search and seizure at the border.

Remember Rosa before succumbing to the temptation of bringing that little piece of hash back from Amsterdam as a souvenir. I know it's hard, but you've got to leave your beloved in Holland, where she belongs. Where she can be free. Travelers returning to the States from countries like Holland, Thailand, Mexico, Jamaica, and, of course, Colombia are automatically suspicious, making a search that much more

Word to the Pill Heads: Made a swing through a Thailand-all-you-can-handle pharmacy during your trip abroad? Importing prescription pills is illegal without a valid prescription. You must declare the medication at the border, have an original container, and have no more than a sixty- to ninety-day supply. A large quantity will look like it's for resale and will result in an arrest on either side of the border, as sixty-six-year-old Raymond Lindell would tell you if he got to know you better. The retiree from Phoenix, Arizona, spent almost eight weeks in a Mexican prison after getting nabbed with 270 Valiums, enough that the federales initially decided it was for sale. (Raymond had refilled his prescription in Mexico after his insurance company stopped covering Valium.)

likely, and federal charges for importing dope. Very bad on your resumé.

Getting Oblivious Abroad

Should you get busted with drugs or doing drugs abroad, lots of luck, Kemo Sabe. There can be no more terrifying experience than winding up in jail in a country where you don't speak the language and have no idea what your rights are or what's in store from the local criminal justice system. (But see *Busted! Backpacker's Edition*, coming soon.)

A couple of general principles to throw out to the mad desperate: Start collecting money and looking for an opportunity to buy your way out of the jam. Any opportunity. Any price. Whatever you have, whatever your companions have, it will be worth it. Nowhere is this more true than Mexican border towns like Nogales and Tijuana, where payment is a simple (one-sided) negotiation but the prisons are hard-core. (My guess is that Raymond of the Pill Heads spent all his money on the Valium or disregarded "Limbaugh Lesson #6," page 265.)

You also need to start stirring the pot. Call the American embassy, or have a traveling companion make the call. Whether the embassy will be able or willing to do much about it depends on what part of the world you're in and what your arrest record back in the States looks like. Whatever the case, contact American lawyers, influential friends, family, priests, rabbis, whatevers, and maybe even your boss to call and bring pressure on the diplomats to pay attention to your bust.

The last thing you should do is assert yourself as an "American." This will undoubtedly result in the worst possible treatment and double the bribe. Americans abroad should always understand that the locals assume you are an arrogant asshole deserving of what's coming until you prove otherwise by speaking their language. You are submitting to a whole new criminal justice system, *Midnight Express* style. Time to adapt. American backpacker types are targets for extortion around the globe and sometimes they really do just want to lock you up.

If nothing else, when in Rome, party with the Romans, keep plenty of cash handy, and hope that someone misses you.

The New Millennium Drug War

On the Internet, on Your Hard Drive, and in the Name of Fighting Terrorism

Doooope . . . in . . . Spaaaace

The Internet is a wild and wooly beast, a lawless, virtually unregulated universe where every nutball with a laptop and a dream has something legal, quasi-legal, or downright criminal to sell you (for free!). All you need is an Internet connection and a credit card to get your party started. We are bombarded with spam daily to buy every prescription drug available to ease the pain, get laid, get wasted, or all three. GHB is available. Ketamine is online. Pot seeds, legal only if they're incapable of germination, are everywhere. The new dope frontier, Salvia divinorum, is coming at you online. (Divinorum is a trippy drug, perhaps

destined to be the first drug to emerge solely from cyberspace into the mainstream.)

But unlike your typical dope deal, where once you've scored, you have probably gotten away with it—there are no cold case files of unsolved dope deals—buying drugs or paraphernalia online leaves a cybertrail, as does everything else you put out into space. The trail itself is generally not significant *unless* you get busted and the police are looking for additional evidence.

Forget the Fourth Amendment online. Like an overheard conversation, you have no privacy rights to anything that you "knowingly expose to the public." Online, everything is exposed to the public, and it will be assumed you do so "knowingly," no matter if the Internet is as baffling to you as sign language to a monkey.

I Just Ordered a Big Bucket of Xanax at SketchyMeds.com and a Brand-New Pipe at Phatbongs.com. Will a DEA Agent Be Making the Delivery?

Since the DEA usually goes after the dealers, and your local sheriff has lots of other problems to worry about, you probably won't get jammed making a buy online, particularly for a prescription med. (As always, absolutely no guarantees, and keep in mind that script fraud is a felony.) U.S. Customs and the Postal Inspection Service often seize contraband and send you a seizure letter in lieu of your dope, which will only leave you hanging and paranoid. More risky is buying paraphernalia, pot-growing material, or a large quantity of pills, and leaving your bloody footprints out there in cyberspace to be collected by the DEA.

For example, during the DEA's crackdown on paraphernalia sold over the Internet, the language quoted in the box was on a DEA website that surfers were rerouted to when they tried to access sites such as Aheadcase.com, which had been targeted. What the DEA's site didn't mention was that it collected the Internet Protocol (IP) numbers of everyone who tried to access the paraphernalia site. (An IP number is your computer's social security number and is considered information that you are know-

> **"By application of the United States Drug Enforcement Administration, the website that you are attempting to visit has been restrained by the United States District Court."**
>
> —Message received by Web surfers shopping for bongs on sites targeted by the DEA's "Operation Pipe Dreams"

ingly exposing to the public.) Buried deep in the DEA's online privacy statement was the following line: "In certain circumstances . . . we may take additional steps to identify you based on [the IP number] and we may share this information, including your identity, with other government agencies." The PATRIOT Act gives the FBI the authority to take those additional steps by demanding that your Internet service provider turn over your name, address, and screen name(s), which can be retrieved through your IP number.

While it should not be comforting to be in the DEA's database as a bong connoisseur, the DEA does not have the resources to devote to busting you on simple possession charges. The feds generally make their point with high-profile busts, like Tommy Chong's (page 44), and raids on medical marijuana clubs in California. But another tactic the DEA sometimes employs amounts to losing the liberty lottery. These are old-fashioned this-could-happen-to-you-lawbreaker! busts, similar to the lawsuits brought by the music industry against a few, biblically unlucky music downloaders, serving notice on the general public to be afraid, very afraid.

A *Busted!* Prophecy: Since the feds have been making script fraud and painkiller abuse much more of a priority, the DEA will take a few pill fiends' scalps in the near future.

For the moment, however, law enforcement is behind the curve online. Cyberspace has no borders and is simply too vast to patrol effectively. Absent a bricks-and-mortar bust that leads to your hard drive, the same principles apply to getting busted online as anywhere else: Do not make yourself a target. Don't launch a legalize-it website, sell dope, or otherwise raise your online profile. And do not send incriminating e-mails to anyone—particularly to anyone who might forward it along.

Confession Confetti

The Incriminating E-mail Scattering Through Space

An e-mail promising your girlfriend to "bring **E**van to the party" will look very bad should she end up in the ER. As our guest guru would counsel you, once you're on police radar, they go looking for e-trails, and they are always out there somewhere. An e-mail feels like a phone call but it lasts like an unfortunate yearbook photo; it's carved in stone, and copies are echoing through Internet service providers, online e-mail services, hard drives of all recipients, backup tapes of networked computers, and anyone it happens to be forwarded to.

> **"Get some more 'little blues.' "**
>
> **"You know how this stuff works . . . the more you get used to, the more it takes."**
>
> —E-MAILS RUSH LIMBAUGH REPORTEDLY SENT TO HIS DOPE SOURCE

The feds recently offered citizens a spooky glimpse of the future of cyberpatrol. They call it Carnivore. This baby allows the FBI to read all Internet traffic in whatever segment of the network Carnivore happens to be devouring. *Agent Smith is among you. You can feel him. You can taste him. But you won't even know he's there.* (A *Matrix* reference for the uninitiated.)

If You're Writing the Dope E-mail Anyway . . .

1. Never use a work computer: When using "your" "work" computer, never send an e-mail that you wouldn't feel comfortable explaining to a DEA agent or to your boss. Networked computers are backed up on tape, which keeps a record of all the e-mails that you send and the Web sites you visit. You don't necessarily have to fall under suspicion for an e-mail to haunt you. Should your company get sued and its e-mails be subpoenaed (very common), your boss is going to have to start reading your mail. The PATRIOT Act, by the way, allows the feds to seize your work computer if they decide it "belongs to the enemy," but the authority is limited to those flashes in history during which the "United States is engaged in armed hostilities."

2. Bland/Blank Titles: Don't put anything in the title of an e-mail that would encourage further reading. You have less right to privacy in the title of your e-mail than you do to its content because it's considered more "knowingly exposed to the public."

3. Trash and Burn E-mail: Trash any incriminating e-mail immediately upon reading and make sure your recipient is doing the same. The longer the e-mail sits in a service provider's system, your in-box, your sent-box, or an archive folder, the less privacy you have over the content of the message.

4. Muzzle the Hard Drive: Follow the instructions below.

Dope in the Hard Drive

It's difficult to get too fired up about the privacy rights of someone diddling little boys or plotting to detonate a dirty bomb at the Super Bowl, so we have the pedophiles and the terrorists to thank for the direction that computer privacy law is going. These are the people with the chat rooms the cops are monitoring and with hard drives stuffed full of very, very dirty laundry. No one has the stomach to stand up for these types when they get busted through information wrested from their hard drives, but the rules the courts are laying down for these trailblazing dirtballs don't apply only to them. They apply to you. And they apply to your mama.

Hello? Where Are You Taking My Computer?

Ripping the computer out of the wall and taking it down to the station for a cavity search usually requires a warrant, and computers and computer disks are routinely included in search warrants, particularly for drug dealers because they tend to keep better records than your typical burnout. The police generally get a warrant specifically for your computer based on some confession confetti that someone blows in their direction, or a nosy computer technician working on your laptop contacts them, or you get busted and the police are looking for more dirt.

But there's always your roommate letting the cops search your computer files while you're not home. Your roommate, your mom, your kids, and virtually anyone who opens the door to the police can consent to a search of your computer if they have access to it or it appears as though they do. The only way to prevent consent is to maintain exclusive control over your computer *and* the computer must be kept in your exclusive space. As to the computer itself, no one else can *ever* use it, you must password-protect all your files, and you must pay the Internet bill.

Your Hard Drive Knows You Better Than Your Mama (And She's Very Disappointed)

You've probably lost a crucial document to the whim of your computer's temperament before. You went searching for it, checking the mysterious "backup folder," which never seems to contain anything whatsoever. You tried the old restart trick, hoping a backup file would magically appear. Maybe you even called a computer nerd to have him run through his bag of tricks. But you didn't find it. It was lost and gone forever.

Nope.

What you needed was a "computer forensic specialist," also known as a cop with a copy of the EnCase program, or a version of the Norton Utilities program that didn't come with your computer. The cop would have no trouble finding anything you lost, or even intentionally destroyed. The simple plug and play programs provide a mirror copy of everything that was *ever* on your hard drive. It's like having a dead body in the house that you can never truly get rid of.

Records are kept of everything you do on your computer; it's a running tape recorder of your life. In a Windows environment, backup files are constantly being created, and they're never deleted. The user.dat and system.dat files keep track of the websites you visit, all your passwords, and all the software you have installed, and can trace messages downloaded from newsgroups.

Feeling paranoid?

Muzzling Your Hard Drive

Once you get your computer out of the box and jump online, your information is out there and it's being collected, probably by people much more computer-savvy than you. The following is about the best you can do without employing the services of a computer ninja.

1. **Zero Out Your Hard Drive:** Right now your free HD space is loaded with all the information discussed above. The only way it will disappear is when you start running out of memory and start putting new incriminating information over it. Zeroing out your HD will replace all those files with ones and zeros. This is not 100 percent effective, but anyone interested in your dirty laundry will have to get very high-tech to get at it now. The only foolproof way to erase the memory is drilling a hole in the HD. That's a little out of hand, though. (Lsoft Technologies Inc., lsoft.net, has a free program to zero out your HD.)

2. **Dump Your Cookies:** As you're probably aware, most websites place cookies on your HD to track you through cyberspace while you're watching all that porn and admiring the bongs. Cookies can be read by other websites and any tech-savvy cybersleuth, and they are almost as revealing as your HD; every site you have visited is right there along with your credit card

information, passwords, name and address. New cookies are attached every time you surf the Net, so you'll have to dump the cookies regularly to keep one step ahead of the information Nazis.

3. Download an Antispyware Program: Cookies are not the only way you can be tracked online; spyware can be attached to your computer like a baby leash. A program like Spybot—Search and Destroy, or one of the many programs available at download.com, can eliminate spyware programs that allow remote access to all your computer files, and these programs will notify you when a remote thread has been put on your hard drive by a tracking Web site.

SANITIZING YOUR HARD DRIVE RIGHT NOW IS JUST PARANOID. AFTER YOU GET BUSTED, IT'S DESTRUCTION OF EVIDENCE.

Vigilante Hackers

The New Millennium Posse

It's hard to imagine the local sheriff handing out Citizen of the Year plaques to citizens who broke into their neighbors' houses, dug through their file cabinets, read their journals, looked through their photo album, and then took anything that they deemed suspicious to the police for further investigation. Here in the information age, however, this gets a from the judge because the hacker caught the feds a dirtbag pedophile. The lone hacker gets a couple of e-mail thank-yous from the authorities to archive for a rainy day and *Hi ho, Silver! Awaaay!*

Never mind that he searched your computer illegally. *Are we going to prosecute the hacker who unearthed a scumbag little-boy rapist, even if we could find him?* No way. It might be different if the hacker had actually broken a window and crawled into his house, but that's not necessary when we have the Internet. The civil libertarians (not that anyone's listening to them) are left to fret about the slippery slope. First it's the pedophiles; next it's the pot smokers, er, supporters of terrorism.

The Drug War and the War on Terrorism

Strangers in the Night, Exchanging Glances . . .

Anyone who got high and watched the 2002 Super Bowl probably remembers when the halftime commercial rolled linking the dime bag you scored to your support of terrorism. And certainly drug money has been used directly and indirectly by a lot of despicable people and organizations, including Al Qaeda, and including the CIA in Nicaragua, Panama, and Afghanistan. But so long as the demand for dope remains insatiable and dope remains illegal—both certainties if history is any guide—drug money, which accounts for 8 percent of international trade, will be used to support any organization that will supply the demand. Ironically, the deposed Taliban regime had one of the world's most effective domestic drug wars, demonstrating that the only effective way to curb the masses' enthusiasm for getting high is chopping off their hands and executing them. (Now that those bastards are gone,

Afghanistan's drug trade has really taken off again, accounting for 39 percent of its gross domestic product in 2003 and breaking all records in 2004. *Democracy, baby!*)

Whatever its merits, the connection between terrorists and casual drug users is being made by the folks in charge of jailing both types, and they have demonstrated their willingness to fight both wars at once. What has civil libertarians concerned (not that anyone's listening to them) is that the laws passed now and decisions being made in the name of fighting terrorism are applicable not only to terrorists. And as we have seen with the "Old-School Antidance Laws" (page 136), once a statute is on the books, its original purpose tends to get lost over the years.

The USA PATRIOT Act, also known as the "Uniting and Strengthening America by Providing Appropriate Tools Required to Intercept and Obstruct Terrorism Act," was the first piece of legislation passed in response to September 11. Passed without debate days after the attack, it takes aim at the Fourth Amendment, giving the FBI, for example, the authority to search your home without telling you about it, and the power to force doctors, libraries, bookstores, universities, and, perhaps most significantly, Internet service providers to turn over your records without a judge issuing a warrant (not that that was ever such a hurdle).

To have a sniff at your dirty laundry, the feds write up a "national security letter," stating that the information is relevant to an ongoing investigation and the information must be provided. *There is no requirement that you be specifically suspected of terrorism, and the gag provision of the PATRIOT Act makes it a crime for you or your attorney to speak publicly about being investigated.* A federal judge in New York has found the gag provision unconstitutional, a violation of the First Amendment. (The ACLU was barred from speaking publicly about its suit challenging the constitutionality of the act during the same period the Bush administration was lobbying to have the law renewed.)

Fundamentally, the PATRIOT Act and the war on terrorism have sped up the direction that the Fourth Amendment was going anyway. The feds were already tracking people through the Internet. In essence, the police could already search your house without telling you (page 101). And racial profiling had already been legalized (see "Bullshit, Er, Pretext Stops," page 143); they've just added a new suspicious shade of brown. What has that fascist, "Let's see your papers" feel are the secret investigations and censorship.

Drug Test?

Why Would I Object to a Drug Test?

Doing dope can of course get you busted, but it can also cost you your job. Most of "The Incredible Shrinking Fourth Amendment" is dedicated to avoiding getting busted by the police, which can cost you your job. This section is devoted to on-the-job drug testing, which cuts out the middlemen.

> **"There is no drug exception to the Constitution . . . [D]ragnet blood and urine testing ensures that the first, and worst, casualty of the war on drugs will be the precious liberties of our citizens."**
>
> —The late Supreme Court Justice Thurgood Marshall

Dedicating all the urine samples to Nancy, Reagan ushered in the era of drug testing in the workplace, and Clinton, still smarting from I-Didn't-Inhale gate, pushed to bring widespread testing to small businesses through his National Drug Control Strategy. (Clinton, by the way, spent more money on the Drug War during his first four years in office than Reagan and Papa Bush spent combined over twelve years.)

Today, the vast majority of companies employing more than five thousand people subject their employees to drug tests, and over 40 percent of companies employing more than one thousand people drug-test job applicants and/or current employees. And they are catching plenty of dopers; in 2002, about 10 percent of the 20 million to 25 million people subjected to a drug test flunked.

Dude, I Am Soooo Fired; Everyone's Gotta Step to the Beaker at the J-O-B. That's a Violation of My Stinking Rights, Right?

So long as you are not singled out because of your race or your sex and you're not horribly humiliated in the sample-collection process, any private employer can require you to submit to a drug test for no particular reason. Aside from the relatively few states that have drug-testing statutes, there are no limits burdening a private employer's right to test their employees. They're bound only by their conscience. (Listen to the evil laughter.) "Public employees"—anyone working for the city, county, state, or federal government—can, however, cling to our emaciated friend, the Fourth Amendment.

A drug test that violates your Fourth Amendment rights will depend on the type of test and your line of work.

Grabbing You by the Short and Curlies

Random, Suspicionless Drug Testing

People who do dope, even on their own time, are assumed to be untrustworthy, irrational, erratic, susceptible to blackmail and bribes, dangerously clumsy, and unproductive when they bother to show up. Gotcha! drug tests therefore get a 👍 anytime the public has some stake in your job performance, a good reason not to want you getting bombed at work. The higher the stakes, the more random and humiliating the testing can be, including "direct observation" of you providing a urine sample—that's next to you, not behind you, for the boys and the girls, although judges sometimes get a little squeamish if your boss looks right at the source.

Contemplate your fascinating job. Do you need to be able to shoot straight? Drive between the lines? Do you have access to the city's water supply? The city's dope? Are you in charge of busting other citizens doing dope? Are you working with, or even near, children? Do you work at a prison? If you were really loaded, could you take a shot at the president without leaving your desk? Is your brain cluttered with state secrets? Are we risking a core meltdown if you nod off at your post?

If you answered yes to any of these questions, you can be required to submit to virtually any type of drug test, unless you're running for office. The Supreme Court decided that there's no "special need" to have dope-free politicians, only the lackeys they appoint.

Drug Testing in the Second Level of Doom

Mr. Johnson, We Noticed You Missed Your Chair When You Tried to Sit at the Conference Table This Morning

Stagger out of the morning office meeting mumbling about the tracers coming off the fluorescents and drug tests are the order of the afternoon. Any unexplained happiness, bloodshot eyes, productivity even worse than usual, napping on your keyboard, calling your supervisor a smelly slut, exchanging blows at the company picnic, and/or hitting the lights, dumping the water cooler over your head, and insisting that everyone get a groove on will all lead to a dope test. No matter how meaningless your job, drug testing based on reasonable suspicion of drug use always gets a 👍, and no policy needs to have been in place.

Testing is of course in order if you actually do your dope at work.

Dope In, Dope Out Ditty: Montgomery County, Ohio, officials noticed that Johnny Pernell's office smelled an awful like pot smoke, and then they found a couple of roaches in his government-issued trash can. This made Johnny's employers suspicious that he was smoking marijuana on county time, but Johnny didn't want to take a drug test, and Johnny don't work there no more.

Assuming you're not so settled into your work routine that you feel at ease throwing your feet up and smoking a fatty at your desk, one of the more common ways employers decide drug tests are in order is through snitches, and the snitches don't have to be particularly reliable types. You can be dimed out by your drug dealer, as Atlanta firefighter Tommy Everett was, or your delusional brother, as prison guard Daryel Garrison claimed. How about your ex-girlfriend who calls your boss to "get even"? No problem! as (ex) Chicago cop Curtis Moore learned the hard way. Spies can also be planted in your office to suggest who ought to step to the beaker, as the employees of Georgia's Board of Lights and Water were unhappy to discover.

Finally, as with everything else in the Drug War, the easiest way to fall under suspicion is to have a prior drug bust on your record that your employer is aware of (see "You Want to Pretend This Never Happened?!" page 323), or a positive drug test in your dark past. For your kind, anything short of punching in at nine and punching out at five without incident will be sufficient grounds for testing.

Postaccident Testing

Ms. Jones, We Couldn't Help Noticing You Ran Over a Bag Lady in the Parking Lot This Morning

Accidents happen, but people who do dope are more likely to get into accidents. This isn't a particularly controversial rationalization for drug-testing employees after they've totaled the company car, although a lot of pot smokers think they're better drivers when they're high because the paranoia makes them cautious. (Not something you're going to want to offer up in your defense.)

Although being involved in an accident doesn't automatically mean that you can be tested, it's a nice start, and a serious on-the-job accident—something like running over a bag lady or derailing a train—is plenty of rationalization. It won't matter if there's no evidence that drugs had anything to do with it. Nor does it matter if the accident was not your fault. It can be a "below the skin search" with no particular basis to suspect you of doing drugs.

Similar to the drugged-driver situation, flunking a postaccident test does not necessarily mean that you were high when the bag lady went down, but that will not get you off the hook. It's accepted that off-the-job drug use affects on-the-job performance. It doesn't really matter how you felt the next morning. All the bumps in the bathroom last night? They count for a few days.

Weeding Out the Junkies and the Dumb Asses

Preemployment and Scheduled Testing

NFL players know when they are going to be tested in advance, yet every year scads of these dumb asses blow millions of dollars because they can't put down the pipe for a few weeks, and their fans are no different, out there risking their crappy little paychecks to get bombed. Judges generally take the view that if you can't keep your shit together long enough to apply for a job or pass a drug test that you know is coming up, they're not going to bail you out, and no one should have to hire you.

Preemployment testing is even easier to rationalize because you won't get fired, you just won't get the job, although if there is no "special need" for sober people to perform the job, you can challenge the testing policy. This will be a losing, time-consuming, *pro se* (without a lawyer) lawsuit, resulting in much agony and no money and no job. No attorney in his right mind would take your case, because you're likely a litigious dope fiend, and they make bad clients.

Finally, one thing to keep in mind while you're lying in your parents' basement, getting blunted and watching TV. Before the unemployment checks run out, you're going to have to put the pipe down and go for a jog. Many employers don't mention the drug test until after they've interviewed you, usually eliminating the need to do the tests, as the junkies tend to slink away or file a lawsuit. On a more positive note, thanks to the Americans with Disabilities Act, an employer cannot ask you about your past use of drugs. A history of drug use is considered a disability; current drug use is a liability.

> **Enjoying Those Sick Days?** Going on medical leave again? Better not be vague or confused about what ails you and better not do dope while you're gone. Unannounced drug tests following medical leave are common. Also beware of testing done by a physician without your knowledge; the results can be turned over to the employer if you have signed a waiver. Check the company policy—it's buried in that book somewhere—particularly if the company is using a self-insured plan.

The Gotcha! Drug Test . . . Take It or Leave it?

If you arrive at work one morning and find a specimen jar attached to a chain-of-custody form sitting on your desk and a wave of panic washes over you, you have a hard decision to make. Been on a bit of jag the last few weeks? Does it take more than one hand to count the substances you've been abusing? If so, you may be better off refusing the test because failed drug tests—even false positives—are very hard to explain away, as discussed below. But if you do refuse to take the test, your only recourse will be to immediately contact an attorney to seek an emergency injunction, asking a judge to bar the drug test until he decides whether or not it would be a violation of your Fourth Amendment rights. This is another of those futile *pro se* lawsuits in which to embroil yourself. The best you can hope for is that there was no basis to suspect you of doing drugs and you are not in a "safety sensitive" position.

The advantage of taking the test is that you can challenge the results, or the manner in which you were tested. Say, for example, your boss locked you in your office and stared at your schlong, tapping her watch while you tried to queue up a sample. Under these circumstances, the manner in which the sample was collected would be "unreasonable" and the test would be thrown out, even if there was a good reason to suspect you of doing dope.

Tips for the Gotcha! Test Takers . . .

1. Do Not Admit Drug Use: Like drug possessors confronted by a cop, dirty urine carriers often abandon any chance of defending themselves when confronted with the odious prospect of a drug test. In a panic, they confess that they're going to fail the test, or they admit drug use after a positive result. Either way, once you have admitted drug use, the test is irrelevant.

2. Do Not Tamper with Your Sample: Toilet water, Visine, loogies, and anything else not originating in your bladder will be detected and reported as a tampered sample, which can make you look worse than actually failing the test. More suspicious employers put dyes in the toilet water.

3. Insist on a Split Test: This means filling two separate beakers so a second test can be performed if the first sample comes back positive. Employers will not usually accept the result of a separate second sample, even if it was only a few hours after the initial sample. If the employer won't have it retested, you can.

THE SECOND SAMPLE IS THE ONE THAT SHOULD BE GIVEN TO THE EMPLOYER, AS THE FIRST OUT OF THE TAP IS USUALLY THE DIRTIEST.

4. List All the "Medications" You're On: You will likely be asked to list anything that might cause a false positive. It's too late to go back and add something to your list after you've flunked a drug test. Nobody's going to buy that you "forgot" about those ludes you've been taking to make it through the agony of your workday. Anything over-the-counter, any prescription pills, and any funky supplements should also be included. In other words, start building your GNC Defense now (page 204).

5. Schedule an Afternoon Test: Early-morning urine has the highest concentration of dope. The later in the day the test is taken, the better, assuming you have something to hide. Suffer from stage fright? That's considered a refusal to provide a sample if you can't squirt one out after three hours and downing forty ounces of water, grounds for a good sacking. And it better be a nice-sized sample, checking in at about ninety-eight degrees with a mellow yellow hue.

But . . . I Can Explain! Ah . . .

A public employee cannot be summarily fired for failing a drug test. You are entitled to some kind of a hearing during which you will have the opportunity to explain why you flunked. Most private employers will also give you an opportunity to get creative, but it is very, very hard to come up with a plausible explanation. Many have tried. Most, like the Drug War casualties below, have failed:

Dr. Bruce Hinkley of Texas: *I had some crack monkeys staying at my house. They must have used the stove to cook their cocaine. The residue from the coke got on my hands while I was cooking and I accidentally inhaled it.*

The Judge: Hmmmm. That's one I haven't heard, but . . . no.

John Wiegant of California: *I was destroying the meth lab in my garage and I inhaled the fumes.*

The Judge: Ah, no.

Tobey Anderson of Wyoming: *I used Mother's Mix mouthwash for my gnarly canker sores and it contains cocaine.*

The Judge: Going to have to call that one bullshit.

Deloris Adams of Louisiana: *I ate some hemp seed oil.*

The Judge: Not unless you were injecting it.

Mario Quintanilla of Texas: *I drank some herbal tea in Mexico called Te Nervioso; I think it's full of coke.*

The Judge: You're fired!

Paul Guitard of Philadelphia: *I ate some funky-tasting brownies of unknown origin.*

The Judge: No.

NFL #1 Draft Pick Darrel Russell: *I inhaled some secondhand bong hits.*

The Judge: No.

Russell: *Uh . . . My drink was spiked with E?*

The Judge: No.

Russell: *How about, I didn't know about the drug test.*

The Judge: And no again.

Passive inhalation of marijuana is probably the most common excuse, but it never works, even in a hot-boxed car or living with a chronic dope smoker blowing bong hits in your ear all night long. Women sometimes claim that they must have absorbed coke through their man's semen, which is actually possible. But if you've absorbed enough sperm to flunk a drug test, losing your job is not likely your biggest problem (or it's a hazard of your profession).

Simply put, there's not much you can say that hasn't been said. While false positives are very common, they are very hard to explain away. And if you miss a scheduled test, à la Darrel Russell, you'd better have a *much* better reason than simply forgetting about it, particularly if you've failed one before. Absent a credible explanation or a violation of your Fourth Amendment rights (random testing without a "special need" or staring at your schlong), there are only a few ways to successfully challenge a positive drug test.

Defending Your Positive Drug Test

The following is relevant for anyone with a job, not just public employees. Also note that these are all nice defenses, but you will be using them in your wrongful-termination suit. A private employer is not obligated to use any particular test or to retest a positive urine sample. She can sack you and refer the matter to the legal department to squash your *pro se* lawsuit like a pesky gnat.

1. The Bogus Test Defense

Like DNA testing, drug tests are often viewed as infallible. The rule of thumb is that dope tests don't lie, dopers do.

Companies that perform the tests are in business to make money, so their testing procedures are touted as 100 percent reliable. Likewise, employers are in business to make money, so they'll often use the cheapest—and most unreliable—testing method available. But like DNA testing, *no* test is perfect; much depends on the method of testing and how the testing was done. Mistakes are common.

A few of the most common types of drug tests and some of the problems associated with them to highlight in your lawsuit:

On-site urine testing, designed to pick up a single type of drug, costs about $3 a pop, so it's gaining in popularity. Accuracy? It's right about half of the time. Hair testing has caused a lot of panic because it can detect your mamma's drug use while you were in the womb. (Actually the testing usually detects drug use for about ninety days, but it can go back as far as four years, depending on how sophisticated the test is.) Your hair, however, is exposed to all kinds of crap, making the tests more unreliable. Worse, African Americans, Asians, and Hispanics are ten to fifty times more likely to test positive than a light-skinned person with the same drug history, because of the differences in hair thickness.

Sweat patches have become the rage in the fun world of parole and probation drug testing. The patches are popular because they're cheap and hard to beat; if you take it off it's impossible to reattach. These too, however, are susceptible to contamination from the environment, but since parolees are the ones most often given a patch, no one really believes them when they say it's lying.

Neither blood nor saliva testing, which can detect drugs

for only about three days after the last line is snorted, are common in an employment setting. Blood testing is rare because you need a nurse of some sort to start drawing blood and it's expensive. Saliva testing is sometimes used by the police to determine if a suspect is high on drugs rather than wasted on booze; it's similar to a field test to determine if a substance contains dope, but it's not common and not particularly reliable.

Laboratory urine testing is by far the most common and reliable test, aside from gas chromatography–mass spectrometry (GC-MS). If they go GC-MS, you're going to need Barry Scheck pounding the podium for you (worked for O.J. on the DNA), or move down to one of the other defenses offered below. Or maybe you can give the lab techs a blow job in exchange for a negative test result. That was the going rate at Bulldog Laboratory in Oklahoma City, according the local district attorney. Before one woman decided she'd rather flunk a drug test than give a lab tech another blow job, Bulldog Lab performed court-ordered testing for probationers and also did the preemployment screening for thirty-eight local businesses. (The techs reportedly accepted cocaine or plain old cash as well before they were indicted on racketeering charges.)

2. The GNC Defense

Athletes are especially found of the GNC (General Nutrition Centers) defense. A GNC defense means that you took some sort of supplement or medication, or ate some very funky food, that explains away the positive test result, or resulted in a false positive. Fancy cocaine tea from Mexico ain't going to get the job done, but if you can establish that the test was a false positive as the result of something you ingested or some medication you were taking, for which you have a valid prescription, you've got a shot. Some AIDS medications have reportedly accounted for false positives for marijuana, but only dronabinol, synthetic THC sold as Marinol, is a surefire excuse for a positive THC test. Cold medication can sometimes cause false positives for meth. Cough syrup can cause false positives for opiates. And finally, if you've got the courage to give it a shot, poppy seed bagels can also explain the presence of opiates in your urine. (If you're going the bagel route, start eating them daily and conspicuously around the office. *"Mmm . . . mmm, how I love these POPPY SEED BAGELS!"*)

3. The "Wasn't Me" Defense

Everything that happens to your urine from the time it leaves your body to the time it gets to the lab for testing is known as the "chain of custody." If there's a break in the chain—some point where it's not clear how your urine got from point A to point B—the sun may shine on your ass, since it's harder to prove conclusively that it was your urine sample, or because it may have been tampered with if no one knows where it was for a little while (worked for O. J.).

To establish the chain of custody, employers will usually seal the urine sample in front of you, have you sign and date the beaker, and then document what happens to the sample every moment until the test is completed and you're fired. Ideally, you want your urine to sit on a shelf somewhere for a couple of weeks before some nameless, faceless piss boy picks it up and ships it to a place like the Bulldog Lab in Oklahoma, which invests about 50¢ on the test, loses it for a little while, and then sends it back with apologies to the piss boy. Federal testing, however, is very meticulous, and the chain of custody will likely not be in dispute.

Beating the Dope Test

I know this is what you've been waiting for: the desperately clever drug fiends ingeniously beating the system by the old switcheroo or by employing the ultimate masking agent. Urine swaps are where the Drug War begins to drive people to the absurdities and humiliation its infamy is built upon. Women will fill condoms with clean urine and stuff it in their holiest to pass the test; men will tape bags of clean urine in their armpits and run tubes through their clothes and into their drawers; some go strap-on, hooking themselves up with a prosthetic penis filled with clean urine. Sixty-five-year-old men bleach their hair blond to foil hair testing. It goes on and on. If you find yourself in the john, dildo in hand, sweating over a bag of someone else's urine, it's time to consider rehab.

Cleaning your own dirty urine is fraught with peril. Anyone familiar with the Balco scandal or who happened to catch thirty-five seconds of the 2004 Olympics is aware that drug testing is an arms race. When the testers come up with a new test, the athletes come up with a new way to beat it. But you don't have access to the nukes employed by professional track athletes to mask the dirt in their urine. You have the wives' tales told over the Internet. Drink pickle juice! Vinegar!

Cranberry juice! Eat vitamin C! These home remedies, alas, are only marginally effective at beating tests for amphetamines or PCP, and suspicions will be aroused that you tampered with your sample, because most people don't sit down with a keg of pickle juice to get sloppy.

Pot stays with you a long time and is one of the more difficult drugs to cleanse from your system. Aside from not smoking any, exercise and lots and lots of water are the only universally accepted methods of flushing out your system. Drink too much, however, and the lab will report the sample as "diluted," which translates as "tampered." Which brings us to our last Internet legend: vitamin B. Vitamin B does not change the content of the urine; it makes it darker and it will appear as though it is not diluted, but if it's tested anyway it will not matter.

> **"Ricky should've taken his own advice and used the proper masking agent."**
>
> —ESPN commentator Sean Salisbury, on Miami Dolphin running back Ricky Williams, who failed his third dope test just before retiring from the NFL.

> **Word to the Urine Donors:** Sacrificing your urine for a loved one is illegal in Texas, Pennsylvania, Nebraska, and South Carolina.

And then there's the endless crap sold over the Internet and at your friendly local head shop. The quality, cost, reliability, and legality of these concoctions vary wildly, so it's always a roll of the dice. Ricky Williams, for a bad example, swore by Extra Clean with a thirty-two-ounce water chaser, but he failed three drug tests during his NFL career. It should be noted that Ricky preferred marijuana to the drug Paxil to treat his social anxiety disorder, which, I imagine, is a tough disorder for a superstar pro football player to manage.

Dope Detection Periods

If you wake and bake every morning, check in at three hundred pounds, never exercise, and have maybe two good craps a week, the dope tends to stick to your ribs. In other words, the length of time a drug can be detected in a urine test varies from drug to drug and person to person. The following are therefore *rough* estimates:

Marijuana	5 to 30 days
Cocaine	Up to 3 days
Opiates	Up to 4 days
Amphetamines	2 to 4 days
Ecstasy	2 to 4 days
PCP	10 to 14 days (up to 30 days if you really dig it)
Barbiturates	14 to 21 days
Benzodiazepines	2 to 4 days
Oxycodone	2 to 4 days

So I'm Officially a Feckless Fuckup; I Flunked My Dope Test and Got Booted. Am I Going to Get Busted Now Too?

Rejoice. You probably will not go to jail after you get fired, because most jurisdictions do not prosecute people simply because there is evidence that they used an illegal drug. Also, the consent-to-test forms generally do not allow a positive test to be turned over to the police for prosecution or to a third party.

However, if your test was done after you ran over the bag lady or there is some indication of criminal activity resulting from your drug use, the DA may be able to get access to the test results because they're evidence of a crime, aside from just doing dope. And if you are out on bond or on parole and have somehow held on to your job, a positive drug test will be evidence that you have violated a condition of your release and your employer may be required to turn it over if the DA requests it.

Finally, if you work for the federal government or for any company receiving federal money and get busted, you must notify your employer within five days of the conviction, whereupon your boss is required to fire you, give you some demerits, or send you to rehab.

FLYING HIGH AGAIN

Priors and the End of the Fourth Amendment As You Knew It

It's fitting to end the Fourth Amendment by having a look at what happens if it happens again. If everything that has been said about the Fourth Amendment thus far has felt like a black hole sucking you toward "Busted!" wait until Daddy gets home and finds out you've gotten busted again; you'll never be able to sit on your Fourth Amendment rights again.

As we have seen when you're "Tipping the Scales of Bullshit" (page 31), a prior drug bust changes everything about how the criminal justice system looks at you. Anyone who has been busted once is simply a more suspicious, feckless, untrustworthy, and unsympathetic junkie forever after, making it that much easier to descend into the dark depths of the Third Level of Doom. And in the age of information, arrest records are at the cops' fingertips, and even if The Computer is wrong—not uncommon—the police are entitled to rely on its bogus information to justify searching you.

How does this play out in the everyday? Get pulled over, the cop takes your license, goes back to the cruiser, swipes the bar code on the license, sees that you've been busted before, and a Pavlovian search instinct grabs hold. A search must follow. Should your crib come under suspicion, the cops will find out who lives there and look up your record. Bang goes the rubber stamp, if they bother asking a judge for a warrant at all. "No-knock" warrants are much easier to attain against someone with a prior because the judge knows that you'll be desperate not to get busted again and be flushing that shit pronto, if you know what's good for you.

Any leeway a judge might give to someone who says the cop intimidated him because he didn't know his rights will not be given to you. You know your rights because you've been busted before. (My clients will read this book with a lot of knowing nods of the head, perhaps a smack to the forehead.) Your consent to search will always be voluntary. Force used during your arrest is more likely to be considered reasonable. You are more likely to be subjected to drug tests at the behest of your employer. You are more likely to be denied bail and jailed for longer periods of time without being charged, and you will absolutely be given a harsher sentence.

Lastly, the first thing criminal appellate attorneys think about when they give (long) odds at getting a reversal: *Let's have a look at his record.*

Take heed of the Seventh Commandment (page 328). Bust you once, shame on the Drug War. Bust you twice, shame on the junkie.

PART 3

Everything that you have read up to this point is aimed at avoiding everything that follows. The pain. The humiliation. The money. The cold, tight handcuffs. The smackdown. The strip search. The cough and squat. The fingerprints. The mug shot. The nights in jail. The sadistic prison guards. The clammy bologna sandwiches. The permanent arrest record. The end of the white-collar era of your employment.

It all starts right here.

Rights? I Got Your Rights Right Here, Motherfucker!

Ah, the soothing melody of your Miranda rights, perfect to ease the transition away from liberty and a must for every bust. You'll likely be calling your lawyer from your holding cell suggesting a lot of reasons why you should be sprung immediately, beginning with the cop's failure to read you your rights. *Aha! Kiss my ass, copper! I'm outta here, baby!*

Unfortunately, this is not one of those get-out-of-jail-free technicalities we'll be searching for. You have no right to have your Miranda rights read to you. Sad and true. For the uninitiated, this is the first glimpse at the dark underbelly of the criminal justice beast, where all those criminals' rights you hear so much complaining about and all those technicalities the scumbags are always getting off on meet bare-knuckle reality.

You are now under arrest. You are powerless. You have no rights. Not even the right to know your rights, and even if you are read your rights, you're not going to be thinking about them. You're going to be thinking, *Holy shit! They're reading me my rights! I'm getting arrested!* Next comes the panic as liberty slips away, followed by a lot of begging, pleading, denying, and lying—all of which are being duly recorded by your arresting officer.

You Have the Right to Remain Silent, Motherfucker!

There is absolutely nothing that you can say that will change a cop's mind once he has decided to bust you, so nothing positive can come from saying *anything*. (Cops are the same way about parking tickets—once the pen hits the pad, it's all over but the whining.) Remember all that advice on being Face-to-Face with the Fuzz, and Answering the Bell and The Roadside Q & A? You can forget that now.

You have failed. You are busted. It is time to *shut the hell up*.

The police are free to demand an explanation as to why you were discovered slobbering uncontrollably, staggering through the aisles of Rite Aid guzzling cough syrup in nipple clamps and assless chaps, but you don't have to answer them. And since this is going to be hard to explain away, you shouldn't try. (Let your attorney give it a shot.)

The right to silence is a widely misunderstood and grossly underutilized right. Fundamentally, it's your right not to incriminate yourself, which is why you never have to say anything, or perform roadside sobriety tests, or admit how many rails you snorted at "The Hard-core House Party" (page 34). But you are free to incriminate yourself all you like. You can run. You can scream. You can resist. You can deny. You can rage against the Drug War. You can plead with the cop, "It's only pot, man!" All you are doing is incriminating yourself.

Put another way, the evidence against you continues to gather long after the bright lights shine, and it's usually the suspects themselves that pound the final nails into their coffins. Picture yourself in one of those wacky Fox police shows where wasted "suspects" engage the fuzz in high-speed car chases, slam into trees doing 150 miles per hour, suffer crippling injuries, and still try to crawl away from the cops like the guy from *My Left Foot*. The video not only makes gripping drama, it's great evidence that the cop's suspicion was justified, and it will be used against you.

DOPE NOTE: THE ONLY INFORMATION THAT YOU MUST PROVIDE UPON ARREST IS YOUR PEDI-

GREE INFORMATION, ALSO KNOWN AS YOUR NAME, ADDRESS, DATE OF BIRTH, AND SOCIAL SECURITY NUMBER. COPS DON'T LIKE IT WHEN YOU REFUSE TO GIVE UP THIS INFORMATION AND WILL LIKELY GIVE YOU A SMACK TO THE HEAD JUST ON PRINCIPLE, SO OUT WITH IT.

Another benefit of silence: The more times you open your mouth, the more times you're going to have to be consistent with what you say. Whatever you blurt out is your story, and you'll have to stick with it to the bitter end, no matter how outrageous it begins to sound. Proclaim "It's only pot, man" when a cop searches your backpack and it will be impossible to blame it on the houseboy later (see page 17), as it will be obvious you knew about it. Nothing said, nothing inconsistent.

While anything you say will be well documented in the cop's complaint report, which is essentially the only record of what happened, the cop's version of events will be very simple and vague. It will have some flexibility. Say for example a cop steps across the threshold of your front door and arrests you without a warrant. That's (probably) an illegal arrest. But a veteran cop is not going to write in his report that he arrested you illegally and hope your defense attorney doesn't notice. The report will simply read that you were busted at your house. At the suppression hearing, the actual arrest will have taken place as you left the house, making it legal and consistent with the cop's notes. (See "The License to Lie," page 273).

Cops are always bellyaching about paperwork not just because it's less fun than busting you, but because it's yet another piece of paper that your attorney will use to cross-examine them if they aren't 100 percent consistent. (They hate that.) With a vague report, all a defense attorney can do is call the cop a liar; he can't claim his testimony is inconsistent with his notes. Rookie cops, however, sometimes learn the hard way not to get too carried away with their note taking.

Dry Heaving Dope Ditty: Although juvenile delinquent "Peter G." was only thirteen years old and weighed in at a ready 110 pounds, he still managed to slam down nine brews one summer evening in California. Another boy happened by and Peter stabbed him in the back with a screwdriver for no good reason. As the victim was running to a nearby police station, he noticed that he still had the screwdriver in his back. He pulled it out and gave it to the cops upon his arrival. Not the swiftest of drunks, Peter was standing outside the precinct when the cops went outside to look for him. "What's that cop doing with my screwdriver?" slurred Peter as he was taken into custody. Officer Joseph Sanchez's notes indicated that Peter was "very intoxicated," and he'd underlined "very." He also reported that Peter was too wasted to comprehend, particularly after he began vomiting and dry heaving during his interrogation. But when the DA wanted to use the statements Peter had made between dry heaves, Officer Sanchez suddenly decided that Peter hadn't been hanging around the precinct in a drunken stupor after all; he was, ah, "faking" being drunk. In light of the officer's notes, though, the California Court of Appeals didn't buy it and threw out the statement. *(Yes, if you're thirteen, barely register triple digits, down 108 ounces of beer, and vomit on* *the cop's shoes while giving your statement, and he writes all that down, your statement might not be used against you.)*

DAs, by the way, don't like a lot of paperwork either because if there's any good news for you in it—say, the lab plumb lost the dope—they have to turn it over to you. (They hate that.)

You Have the Right to an Attorney! (And you'd better ask for one.)

No matter what the police are accusing you of, or what kind of intimate showers they're promising you in Boys Town, the only thing out of your mouth upon your bust should be a *polite* request—not a belligerent demand—to speak to an attorney. No one, least of all your arresting officer, is going to run right out and get one for you, but the police are not authorized to question you after you've asked for an attorney. This of course doesn't mean that they won't, but your answers cannot be used against you. *Strike a blow for liberty!*

DOPE NOTE: *EVEN IF SOMEONE HAS RETAINED ONE FOR YOU, YOU DON'T HAVE THE RIGHT TO SPEAK TO YOUR ATTORNEY UNTIL THE BAIL HEARING, WHICH MAY NOT BE FOR A COUPLE OF DAYS. THESE COUPLE OF DAYS WILL BE PASSED IN JAIL.*

Can I Get a Witness?! Where My People At?!

Your only power during your bust is your power to observe. Where are you? Where were you when the cop came up to you? What time was it? What are the lighting conditions like? What time did you get to the precinct? This is all information that may be useful to your attorney when you finally get to meet him. Also note the badge number and the names of the arresting officers and, if at all possible, get the names of anyone who witnessed your arrest. Your cop will always have a witness—his partner—and if he's solo, backup is on the way. Like a good defense swarming to the football, cops swarm to any arrest situation. When you see five cops taking one person into custody, or three cruisers stopped for one miserable little meathead in a Pinto, it is not necessarily because the bustee is a particularly dangerous or loathsome criminal, it's because cops back each other up, with a nightstick if necessary, and on the witness stand if necessary.

Should you be so fortunate as to get busted with friends not also collared, make sure they're taking good notes, contacting an attorney, and following you to the precinct. These people are your only contact to the outside world, and you're probably going to need them. The Department of Corrections in your hometown is likely held together by a couple of Commodore 64s and a lot of late-night bus rides; it's easy to lose someone for a weekend, maybe more; much depends on how hard someone else is looking for you. A witness will also be able to testify as to how cooperative you were during the arrest, and you *will* be cooperative, one way or another.

Resisting Your Arrest and the Excessive-Force Experience

When the bright lights shine, put the lighter down, step away from the bong, and come out with your hands up. The police have the authority to beat you senseless if you resist arrest, and what constitutes "resistance" is very, very liberally construed. It is therefore essential not to offer *even verbal* resistance to your arrest. The police do not have to wait for you to physically resist; start making noises like you're not going down without a struggle, and they can bring preemptive pain.

Nightsticks, pepper spray, stun guns, choke holds, hog ties, shots to the groin, and good ol'-fashioned knuckle sandwiches like the one Ms. Alberts experienced have been given a 👍 to subdue anyone resisting arrest. Force is not required to be even roughly equivalent to your level of resistance. (Rodney King was resisting arrest.) And even if your arrest was completely bogus, you can still be tried and convicted for resisting your bogus arrest if the police discovered you wandering in the darkness of the Third Level of Doom. That is, they had probable cause to believe you had committed *any* crime, even if it turns out that you hadn't actually broken the law. So break the Sixth Commandment—Thou Shall Not Piss Off the Police (page 328)—at your own peril.

"At this point, to restrain the plaintiff, [Officer] Ogletree punched Ms. Alberts with full force on her left cheek. This blow quieted the plaintiff. She was then placed under arrest for disorderly conduct, harassment of an officer, and resisting arrest, and transported to the 34th Precinct."

—A U.S. DISTRICT COURT JUDGE, SUCCINCTLY SUMMARIZING THE TYPICAL RESISTING ARREST EXPERIENCE

It would be nice if the police did give you a good working over, then the charges against you would be thrown out. Seems fair. A caning ought to be sufficient to repay your debt to society. But it does not matter how much force it took to get you in front of the judge to answer for your dope; your crimes will not be forgiven. The thinking is that it's better to lock you up than to let you walk just because you took a couple of shots to the dome that you probably had coming. And you have a remedy. *Sue the sons of bitches!* A favorite pastime among our nation's incarcerated citizens. (Not that anyone's paying attention to them.)

An excessive-force experience will not only change how you feel about criminal defense attorneys, the guys who can get you out on bail; it'll also give you a new appreciation for personal-injury lawyers. The slip-and-fall guys can get you paid. And if you are looking to get paid, a great way to provoke a beating and beef up that pain-and-suffering award is to indulge in a lot of cursing and vows to sue while you're getting busted. Cops hate being sued.

"I SWEAR ON ALL THAT'S HOLY, I'M GOING TO SUE THE SHIT OUT OF YOU TWO BITCHES, I SWEAR, I SWEAR, I SWEAR TO GOD!" So swore Arthur Lockett just before the bitches allegedly gave him a couple of shots to the head and Officer John Stuewer inflicted "a series of wicked body blows." Meanwhile, according to Lockett, Officer Karen Thomas kneed him in the thigh and choked him. Lockett's lawsuit was summarily dismissed, but it certainly had the ring of truth. He did sue the bitches after all, and the capitals in Lockett's holy vow are not mine; the judge included them in his opinion to add a little flavor.

Excessive-force suits like Lockett's are dogs because police officers are immune from suit unless they gratuitously beat the piss out of you, and also because you'll be filing your suit after you have been convicted of possessing the drugs for which you were busted. Fairly or unfairly, the drug bust costs you your credibility with your typical judge, as the quote in the sidebar demonstrates. Thus, you have little shot at winning an excessive-force suit without getting the charges against you dismissed (or if you're charged only with resisting arrest). You'll also need medical records documenting at least one badly broken bone; scarring is also good, a limp is excellent, but none of that "tingling hands" nonsense. A videotape of the incident and/or a credible witness is probably going to be necessary as well.

"The habit of lying comes doubtless from the fact that users of . . . narcotics pass the greater part of their lives in an unreal world, and thus become unable to distinguish between images and facts, between illusions and realities."

—The D.C. Federal court, on doper credibility

But even with all these excellent facts on your side, a typical trial judge will take a look at everything you scribbled down on the toilet paper in your cell and decide that even if everything you say isn't total bullshit, you still have no case. Like O. J. "wrastling" with Nicole, your beating will be characterized as "a scuffle," during which your various body parts "came in contact" with various inanimate objects and parts of the officer's body, like his fist, elbow, knee, etc.—all caused by your resistance to the arrest. (See the San Diego judge's description in "Can They Force Me to Give a Blood Sample?" page 161.)

Sometimes, however, an appellate judge will have pity and allow a bustee's side of the story to see the light. Compare how the trial judge presented Edward Arthur Jones's pathetic pile of facts in his excessive-force suit with how the appellate judge presented them.

The He Said, She Said, You Must Be High Dope Ditty: One thing both judges agreed on was that on the morning of November 3, 1999, Edward Jones started getting cabbaged like there was no November 4.

What were the circumstances of the boozing?

He said [trial judge]: At 8:00 a.m. Jones "began drinking straight whisky in preparation for his day at work as a carpenter." By 8:30, he had had about three shots and "[d]uring the drive to work [he] had as much as another 6 ounces of Canadian Mist Whisky." Jones then "decided to go hunting instead of to work." On the way home, however, Jones "purchased another fifth of Canadian Mist. Apparently having finished off the first fifth, [and] started drinking from a new bottle around noon, and [to quote Jones]: 'I sat right there at the house and drunk most all of it.' "

She said [appellate judge]: "On the morning of November 3, 1999, Jones began drinking Canadian Mist whiskey, and he continued doing so throughout the day."

Both judges also agreed that at some point, wasted as he was, Jones realized that he had a court date the next morning, and decided his "best bet" was to call 911 and have the cops take him to jail so he'd have some first-rate documentation that he had stopped drinking at some point and he'd make his court date.

How did the 911 call go?

He said: "[to quote Jones], 'Shoot, I was pretty well drunk by then. You know, I couldn't tell you exactly what [the dispatcher] said or nothing.' "

She said, quoting Jones: He said that he was "drunk" and would like "for an officer to come and get him and take him to jail so he could get sober."

No one doubted that the police showed up at Jones's house at some point and took him to jail in the back of their vehicle.

How did Jones get in the police cruiser?

He said: Jones "was escorted to the sheriff's vehicle where he passed out."

She said: Although Jones had not committed a crime, he was cuffed behind his back before he was put in the cruiser. Nonetheless he was polite, "answering 'yes, sir' and 'yes, ma'am' to the [officers'] questions."

How did Jones get out of the car?

He said: "Upon his arrival at jail, [he] recalled someone saying, 'Get out of the car,' but he wanted to lie in the back seat and sleep instead."

She said: "[O]ne officer told Jones to 'get out of the car.' Another 'grabbed' Jones by the 'center part of the handcuffs' and 'got him out of the car.' "

Why did Jones start cursing at the cops?

He said: He was "drunk and got to cussing."

She said: Jones was in pain from being "jerked" out of the cruiser by his handcuffs and "slammed down in the chair" at the precinct, and he began having trouble breathing because of the way he had been cuffed behind his back in the chair.

How did the officers respond to Jones's complaints?

He said: The police "asked Jones to be quiet several times, with no positive result."

She said: The police "told him to shut the fuck up."

How did Jones's nose get broken?

He said: After Jones took a swing at one of the cops [*with his hands cuffed???*], the officer either "miscalculated" when he was "utilizing a restraining hold" and [*oops!*] broke his nose, or it may have "been broken when it contacted the floor—a scenario which finds no evidence in the medical record."

She said: Jones attempted to stand up from the chair, whereupon the cops "knocked him to the floor and jumped on him"; a knee was in his back and Jones "felt his nose go 'whaa' and saw a puddle of blood."

What happened in the holding cell?

He said: Jones continued to "violently resist" and "brutally kicked a female deputy." It "took four deputies to get him handcuffed and shackled."

She said: Jones was thrown into the holding cell, smashing his head on the wall. Shortly thereafter, he was observed "lying on the floor in a fetal position," weeping. There was a "basketball" sized puddle of blood "on the floor next to his head and big clots of blood coming out of his nose."

What happened next?

He said: Jones was taken to the hospital.

She said: The cop came out of the holding cell "shaking his hand," commenting that Jones "got a tough mouth," and "that his knee accidentally hit Jones's nose."

How bad were Jones's injuries?

He said: He had some "small facial cuts and a nose broken in a manner consistent with an inadvertent blow," caused by his own resistance.

She said: Jones's nose was "splintered or crushed into numerous pieces." He also had a "1.5 centimeter laceration over the bridge of his nose," a "gaping" laceration of his "upper lip" that required ten stitches to close, and bruised ribs, and he had to have "surgery to repair his severe, significantly displaced nasal fracture."

So did the cops use excessive force?

He said: "The evidence indicates that [Deputy] Keller exercised incredible restraint in not applying greater force."

She said you must be high: "Jones has presented evidence that he voluntarily came to the sheriff's department and was never under arrest or suspected of any crime." But "in order to quiet him down . . . Deputy Keller knocked Jones to the floor and then jumped on him, crushing his nose, lacerating his nose and lips, and bruising his ribs."

While the reversal of the trial judge's decision is virtually unheard of, the open disgust he showed for Jones, whose blood-alcohol content was a meaty .45 percent, was not. Basically, he decided that it wasn't unreasonable to beat the snot out of any asshole who calls 911 because he's too wasted to get to court. But the appellate judge decided that while Jones may be an asshole, you can't just beat the snot out of him in the name of resisting arrest. (Jones, you'll notice, had what he needed for his suit: he had committed no crime; and he had a witness; a nicely documented, severely broken bone; and some excellent scarring.)

Carving Your Drug Bust in Stone

Booking

After you have been subdued—one way or another—you'll be taken to the precinct to get booked, making your bust official and getting the ball rolling toward your inevitable guilty plea. As anybody who has been subjected to a "perp walk" or had his drug bust shamelessly exploited in a book like this would tell you, getting arrested is a very public, humiliating, sometimes painful gauntlet to endure.

That doesn't mean that it can't be used for public entertainment, as the judges of Manhattan's top federal court noted in the quote to the right. This is true even though you have not been convicted of anything, and it's still true if you are never convicted of anything. *Piss on your presumption of innocence!* The presumption of innocence does

> **"[P]erp walks are broadcast by networks and reprinted in newspapers at least in part for their entertainment value."**
>
> —Court of Appeals for the Second Circuit, deciding that a little public humiliation is good for the soul

nothing for you during the arrest process, although as "Jail/Holding Cell Hell" (page 237) makes clear, it will feel like you've already been tried and convicted and punished in the extreme for your "alleged" crime.

During booking, you must provide fingerprints and a mug shot. And you *must* continue to keep your mouth shut. All too often arrestees learn what they're being charged with and end up making an incriminating statement. *"What!? I wasn't selling that dope! I gave it to her!"* (An admission of both possession and distribution.) Everyone in the precinct is out to get you. They're supposed to be out to get you. The criminal justice system is adversarial. The desk sergeant, the mug shot photographer, the fingerprint guy, and anyone else within earshot—their jobs are to put lawbreakers like you in jail.

Ready for your close-up?

Like everything else during booking, your mug shot can be used against you. It's not helpful if you look like you were out of your mind. Some people smile, which is weird and too much of a wild card, so I advise against that. A blank stare is ideal. Don't look defiant or smug, as that will be the judge's impression when he's looking at your file, and smug, defiant types get extra pain. If possible, check your look in the mirror and comb your hair before the photo is taken. If nothing else, your mug shot is less likely to be put in wide circulation if it's a nice, boring, sober-looking shot, unlike our friend Mr. Nolte (page 164), whose credibility really took a blow after his close-up made the rounds.

Now You Want a Phone Call, Motherfucker?!

Three rights that everyone knows they have when they get busted: the right to have your rights read to you (wrong), the right to an attorney (wrong), and the right to a phone call (wrong again). There were no phones when they were writing the Constitution, and no judge has seen fit to read a right to a phone call between the lines, although most states have statutes allowing bustees to make a call after booking. But there are no guarantees; it will depend on the circumstances of your bust, and it's not a get-out-of-jail-free technicality if you're denied a call.

Sometimes a cop will deny you a call just to be a dick. Sometimes the only phone is a broken pay phone in the holding cell, or it will work but one of your new roomies will have stolen all your money. Get busted with a lot of other people during a club crackdown, a "quality of life" crime sweep, or a "fuck the police" protest, and you may not get a call at all, or it might not be until the next day (particularly in the last type of bust).

Should you get a phone call, don't call someone who cares. Call an attorney. It's understandable that you would want your mama after you've been arrested, but the only person who can help you now is a criminal defense attorney. Most criminal attorneys, unlike your slip-and-fall guys, have emergency phone numbers, and, unlike your mama, a defense attorney won't waste your time with irrelevant questions. *What were you doing in nipple clamps at the Rite Aid?!* If you don't know a criminal attorney, call someone who will get you one. (You may now be obliged to call your mama.) As discussed below, simply having a private attorney at your bail hearing betters the odds of getting sprung. (For tips on choosing an attorney, see "Limbaugh Lesson # 5," page 260.)

The Phone Call Script

1. Get the Facts Before You Call: Make your call count. You never know when you'll be able to speak to the outside world next. At minimum, you'll need to be able to relate the following: (1) where you are, (2) how long you have been there, (3) what you have been charged with, and (4) your booking number—the number on that little sign you'll be holding in your mug shot. If you don't know these basics, you'd better ask somebody. You have the right to know what you are being charged with.

2. Deny, Deny, Deny: Do not implicate yourself during your call. Jailhouse phone calls are recorded. Admit nothing. Tell your attorney/mama, "I have been accused of blah, blah, blah. But it's all bullshit." And do not discuss your immigration status over the phone if it's anything short of full citizenship. A miserable little dope bust can get you deported. (See "Now We Bring the Pain," page 311.)

3. Spread the Lie: Time to invent a cover story as to why nobody's heard from what's-her-name lately. It's never certain how long you will be in custody, and you're going to need some time to regroup anyway, so have someone call in sick for you at work and clear the calendar for the next few days. Do not call yourself. The background clamor and wails of pain in jail are very distinctive and hard to explain away.

4. Raise Money: Time to kick off the won't-you-please-save-this-junkie's-ass telethon. You're going to need money to retain an attorney and to post bail if you're not released on your own recognizance. Don't ask your drug dealer for bail money because it's possible that whoever posts bail will have to testify under oath as to where the money came from. Judges are reluctant to take drug money to let bustees out of jail.

5. Find Out Who Your Friends Are: Get character witnesses for the bail hearing. Family is good; priests/rabbis/whatevers are always nice, as are landlords you haven't outraged, and business associates, unless that's what landed you in the joint to begin with.

6. Get Your Paperwork: Depending on how serious a drug bust you're facing, you're going to need to establish your community ties, particularly if you can't find a character witness, aside from your mama. Deeds, leases, rent receipts, utility bills, school records, and the like are excellent to show you're not such a drifter scumbag after all. If there is no time to get these documents together, ask your attorney to make a couple of calls to verify your employment and/or residence. Because your defense attorney is an "officer of the court," her word will be credited by the judge, however reluctantly.

After booking, the best-case scenario is that you'll be issued a summons, ordering you to appear in court for arraignment, where you will enter a plea of guilty or not guilty. In most states, if you have been busted with any illegal drugs or on a DUI charge, you will not go home. Instead, you'll be taken to jail at least until you are arraigned or detoxed. If you're charged with a felony, it is not uncommon to be held in jail until you wise up and Beg for Mercy, Punk (page 287), or until your trial, which will not be for many, many months.

Time for a Squat and Cough

A search Into Your Ass (page 95) by a cop is not routine, but it's like shaking hands to a prison guard, and drug offenders like you are the top candidates for body cavity searches because drugs are easier to hide up your ass than, say, handguns, and no one is worried about your rights anymore. Supreme Court justice Thurgood Marshall aptly described a typical jailhouse search: "[A]n inmate must remove all of his or her clothing, bend over, spread the buttocks, and display the anal cavity for inspection by a correctional officer. Women inmates must assume a suitable posture for vaginal inspection [often accompanied by a 'squat and cough' order to dislodge contraband], while men must raise their genitals. And . . . because of time pressures, this humiliating spectacle is frequently conducted in the presence of other inmates." The humanity of this practice notwithstanding, courts have given this very thorough procedure for ensuring a drug-free environment a 👍 (Justice Marshall was dissenting), and it will likely be done more than once during your stay.

> **DOPE NOTE:** ANOTHER GOOD REASON NOT TO RESIST ARREST. IT MAKES A STRIP SEARCH MORE LIKELY, NOT ONLY BECAUSE YOUR ARRESTING OFFICER WILL NOW ENJOY SEEING YOU SUFFER, BUT ALSO BECAUSE IT IS ASSUMED THAT THOSE WHO RESIST ARREST ARE MORE LIKELY TO HAVE SOMETHING TO HIDE.

Jail/Holding Cell Hell

Jail is not for sissies like you, it's for murderers, rapists, and stickup punks. Alas, there is no sissy jail. There's only regular old jail, and every dirtbag the police pick up is sent there and packed into the same sweaty holding cell with you to wait for arraignment (some will be waiting for their homicide trial, or serving shorter sentences). Here again is where you'd like that presumption of innocence to kick in, so you could get out of jail or at least go to a jail for people who are simply waiting to be formally charged with a crime. But no distinctions are made—and you can be incarcerated just on a cop's say-so for up to forty-eight hours, longer on the weekends and holidays, or if you get "lost."

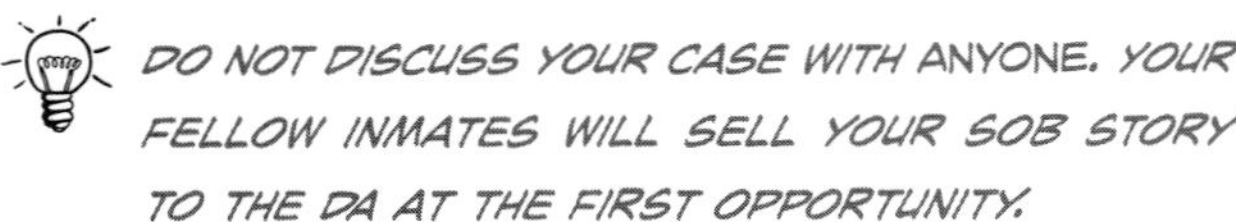

"Jail" is often more brutal and revolting than "prison," where you go after you've been convicted; so much so that bustees who've been through the system before are often anxious to plead guilty just to get the hell out of jail and start doing their time in prison, where there has been some effort to separate the homicidal, ass-raping, gang-banging, car-jacking, wife-beating pimp rollers from the *very sorry* dope smokers.

So what's jail like?

Vomit will be strewn. Some here. Some there. Cockroaches will be riding rats bareback over piles of feces. Junkies ripe with disease and suffering from withdrawal will be howling in agony. Drunks will vacillate between shouting obscenities, weeping hysterically, and expelling the odd fluid. The anxiety of the mentally ill, who account for about 10 percent of the prison population and at least as much in jail, is exacerbated by the stressful conditions, making their behavior odd and unpredictable, even by jail's bottom-of-the-barrel standards.

You will not sleep. You will not smoke. The cell will be

"[T]he noise seemed to increase after midnight . . . a deep-voiced inmate, evidently deranged, shouted an obscene, incoherent monologue, beginning, 'Ah want mah beer, you hear? Ah want mah beer . . . ,' over and over like a broken record."

—A FEDERAL JUDGE IN BOSTON DESCRIBING A NIGHT HE SPENT IN JAIL (OBSERVING) packed like a mosh pit, particularly if you get busted during Amateur Hour (page 82), which is likely, since this is when you're most likely to get sufficiently wasted to attract police attention. If it's winter it will be colder than the prison guards. If it's summer it will smell like a homeless Roman orgy in a cesspool. The food will taste like ass-wiped bologna. And if you're white, you'll be feeling mighty conspicuous. (See "Now We Bring the Pain," page 311, for sentencing disparity between black and white people.)

Sound good?

> **"Once I found a cigarette butt inside a meatball I was eating."**
>
> —A FORMER INMATE ON JAIL CUISINE

Time for a Crap?

Murderers, rapists, and stickup punks have been down this road before and have adapted to institutionalized shitting. Shitting will be a challenge for you. In your cell, there will be a community toilet. It will not have curtains and probably won't have toilet paper. If there is toilet paper, the chances are good that you're not man enough to fight for your square. The toilets themselves will not have seats, and even if they did you would not sit on them, because the toilet will be overflowing with its unmysterious contents.

Phoenix, Arizona, sheriff Joe Arpaio—an infamous asshole who, among other indignities, forced inmates to wear pink underwear—kept the toilets so revolting in the Maricopa County Jail that he featured them on his now defunct Web site, crime.com, to deter people from doing dope.

Is it working? I didn't think so.

Please, Mister, I'm Begging You, I Need Some Clean Drawers

Try not to vomit on yourself or shit your pants during your bust because you're going to be in those clothes for a spell, unless they're so snappy one of your fellow inmates just can't be without them. You're unlikely to be outfitted with one of those striped prison jumpers you always imagined, or one of those eye-grabbing Day-Glo numbers that chain gangs wear in the South. You will instead be jailed wearing the clothes in which you were busted. To avoid the temptation of hanging yourself, your shoelaces and belt will be taken away. So you will shuffle about your cell holding up your pants for dear life. Women will give up wired bras, since they make such nice shanks.

Prison Guards

High Risk + Low Pay + No Respect + Awesome Power = Beatings. A Whole Lot of Beatings.

Anyone who has worked in the criminal justice system or done time was not stunned that one of the prison guards at the Abu Ghraib prison in Iraq was employed in the same capacity here in the States. Prison guards have one of the most loathsome, dangerous jobs in the world—the only true perk is that they get to beat the shit out of anyone who irritates them at work. Therefore, under no circumstances should you aggravate a guard. No whining about food, toilet paper, noise, smell, or fellow inmates, or nagging them about when your arraignment will be. Absent a threat to your life or your manhood, you should not speak to the guards unless spoken to. And if you are spoken to, do your best to make friends because a corrections officer can affect how long you will be held prior to your arraignment/bail hearing. Piss off a CO and he could plumb forget to put you on that DOC bus, costing you an extra day or two in jail. Days in jail are dog years on your soul.

"[The prison guard] went to the yard and requested that additional officers join him. While he waited for backup, he noticed [the] defendant swaggering in a 'gangster' fashion. He searched defendant and found a razor blade."

—A California judge, on the Third Level of Doom in jail. Should someone start gangster swaggering in your direction, it's time to nag a guard.

Should you survive your night(s) in jail, someone from "pretrial services" will interview you before your bail hearing to prepare a little memo on your shady past and suspicious source of income for the judge. Be cooperative with this person, answer the questions, and no matter what, *do not tell any lies*. The report can come back to haunt you. If you testify either at your suppression hearing or at trial, you can be cross-examined about a statement you made during your jailhouse interview. *Anything* that can be made to sound inconsistent will be exploited to make you sound like a low-life lying bastard.

Defending Your Life

Bail Hearings

Here in this life, the nearest approximation of a heaven's gate experience is an arraignment/bail hearing. How you've been living your life up to the point of your drug bust will be coldly weighed to determine whether you are fit to reenter society pending resolution of the charges. Do you have a job, education, money, respect for the law? Do you beat your wife, kids, dog? Have you done drugs, prostitutes, dirty business? Are you pissed, wasted, dirty, deranged, feckless? Your dirtiest laundry is taken out and dumped before the judge to sniff, and it will take her about five seconds to decide—it's the judicial equivalent of driving by a straggly-looking hitchhiker and deciding in those few seconds whether to give him a ride.

But you won't be hitching alone. Somebody will be standing next to you in a suit, trying hard to make you look like a good candidate for a ride (even if she's not 100 percent certain herself). Enter, at last, the defense attorney: on your side no matter how much of a junkie scumbag you are.

You are entitled to a public defender at your hearing if you can't afford an attorney, but that does not necessarily mean that one will be available, and you may be denied bail simply because there are no attorneys available. It happens. In 2004, poor bustees in Boston routinely sat in jail for weeks waiting for their bail hearings because the state paid the attorneys so little money to take the cases that it couldn't find anyone to represent them. The presumed innocent were sent back to jail until the court could find some slob willing to stand by their side for five seconds at the hearing.

But one way or another, you will have an attorney at your bail hearing. If you were denied a phone call or have otherwise been unable to retain counsel, the lawyer will likely be a public defender. The PD will also be representing that dude who stole your pants and the stickup punk you were chained to when you shuffled into the court's holding cells, "bullpens" in New York. The bullpen is where you are likely to meet your attorney for the first time. This meeting will last about five minutes, and if he's a PD it's likely the last time you will ever see this person again.

While it is essential to be straight with your attorney, it's not necessary to confess. He won't care if you do dope or not. He'll be happy you didn't whack someone. A few things you should tell you attorney, though: If you have the type of drug problem that will make it difficult to put down the pipe should you be released, tell him, because drug testing may be a condition of bail. Also—this will be instinctive—should you get jackbooted by the police, guards, fellow inmates, or all three, your attorney can present your pain to squeeze a drop of sympathy from the judicial stone.

Your attorney should be interested in your version of the events, including whether the search was obviously illegal. Nobody is going to be interested in your guilt or innocence, but the weaker the evidence is, the more likely you will be released. Hopefully, you have followed "The Phone Call Script," and you will have some witnesses the attorney can speak to and some documents establishing your good community standing.

The judge will decide whether to release you and how much, if anything, it will cost you, but that's not all. While bail is not supposed to serve any purpose aside from assuring your reappearance in court, bail conditions are often similar to parole conditions, even though you have not been convicted of anything. You can, for example, be subjected to random drug testing, particularly after a drug bust. Notwithstanding the outstanding efforts made by people like Edward Jones to make their court dates, (page 227), drug tests are fashionable because it is assumed that those on dope are less likely to show for court, and if you fail a drug test you will have committed an additional crime: bail jumping. *(Yes, you can "jump" bail just lying on your couch and getting baked.)* You can also be required to give up your Fourth Amendment rights altogether as a condition of bail, allowing the police to come search your crib, car, and person whenever the spirit moves them.

Poor in the Drug War: Perhaps no other aspect of the criminal justice system so unfairly impacts the poor as the bail system. Living around the poverty line means you are likely unemployed, your living conditions are more likely to be unstable, you are more likely to have priors, your family is unlikely to be able to take off work to attend your bail hearing, you're not going to have a snappy suit for your hearing, you're less likely to have an advanced degree, and even a modest amount of bail will be excessive.

The bail hearing will be the first opportunity the DA has to get nasty with you. She will be highlighting the massive amount of dope you had, that there were kids near the drugs, that you don't even have a freaking GED, that you resisted arrest, and anything else in your history suggesting that you are the type of hitchhiker likely to shank the judge in the gut and steal his wallet for more crack if given a lift.

You need to make her sound absurd.

Acing Your Bail Hearing . . .

Your bail hearing will probably be the most important hearing of your entire case because beating the rap or getting a reasonable deal hinges on getting released on bail and waiting it out (see "Limbaugh Lesson # 7," page 266). Studies have shown that 64 percent of bustees who don't make bail are ultimately sentenced to prison time, while only 17 percent of those who get sprung ever set foot back in the joint. It is therefore *vital* to make a good impression.

1. Look Sharp

Try to get in front of a mirror before your appearance, tie your shoes, tuck in your shirt, comb your hair, etc. Obviously, if you haven't been in jail, wear a suit to your initial appearance. If don't own a suit, or if you're such an outrageous-looking individual that you look ridiculous in a suit, be sure to appear as though you are making an earnest effort to dress appropriately for court. Unless you break out something Michael Jackson might wear for trial and make a mockery of the proceeding, it's always okay to overdress for court; it demonstrates that you understand the gravity of your situation and shows your respect, even if you don't have any.

Off with the bling! A lot of ropy gold chains, diamond watches, and Cadillac medallions will not only scream gangster to the judge, but might cost you your public defender, since it will appear as though you have plenty of scratch to blow on things other than the rent. As always, take out the piercings and cover the tats.

2. Clean Up Your Body Language

Pathetic and scared is the look you want to convey to the judge. Hard to pull off when you're enraged, handcuffed, exhausted, hungover, smell bad, and wearing someone else's pants, and while listening to the DA call you a lying junkie swine. But still you must, beginning with your posture. Stand up straight. Don't cross your arms over your chest or otherwise appear defiant. Look the judge in the eye, not around the courtroom, or at the weirdos who like watching miserable bustees shuffle in and out of court all day, or at friends/family who (hopefully) came to the hearing. A wandering gaze is a sign of disrespect, disinterest, and/or debauchery; it's not pathetic and scared.

3. No Talking

Your lawyer is there to do the talking for you because he's smarter than you are. He knows the law. He knows how to present you in the best possible light, and the judge wants to hear your attorney say it. If he wants your opinion about you, he will ask for it, but he will not want to hear about what a bunch of shit your charges are, only how closely tied to the community you are and how obvious it is that you are not going to head for the border in a white Bronco with a fake mustache and fifty Gs. (Notice that O.J. spent his entire trial in the L.A. County Jail.)

Word to Friends and Family: If you're attending a loved one's bail hearing, you also must keep your mouth shut. You are there to illustrate what a stable, God-fearing, law-abiding environment the bustee resides in. Do not call attention to yourself—that's the lawyer's job—and comments from the nut gallery are never welcome, and can lead to contempt charges if you get out of hand. Should the kids require a beating, be sure that it is done outside of the judge's presence.

If you are called upon to speak or feel compelled to do so, check yourself before saying anything to the judge. It is a crime to be disrespectful to a judge: the more disrespectful, the more time. And you will be tried, convicted, sentenced, and sent to jail for your crime quicklike. Pissing matches with a judge are similar to getting slapped with extra detention in *The Breakfast Club*.

Consider the year and three months that Hartford, Connecticut, man John Bailey talked himself into at his bail hearing:

The Judge: Well—OK. Just remember, you're in a courtroom, Sir.

Mr. Bailey: I wouldn't give a fuck about your courtroom.

The Judge: OK. [Bailiff]—bring him back. For that statement, I'm finding you in contempt of Court, for saying an obscenity in this courtroom. Do you understand that?

Mr. Bailey: So what? So what?

The Judge: Do you have any reason why I should not find you in contempt? OK.

Mr. Bailey: Why shouldn't you?

The Judge: OK. Ninety days for contempt.

Mr. Bailey: Suck my dick for giving me another 90 days!

The Judge: Six months consecutive for contempt.

Mr. Bailey: Fuck your mother with a stick!

The Judge: Another six months consecutive for contempt. OK. Take him out of here now. Make sure the contempt reads "consecutive," three contempts.

The Clerk of Court: The total was a year and three months?

The Judge: A year and three months.

As Mr. Bailey would probably tell you now that he's had fifteen months to reflect on his crime, you must be humble before the court. No one else on the planet has the power to send you straight to jail for six months without so much as a hearing for calling him an asshole.

DOPE NOTE: *IT'S UNCONSTITUTIONAL TO GIVE ANYONE MORE THAN SIX MONTHS WITHOUT A*

JURY TRIAL, WHICH IS WHY MR. BAILEY GOT THREE SEPARATE CHARGES: NINETY DAYS FOR "FUCK"; SIX MONTHS FOR "SUCK MY DICK"; AND SIX MONTHS FOR "FUCK YOUR MOTHER WITH A STICK."

Not Guilty!

These two words will likely be the only thing out of your mouth at arraignment, and alas, that will likely be the last time you will hear them in reference to your drug bust. If you have a public to concern yourself with it's sometimes nice to thrown in a little "Absolutely 100 percent" with your "not guilty," à la O.J., but a simple "Not guilty" will always get the job done.

Assuming you don't cop out immediately (see "Pleading at Arraignment," page 300, for when this is wise), it's time to start fighting your drug bust.

PART 4

FIGHTING YOUR DRUG BUST

by Rush Limbaugh (Not Really)

FIGHTING YOUR DRUG BUST

by Rush Limbaugh (Not Really)

Rednecks love him. His bust is on the mantel of any self-respecting promoter of the "pure race." Papa Bush carried his bags into the Lincoln Bedroom. Junior called him a "great American." And now he can be your hero too.

No drug bust in American history brought more joy to more people than Rush Limbaugh's. "Hillbilly heroin junkie" has replaced "fascist swine" as a prefix to his name, but Limbaugh must be studied and devotedly followed like the Guru he is, a sage Drug War Buddha. Deep wisdom can be achieved by following Rush's teachings on doing the right kind of dope, evolved methods of scoring dope, protecting your privacy rights, and fighting drug charges to the bitter end without sabotaging your shot at making a good deal if all else fails.

The Limbaugh Lessons are here like a final prayer between "Busted!" and your suppression hearing to demonstrate a masterful maneuvering of Part 1 (how not to possess) and Part 2 (how not to get nabbed possessing); and although he succumbed to Part 3 (he got busted), the Guru still guides you through the darkness of your drug bust.

A true guru must of course be imbued with foresight, an ability to understand what lies ahead before leading his flock over precarious terrain. Our Guru had the foresight and the wisdom to understand that Drug War battles are won and lost long before you engage the enemy. The battle begins with your choice of dope.

Limbaugh Lesson #1

Choose Your Dope Wisely

There are 178 different illegal drugs with which to anesthetize yourself in this country. Each offers its unique buzz, addictive qualities, risks associated with scoring, and criminal justice consequences. Go with crack and the stakes are high on all fronts. Our Guru went with pills. A whole lot of personal choices . . . er, pills. While pills will undoubtedly get you more than sufficiently wasted, and they're crazy addictive, they are nonetheless the white-collar crime of the Drug War, and white-collar criminals are always treated more gently than blue-collar criminals.

"The first time you reach for a substance you are making a choice. Every time you go back, you're making a personal choice."

—Rush, quoting Phoenix Suns owner Jerry Colangelo

Anytime you get busted, pity is what you need from your judge. A traditional white-collar criminal who goes through Part 3 doesn't need to be told to look pathetic and scared at his bail hearings, and he's more sympathetic because he usually stole the money by making chop suey of the books. Judges tend to take a more charitable view of stealing if you don't put a gun in someone's face. The visceral distinctions between the two theft crimes are similar with drug possession crimes, particularly pills. A white-collar criminal sends the maid to the pharmacist for his back pain; a blue-collar guy gives his rent money to a dope-dealing lowlife to get *fucked up, man.*

Not only are pills safer in a criminal justice setting, they're safer in an employment setting; a positive drug test for prescription meds will not automatically get you fired. (See "Drug Test?" page 191.) Indeed, Rush was hired right back after his (third) stint in rehab. Of course, there's only one Guru; blue-collar dopers like you are a dime a dozen.

DOPE NOTE: IF YOUR DOCTOR STARTS GETTING RELUCTANT AND YOU START GETTING NEEDY, BE WARNED: "DOCTOR SHOPPING" AND SCRIPT FRAUD ARE FELONIES. GET BUSTED AND THE DA GETS NASTY—AND HE USUALLY DOES—YOU MAY BE IN OVER YOUR HEAD, PARTICULARLY IF YOU SOLD ANY PILLS OR POSSESSED ENOUGH TO ASSUME YOU WERE DEALING.

Aside from having your Dr. Feelgood prescribe your dope, pot is the wise dope choice, assuming you must have dope. Marijuana, particularly first-time, personal possession, is usually treated differently than busts for all other drugs. There's still room for pity with pot. Many DAs who would otherwise be anxious to lock you up are willing to cut you a little slack, at least the first time. Keep crawling up the ladder of inebriants that state legislatures consider harder drugs (smack, crack) or bigger problems (Ecstasy, meth) and everything gets more painful, from your bust all the way through your appeal. The wrong dope choice plus a prior, and you devolve from the Guru to Robert Downey Jr., and we all remember the orange prison jumper he ended up in.

That said, check "The Dope Law Index" (page 331); pot has not been decriminalized in this country, don't believe it, if you hear it. There's virtually no city where everything that happened in "Busted!" (the chapter) can't happen to anyone caught with a small amount of marijuana, especially if you're caught in a car, and there are just as many DAs who view all drugs as an evil scourge upon society, and will not care that it was "only pot." And no pity for you if you violate the Third Commandment (page 327)—Thou Shall Not Covet More Than a Misdemeanor Buzz—and start buying in bulk.

Limbaugh Lesson #2

Protect Your Privacy

Had Rush been pulled over with a fatty burning in his ashtray, he'd be just another Dope Ditty squashed along the Drug War highway. But the Guru, through his dope choice, protected his Fourth Amendment rights better than the unenlightened out there getting scraped off the pavement and disposed of like so much roadkill.

The advantage that pills have over their dirty stepsisters is that much of the evidence of your illegal activity is in your medical records, which are harder to get at than the dope growing in your backyard or burning in your ashtray. It's not just the civil libertarians who are concerned about the privacy of their medical records. *Everyone's* got a little something hiding in there. *Remember that night you checked into the ER without your eyebrows (page 65)? The mysterious pus a few years back?* Also, statements you make to your doctor in the course of seeking treatment are protected by the doctor-patient privilege. *Unless,* that is, you were lying to your doctor simply to score dope. *But who the hell are you to tell me I'm not in pain? That's right, I'm anxious too, goddamn it!*

The prosecutor went after Rush's medical records, arguing that they were loaded with evidence that could put him in the slam for more than twenty years, but Rush deftly countered that the bastards violated his right to privacy when they seized his medical records and didn't follow the guidelines set up by Florida's medical records statute. Although his suppression hearing went the way most do—the Guru went down (See "Trial?" page 269)—he got the records resealed and he is still fighting to keep the DA from using his medical records on appeal because if there's no violation of his privacy/Fourth Amendment rights, it's all over but the begging for mercy (see page 287).

> **"There is no right to privacy specifically enumerated in the Constitution."**
>
> —Rush

Limbaugh Lesson #3:

Distance Yourself from Your Dope Supply

The evolution of scoring dope in the Drug War has been great for the middle and upper-middle classes, making them much less likely to get busted than poor people. For example, WeeDeliver services (think Domino's for dope) are safer alternatives to buying hand to hand in open-air drug markets, where poorer people are often forced to do their shopping. But the most evolved method of scoring is of course having someone else to do the wet work. The Guru wisely had his (poor Latina) maid score for him. Although the strategy backfired because she narked when she got caught (*curses!*), the more people you can put between you and your dope source, the easier it is to avoid stepping in shit. Rush's notoriety became a liability; under normal circumstances, the maid, as the supplier, would have been in a more serious jam than her customer.

"Too many whites are getting away with drug use . . . The answer is to go out and find the ones who are getting away with it, convict them and send them up the river, too."

—Rush

Another enlightened scoring strategy that Rush employed was based on an old-school hustle, the shell game. He was reportedly into OxyContin, Lorcet, Xanax, and hydrocodone, scored through a variety of doctors, making tracking his habit a little more difficult, even though he made about twelve thousand personal choices over a four-month period in 2001. *Yee haw!*

Limbaugh Lesson #4

Once Busted, It's Time for Rehab, Baby

Even if you don't have a problem, admit you have a problem, check yourself into a clinic for a spell, and *stick with the program.* Announcing to his devoted flock, "I refuse to let anyone think I am doing something great here," Rush heroically checked himself into rehab again when he was nabbed. Not only was this a wise health decision, but at some point Rush will likely face a judge, and when you get busted for drugs, you need to demonstrate that you have gotten your shit together and want to put your criminal past behind you. You understand that drugs are bad. Bad things happen to people who do drugs.

> **"Okay, as you will recall . . . conditions of bond were to, not violate any of the laws of the State . . . and to report for drug or alcohol testing as a condition of bond. Today we are going to do drug tests on all Defendants that are in the room. . . . So after we do your final Pre-Trial, then you'll exit by this door, and you'll meet with the Probation Officers, and they will be doing urine tests, at this time."**
>
> —Judge Cecile Blau, sending a courtroom full of dopers into cold panic and drawing futile objections from their attorneys

Should you be standing in court and hear something like the quote in the box come out of your judge's mouth, you don't want to be one of the wide-eyed, pounding on the table and frantically objecting. A drug test can be sprung at almost any time, including during trial if submitting to drug tests was a condition of your release, assuming you were released. But even if testing is not a condition of your bail, you must stick with the program because the DA may offer you your best deal at a later court proceeding *if* you can pass a drug test. Right here. Right now. If you can't pass, it's hard to argue with much conviction that you have learned your lesson.

DOPE NOTE: ANOTHER GOOD REASON TO GET OFF THE PIPE FOLLOWING A DRUG BUST IS THAT A CONVICTION CAN RESULT IN YOUR BEING THROWN OUT OF PUBLIC HOUSING. HOWEVER, PROOF THAT YOU ARE RECEIVING TREATMENT MAY PREVENT AN EVICTION. (SEE "NOW WE BRING THE PAIN," PAGE 277.)

Limbaugh Lesson #5

Hire Top Talent (Or the Best You Can Do)

Rush is of course going to be able to accomplish some feats that most of his followers will not be able to emulate, including paying a guy like Miami-based attorney Roy Black by the hour. Don't despair. This is not fatal to your defense. But if you've got the money, or you're being made an example of, or your bust has gotten a lot of media attention, a well-connected, top defense attorney like Mr. Black, who also defended William Kennedy Smith and Marv Albert, will make the DA's usually very easy job of convicting you much, much harder. While Marv copped a plea because the whole panties thing was getting embarrassing, Smith skated, and Mr. Black once got Miami coke dealer and powerboat racer Salvador Magluta acquitted, despite twenty-seven witnesses swearing that he and his partner were the CEOs of a $2 billion cocaine cartel. (Bribing a couple of the jurors helped, but Sal didn't need Mr. Black for that.)

The difference between going to court with Roy Black on your arm rather than a local jack-of-all-trades attorney is not unlike going to a club with your devoted date, Beyoncé. Yes, the club is the same, the music is the same, the drinks still get you wasted, but the cat with Beyoncé is not waiting in line, he's probably going to have a better time than the sunglasses-at-night types standing outside the velvet rope, and he's not going to get a lot of attitude from the staff. (But it's going to cost him plenty.)

Although a high-profile lawyer is not necessarily better than any other lawyer you might stumble upon in the Yellow Pages, he puts pressure on the judge and the district attorney. The typical wham-bam-to-the-slam criminal justice machine slows down. Everything is scrutinized more closely; the judges are more careful with their decisions, and the DAs are not so quick to bust you (Rush hadn't even been charged with a crime at press time). In other words, you're going to be treated better by the staff. (And it's going to cost you plenty.)

Go to any trial court in the country and watch a typical hearing. The attorneys are routinely cut off, particularly the defense attorneys, the galleries are half full with winos, the judge will be reading something unrelated to the case, and clerks are coming up and whispering in her ear. But go to any trial court and watch a high-profile attorney argue; the judge is completely focused, allowing the attorney to go on and on and on, no lackeys are puttering around the bench, and the gallery is alert. When the Guru's attorney steps to the podium, the judge is going to listen to what he has to say, and any motion he files will not be summarily dismissed, as is the norm. The judge, in short, will actually listen to your attorney whine about your constitutional rights.

Choosing a Drug Bust Attorney

Assuming that you will not be in the market for a Humvee like Mr. Black, a solid, low-mileage Jetta should be able to get the job done, *if* you shop around. First, put the Yellow Pages down. Deciding whose hands to place your life in should not come down to whoever has the snappiest ad.

1. Investigate the Local Public Defender's Office

One of the great misconceptions about the difference between hiring an attorney and going with a public defender is the quality of the lawyers. There's no guarantee that the most expensive attorney you can afford is the best your money can buy. The very top law schools in the country are well represented in the public defenders offices in major cities, particularly in left-leaning cities. In Washington, D.C., New York City, and San Francisco, the PD offices have excellent reputations and are just as capable, if not more so, than any local attorney at handling a low-level drug bust.

However, in many, if not most, other cities, the PD's office is despised, underfunded, and overwhelmed. Your attorney will be handling hundreds of other cases, many of them serious violent crimes, and he will not have time to hold your hand through your miserable little bust. However, if you've been charged with a misdemeanor and have no money and no priors, and you're simply going to cop out at arraignment or shortly thereafter, you will have little other choice. (See "Pleading at Arraignment," p. 300.)

Many jurisdictions do not have a public defender's office at all. Instead, local attorneys are on contract with the court to handle all indigent bustees for a flat fee. Some of these people are out there fighting the good fight, but many are making their money in private practice and are not interested in doing more than the bare minimum on their contract cases, since they have no incentive to do so. If you're nabbed in one of these godforsaken counties, start shopping.

2. Get References

An attorney is only as good as his reputation, but unless you're in the Roy Black market, that reputation is truly known only inside the small world of the local courthouse. A reference from another attorney—any attorney, but hopefully one you know and can trust—is the path to a reputable corner man. Law schools churn out all kinds of attorneys and they spread like weeds across the county, practicing all kinds of law. *Nobody can stop them!* Chances are good that someone will know someone who can recommend a criminal attorney, no matter where you are. A reference also puts pressure on your man to pay particular attention to your case because he'd like to get additional clients sent his way, and he won't want to embarrass himself.

Call the local bar association and check NORML's website for references if you have no other options.

3. Ask Questions

Some fundamentals you want to know about anyone you hire:

A. How many cases has she tried? If your attorney never goes to trial, there is not much pressure on the DA to make a reasonable offer because he knows that your attorney is never going to try the case. You want someone who is ready to throw down when the gloves are off.

B. Is criminal law the attorney's area of expertise? A jack-of-all-trades attorney is fine if you're probating a will, setting up a trust, suing the sons of bitches, that kind of thing. If you might do time, you want a pro. There are essentially three ways to gain criminal experience: in the district attorney's office, the public defender's office, or hanging out a shingle and lettin' 'er rip. You want one of the first two because they have usually received extensive training before they set foot inside a courtroom. A former prosecutor should have contacts inside the DA's office, which may mean a better deal, if the attorney is willing to call in a favor on your behalf. Here is where it is helpful to have been referred by someone he knows. It will also help if you're not a total burnout, making you a less attractive candidate for a nice slap on the wrist.

C. How long has she been practicing in that jurisdiction? The luck of the draw plays an important role in any bust, but since you will not have any idea whether you've been dealt a sadistic prosecutor and/or a maniacal judge, you want someone who does. The more time your attorney has spent practicing in the same courthouse, the better she knows the players, giving her some contacts and insight into what to expect from the people seeking to punish you. (A public defender benefits from institutional knowledge because someone in the office will have been before your judge and dealt with your DA.)

4. Watch for Warning Signals

Got the feeling this cat's a shyster? Trust your gut. Always plenty of attorneys out there. Anyone who guarantees any particular result is full of shit. Nothing in the criminal justice system is guaranteed, save pain and suffering. Defensiveness about bona fides sends a bad message; and anything aside from a flat fee, at least initially, and you should keep shopping. Flat fees to handle low-level drug busts are the norm.

LIMBAUGH LESSON #6

ABANDON PRINCIPLE

When the stakes are jail time, you have no politics, no philosophy, no pride, no loyalty, and no religion. The Guru ain't going to go marching off to jail preaching "personal choice"; he won't be sticking by the whole "no specifically enumerated" right to privacy thing; and he'll probably be okay with another white guy getting away with doing a little dope. And *hell yes!* he supports the ACLU.

As the wise man of the Drug War, Rush understands that anyone willing to get in the foxhole with him to help beat the rap must be taken to the bosom in a passionate embrace. He embraced the ACLU, and they're helping to fight his drug bust (although they have announced that they're not so concerned with whether he goes to jail or not; it's a principle thing). Rush and the ACLU are not an unholy marriage in the Drug War; they're like chocolate and peanut butter.

Not only must you form uncomfortable alliances, you may also have to sever alliances and rat out your junkie friends and/or your supplier. Providing "substantial assistance" to bust someone else is essentially the only way to escape the death trap of the federal sentencing guidelines. (This is how all those mob hit men skate after admitting that they whacked every greaseball in Jersey.) Or consider Tim Allen, of *Home Improvement* fame. Once busted for dealing about a pound and a half of coke, he got with the Limbaugh program, rolled over on a fellow dealer, spent a couple of years behind bars, got out of jail, and now makes irritating Christmas movies. The alternative was a mandatory *life sentence, no parole*. Yes, you read that right—a life sentence—which is why the First Commandment, Thou Shall Not Deal (page 327), is first.

> **DOPE NOTE:** WHEN IT'S TIME TO ROLL, BE THE FIRST TO THE DA'S DOOR. OTHERWISE, YOU MIGHT GET ROLLED OVER.

Anything you have to do and any coalition you have to form in order to minimize your jail time is a viable option. As your in-house counsel, I advise you to look out for number one and make peace with your karma from outside prison walls. (After spending a couple of nights in jail, you will probably not need this advice.)

LIMBAUGH LESSON #7

WAIT IT OUT

The pill probe against Rush began in earnest in early October of 2002. At press time, Rush was still at large, so to speak, and he will wait through eternity for this matter to pass and keep fighting for his privacy for as long as the judges are still listening; "closure" is not necessarily what you're looking for in a drug bust, particularly on the DA's terms.

So long as you get your ticket punched at the bail hearing—or they hold off on arresting you, as they've done with Rush—time is on your side in the criminal justice system. You are essentially on parole already. The more time that you spend out of jail, not getting busted again, staying sober, punching in at nine and punching out at five, the better your chances are of never going back to jail. A year or two of clean living can do wonders for the complexion of your case.

Wait out a bust long enough and sometimes it just goes away.

Most states have speedy-trial statutes, mandating a trial within a certain amount of time after your bust or the charges will be dismissed. In New York, for example, the DA must announce that he is ready for trial within 180 days of arraignment. Announcing "trial ready" is the DA's check's-in-the-mail put-off; there will be nine thousand adjournments of your case before anything gets done. "Adjournments" are, in essence, a couple of lawyers standing in front of a judge asking her if they can't just do this later. The judge blames one side or the other for the delay, sets the date for the next delay, and it's on to the next. Enough of those delays get blamed on the prosecutor, the case will be dismissed, and you'll slink out of the criminal justice system.

But *you must make every court appearance.* Miss one, and there will be a warrant for your arrest, bail will be revoked, and your case becomes a higher priority. Failing to appear in court will also cost you any chance at a reasonable plea. In Colorado, for example, first-time misdemeanor pot possession is not punishable by jail time, but failing to appear after making bail makes the same offense punishable by six months in jail.

While a big fish like Rush is not going to get his case dismissed on speedy-trial grounds, that doesn't mean that waiting it out is not still an enlightened decision. Memories fade, maids get deported, evidence gets lost, more serious crimes become the DA's priority; all kinds of good stuff can happen if you wait it out.

Poor in the Drug War: Waiting out a drug bust is not usually an option for the poor. First, no bail. But even if they make bail, getting to all the adjournments is much more challenging because poor people always have transportation issues, often they have no one to watch their kids, and if they have jobs they're not usually the type you can slip away from for a quick court appearance. The choice is having a warrant issued for their arrest, or getting fired.

Limbaugh Lesson #8

Make a Deal

You won't have any choice but to make a deal, but following the Guru's path will ensure the best deal if all else fails. Rush's attorneys had the courage to suggest a plea that included no arrest or any of the traditional trappings of the criminal justice system. Just a little (more) rehab to make everything go away. The fuzz didn't go for it, but Rush was wisely looking for a deal before the Fourth Amendment issue is resolved because, as noted earlier, there's not much left to argue about if there's no privacy issue anymore. If you don't have much to argue about, you don't have much leverage, other than that the DA's loath to go to trial—not to be understated.

And so before jumping into the Drug War, always remember to ask yourself, "What would the Guru do?"

PART 5

TRIAL?

You Don't Get No Stinking Trial!

The Suppression Hearing

Some of the more powerful rights in your corner during a jury trial are that the DA has to prove you guilty beyond a reasonable doubt, a jury decides if the cop is lying, and hearsay from anonymous sources is inadmissible. None of this is true at a suppression hearing. *You* will have to prove that the police violated your rights. A judge—not a jury—decides whether the cop is lying. And there are essentially no rules of evidence: anything anyone allegedly said to the cop is fair game until someone (*who, you?*) proves him wrong.

Your suppression hearing is your trial in a drug possession bust because this is where the judge decides if the cop searched you illegally, rendering a trial essentially pointless (see "Your Quick and Painful Jury Trial," page 303, for confirmation).

A rough script of 99 percent of suppression hearings, picked up where the officer who busted you takes the stand:

> ***The Prosecutor:*** Officer, you didn't violate the defendant's stinking constitutional rights, did you?
>
> **The Cop:** No, ma'am.
>
> ***The Defense Attorney:*** Admit it! Admit it, you lying bastard! You violated my client's Fourth Amendment rights, didn't you?
>
> **The Cop:** No, sir.
>
> ***The Defendant:*** [That would be you, sitting there dejectedly, on the wrong side of the table, shaking your head in despair at all the lying. Then maybe you'll take a stab at testifying]: *I didn't smell like dope! He just thrust his hand in my pants!*
>
> **The Judge:** Ah, let's see. You did have the dope, didn't you? I'm going to have to go with the officer on this one. That's a big 👍!

This admittedly condensed hearing illustrates the fundamental problem with squeezing some justice out of the Fourth Amendment: the people in charge of protecting your right to be free of illegal searches (the DAs and the judges) are the same people in charge of putting you away after the cop finds the dope during his illegal search. The latter is unquestionably the higher priority. Not surprisingly, then, suppression hearings ain't no search for truth, like they sometimes tell trial juries; suppression hearings are searches to find a plausible reason—any reason—not to suppress the evidence against you, even if the search was illegal. Everyone's on board: the lying cops, the prosecutors who love them, and the judges who believe them.

THE LICENSE TO LIE

> *[W]hen officers unlawfully stop and search a vehicle because they believe it contains drugs or guns, officers will falsely claim in police reports and under oath that the car ran a red light (or committed some other traffic violation) and that they subsequently saw contraband in the car in plain view. To conceal an unlawful search of an individual who officers believe is carrying drugs or a gun, they will falsely assert that they saw a bulge in the person's pocket or saw drugs and money changing hands. To justify unlawfully entering an apartment where officers believe narcotics or cash can be found, they pretend to have information from an unidentified civilian informant or claim they saw drugs in plain view. . . . To arrest people they suspect are guilty of dealing drugs, they falsely assert that the defendants had drugs in their possession when, in fact, the drugs were found elsewhere where the officers had no lawful right to be.*
>
> —*The Mollen Report, 1994 City of New York Commission to Investigate Police Corruption*

Cops and defendants are notorious liars. They lie to each other in the street and then they lie about what they lied about under oath in court. When defendants lie it's because they don't want to go jail. When cops lie it's either because it's obvious that you're guilty and there is no way in hell that your rights are going to get you out of jail free, or because they're jackbooted thugs. Everyone more or less plays along with the former variety—the day-in, day-out perjury cited by the Mollen Commission—unless the bullshit gets truly ridiculous, so absurd as to be hard for even the most dutiful of the rubber stamps to ignore. Then they have to let at least one guy get away. A jackbooted thug's testimony typically gets rubber-stamped for a few years before things get really out of hand. Then they have to let a few of the (usually black) people he put away out of jail and replace them with the lying cop(s). Then everyone will settle down until the lying gets out of hand again. Call it battered citizen syndrome. I mean, we gotta have cops, *right?*

The Jackbooted Thug Variety

Lying cops are the dirty bombs of the criminal justice system. Just one can destroy thousands of lives and wipe out an entire neighborhood. Nowhere is perjury running more wild and free than out on the Drug War battlefield, where the drugs and money flow, the Fourth Amendment is your only defense, and juries almost never pass on police credibility.

A single cop (and Ku Klux Klan member) in tiny Tulia, Texas, put away thirty-eight people, all but three black, and all on drug charges, on the strength of his lies alone. In Philadelphia, *283 drug convictions* were at last overturned when the lies of six cops got sufficiently out of hand for people to start noticing. The Rampart scandal in L.A. was one of the more outrageous scandals in recent memory. An entire antigang squad set upon the streets of East Los Angeles and descended into lawlessness, selling drugs, shaking down drug dealers, framing gang members, and reportedly killing people. More than 100 convictions have been overturned, more than two dozen cops resigned or got fired and the city anticipates paying out over $100 million in lawsuits.

Aside from the automatic 👍 given to their testimony at suppression hearings, the real problem with the jackbooted thugs is that their victims usually have records, which, as has been said here before, destroys credibility. A judge listening to a veteran cop testify that he found six Baggies of smack and a Glock 9 in a defendant's glove compartment is not going to believe it when an inmate bused into court from the L.A. County Jail, who already has a couple of drug convictions, testifies that the cop planted that evidence on him.

It's that simple.

The Wink-and-Nod Variety

Scandals like those in L.A. and Philadelphia make blaring headlines around the country, but the cops involved in those are the exception, although the effect of their lies is devastating and far-reaching. It's the subtle lies, the winks and nods, that will do you in, and they are *routine* at suppression hearings. In the words of the former chief of police in Kansas

City and San Jose, "hundreds of thousands" of cops commit this type of "felony perjury" every year testifying in drug cases alone.

These liars, most of whom aren't of the jackbooted persuasion, view the Fourth Amendment's search and seizure law as a lot of annoying little rules that get in the way of busting you, but they know those rules; they get extensive Fourth Amendment training at the police academy and regular updates on changes in the law down at the precinct. (You only have *Busted!*) Changes in the law, however, do not alter the way the police have always gone about their business; if they're suspicious that you've got dope, they are going to search you, one way or another. All that changes with the wink-and-nod cops is how they testify at suppression hearings.

All the bullshit started to pile up after the Supreme Court decided that evidence discovered during an illegal search would be thrown out. Drug War kryptonite. No dope. No collar. The answer? Lies. Lot and lots of lies. Shortly after the Supreme Court dropped this bomb, a study found that the number of cases in which NYPD officers claimed that a suspect abandoned his dope when he saw the cops coming went up nearly *80 percent*. Cops call this type of perjury "tightening up a case," and most make no apologies for it, looking at it as the reality of the street, as opposed to the Never Never Land of a courtroom. The facts of an illegal search are "tightened up" to fit into one of several defined categories of busts that will make the search legal.

I smelled it. "The defendant smelled like she'd been bathing in bong water, so I proceeded to search her and her backpack. Yes, I am an expert on the smell of bong water." (See "Oooh That Smell," page 111.)

I saw it. "He was driving with a kilo of cocaine between his legs, scooping out bowls with his crack pipe. Yes, it was in plain view. I could see in my rearview mirror." (See "Packing for Your Drug Trip," page 148.)

I heard it. "I knocked on the door and announced that I was a police officer, and someone yelled to come in. I entered and observed the defendant naked, eating marijuana and standing over a pile of cocaine." (See "Come On In, Officer!, We're Getting Wasted!" page 105.)

I felt it. "For my own safety, I patted the defendant down and felt what appeared to be a Rambo-type dagger. I removed it and it turned out to be a Baggie of dope." (See "Fraidy Cops," page 94.)

The old reliable "I smelled pot" is such a common lie that Utah—that's right, Utah—makes the cops prove that they smelled dope by actually finding some during the search. No dope equals illegal search. But laugh-out-loud lies are served up and credited by judges at suppression hearings all the time. A New York City judge, for example, credited an officer's testimony that he observed the defendant holding a two-inch glass vial, from seventy-four feet way, from a moving patrol car, after dark. Consider the mustard Officer Daniel Jankowski put on his dog at Andrew Thomas's suppression hearing:

The Sound of Falling Grass: Officer Jankowski was conducting surveillance on Andrew Thomas's house in southern Arizona one afternoon. When he saw an El Camino pull into the garage, he crept up to the house, placed his ear to the wall, and . . . *thump!* . . . he heard the telltale sound of a bale of marijuana hitting the ground. Based on the sound of the dope, Jankowski pulled the El Camino over when Thomas drove it away, and he found twelve pounds of weed screaming in the trunk. The judge at Thomas's suppression hearing liked the sound of that, and gave the search a 👍. But a federal judge, not buying Jankowski's "incredible claimed powers of auditory recognition," at last shined the sun on Thomas's ass, deciding that weed "has a distinctive appearance, taste[?], and odor, and perhaps even feel, but it does not have a distinctive sound." So they let this one get away. (Of course, Thomas had already served a couple of years, since his suppression hearing went the way most do.)

Police would not lie if they were not rewarded for lying. There are no medals handed out for the most honest cop of the year, the one that had fifteen of his busts thrown out at the suppression hearing because he admitted that he violated your stinking rights. The medals are handed out to the guys making busts that stand the test of time.

The same motivation can be attributed to the prosecutors who put the lying cops on the stand, knowingly, or unknowingly, or in the great gray ocean in between.

The Wink-and-Nod Prosecutors

The prosecutors know all about the License to Lie problem. This is not a startling phenomenon, revealed for the first time in the pages of this book. It is well known and well documented, and everyone practicing criminal law is intimately familiar with the routine. (Only you, sitting meekly at the defense table, will be surprised.) But as any *Law & Order* fan would tell you, the prosecutors have an intimate working relationship with the police, and that relationship would sour if the DAs were constantly calling their colleagues lying bastards. So like a Jesus freak proclaiming that God said it, I believe it, and that settles it, a prosecutor is not going to be grilling a cop about how your bust went down. It happened the way the cop says it happened.

Flip back to "The Sound of Falling Grass." Some prosecutor put Officer Jankowski on the stand and let him go off. If he had reason to know that Jankowski was lying, the prosecutor was suborning perjury. Out there in the gray ocean between knowing and unknowing, however, is suspicion. And you can't be suspicious of the ones you love. Not unless you've lost your zest for taking scalps. After all, as the rationalization goes, Thomas did have twelve pounds of pot, *didn't he?*

Willfully plugging your nose to the bullshit being shoveled is one thing; implicitly encouraging a cop to tighten up her testimony is another. Now we have a wink-and-nod conspiracy. It's unnecessary with veteran cops, but a prosecutor with a particular fondness for your scalp may just lead the officer to the lying while prepping her for the suppression hearing:

> ***Prosecutor:*** Officer, were you concerned for your own safety when you frisked that junkie scumbag?
>
> **Cop:** Oh, yes.
>
> ***Prosecutor:*** And did the dope in that scumbag's pocket feel like a weapon?
>
> **Cop:** Ah, sure.
>
> ***Prosecutor:*** What did it feel like?
>
> **Cop:** A gun?
>
> ***Prosecutor:*** Any question in your mind about that?
>
> **Cop:** No question.

By an "officer of the court," this "tightening up" of an illegal search crosses the line into plain prosecutorial misconduct. Your little drug bust isn't likely to warrant this type of bare-knuckle, cheap shot to the groin unless you distinguish yourself somehow. Say by getting busted again while out on bail, flunking a drug test, balling the DA's wife, that kind of thing. But you will never know about it because it's impossible to prove. You'll be out there drowning in the gray ocean of suspicion unless your lawyer eviscerates the cop on cross-examination or a judge like J. Skelly Wright comments out loud that the DA's laid the same turd too many times now.

The Wink-and-Nod Judges

"For some time now I have been curious and concerned about evidence offered by the Government, appearing again and again in criminal case records, showing that the defendant . . . had, while in the presence and custody of the police, 'spontaneously and voluntarily' apologized for his misdeed. . . . [I]t appears to me that the time is ripe for some soul searching in the prosecutor's office before it offers any more 'spontaneous' apologies in evidence."

—The late D.C. federal judge J. Skelly Wright in a stunning display of judicial candor

Judges are relied upon to be "neutral and detached" arbiters of the law and the facts, but they are political animals. Like any other candidates for office, they raise money, pander to the voters, and clamp down on crime—no politician interested in winning an election runs on an "It's Time to Get Softer on Crime" or a "Let's End This Silly Drug War" platform. And no judge wants her constituents to read an outraged headline like JUDGE JUST-LET-'EM-GO JULIE ACCUSES VET COP OF PERJURY: THROWS OUT 605 KILOS OF COKE FOUND ON DRUG-DEALING SCUMBAG. In the Age of the Orange Alert, the cop shall be believed as if he has X-ray vision, supersonic hearing, and can leap tall projects in a single bound.

Federal judges, on the other hand, are appointed to the bench and enjoy life tenure, which theoretically immunizes them from political pressure; but they feel it, and it gets hot as hell if they start questioning the veracity of the known liars. The Honorable Harold Baer of federal district court in lower Manhattan felt it in 1996 when he credited a defendant's testimony over a cop's in a suppression hearing:

"The great enemy of truth is very often not the lie—deliberate, contrived, and dishonest—but the myth—persistent, pervasive, and realistic." Judge Baer began his opinion by quoting this line from JFK's 1962 commencement speech at Yale. He went on to quote Thomas Paine, and referred to the cop's testimony as "gossamer" (bullshit), "incredible," and "at best suspect." Citing the Mollen Commission report regarding police misconduct and brutality, largely in Washington Heights, a predominantly minority neighborhood in Manhattan, Judge Baer wrote, "What I find shattering is that in this day and age blacks in black neighborhoods and blacks in white neighborhoods can count on little security for their person." In light of the police mistreatment visited upon the locals, Judge Baer found that it was not necessarily suspicious if the residents ran from the cops when they saw them coming, and he therefore suppressed thirty-four kilos of coke and two keys of smack found in the trunk of a Chevrolet Caprice driven by Carol Bayless, whom he referred to as a "middle-aged black woman," noting several times that she was a mother.

Then came the outrage. Demands for Judge Baer's impeachment. President Clinton publicly criticized him. The cops went ape shit. Letters to Congress poured in. *Hmm, perhaps we should have another suppression hearing,* thought Judge Baer.

On the second thought. Those Kennedy and Paine quotes? That cite to the Mollen Commission report? Ah, that was all "hyperbole" (bullshit) and "dicta" (bullshit) and "regretfully may have demeaned the . . . vast majority of the dedicated men and women in blue who patrol the streets of our great City." Ms. Bayless? Well, she's just the "defendant" now, working with "the dealers," and I find her story "unbelievable." And Washington Heights? "[I]t has now been shown that the area of Manhattan about which we are concerned . . . is known amongst law enforcement officers as a significant center of narcotics trafficking." I am therefore unsuppressing the dope and busting the middle-aged black mother, er, defendant, for all she's worth.

On the flop side of his flip-flop, Judge Baer noted one of the bitter ironies of the criminal justice system, Drug War style: a judge's determination of police credibility at a suppression hearing is subject to almost no scrutiny by any other judge. Judge Baer understood that if he didn't slink away from his first decision like it was a fart in an elevator, it would never be reversed. All the appellate judges up the line are required to defer to Judge Rubber Stamp's decision that the cop wasn't lying, and the rubber stamp is supposed to defer to the cop.

Aside from political pressure, wink-and-nod testimony is credited because no judge is eager to let a guilty defendant skate no matter how obvious the violation of her rights, and because the perjury is generally impossible to prove and hard to detect. The police officers are professional witnesses; they aren't going to break down and sob like a sissy under cross-examination. Finally, while judges are not supposed to consider your criminal record, they have the report that was prepared for your bail hearing, and a couple of priors are impossible to ignore.

Thus, unless the lie makes you laugh like hell, there is no chance anyone will ever openly doubt a cop's testimony, although everyone is aware that perjury is routine. The only effective way to end all of the lying would be to admit, at last, that there is no Fourth Amendment. The cops can search anyone they want, whenever they want, for no reason at all. While the Supreme Court has been working on it, these things take time. For now, we'll go through the motion of a suppression hearing. . . .

. . . But You Can Win, Grasshopper

This is depressing stuff to read if you, like most convicts, start getting curious about criminal law after you got busted, likely by staggering into your bust, pissing away your rights, and relieving the cop of the hassle of the wink-and-nod routine. As a *Busted!* disciple, however, you have gathered enough wisdom, skill, and paranoia to walk the Drug War battlefield lightly, leaving no footprints, and are unlikely to get busted to begin with. If you do, you still have a shot at winning your suppression hearing, for the following reasons:

1. The Search Was Illegal

"The Incredible Shrinking Fourth Amendment" is designed to protect your rights when confronted by the police and to discourage the typical just-begging-for-it behavior that leads to most low-level drug busts. Heed the good word and the search will have to be illegal to bust you, and it will be a fairly obvious violation of rights; the lies start sounding like falling grass, and you're relieved of the temptation of lying yourself.

2. You Were Not Dealing

The First Commandment is first because in the Drug War, the rules, written and unwritten, are different for the dealers than for the users, particularly the recreational users. (Addicts are not pitied and usually have a couple of priors.) The dealers never get the benefit of any doubt and they do not make sympathetic defendants. It's easier for everyone to rationalize a little winking and nodding when it gets a dealer off the street.

3. You Were Nabbed with Misdemeanor Weight

The more dope you have, the less likely it's going to be suppressed. If Ms. Bayless had had an eight ball of coke and a couple of jays in the trunk, no one would have made such a fuss about suppressing the evidence. Once you move into felony weight, the bust becomes more significant to everyone involved. The same is true with other types of drug busts that can lead to felony charges. (See "She Looked Eighteen to Me, Officer!" page 26, and "Hookin' a Brother Up," page 53.)

4. You Will Testify

Most defendants do not testify at suppression hearings because they do not want to be subjected to cross-examination concerning the bust and they don't want to be asked where they got all that dope. You will have a chance because you do not need to lie, you do not have any priors (see the Sixth Commandment, page 328), you did not resist arrest (see "Resisting Your Arrest and the Excessive-Force Experience," page 223), you have been living the clean life after making bail (see "Limbaugh Lesson #4," page 259), and you will hopefully have a witness to corroborate your testimony (see "Can I Get a Witness?!" page 222).

You, Grasshopper, are a Drug War ninja. The time has come to snatch the pebble from my hand and beat the rap. If you cannot, the time has come for you to. . . .

Beg for Mercy, Punk

Pleading Guilty

The criminal justice system is a perfect eating and killing machine. Like a shark moving through the ocean, it never stops; its only goal is to process prey efficiently and keep eating. This means guilty pleas, not jury trials. Guilty pleas are processed prey for the shark—junkie McNuggets to pop in its mouth. If you don't present an easy McNugget for the shark, and insist on presenting yourself as a live chicken that it will have to pluck, debone, and deep-fry, the shark gets very angry and will make your death slow and painful. In the face of this gruesome reality, you, like 95 percent of federal bustees and nearly as many in state courts, will plead guilty if you lose your suppression hearing (and you might not even bother with a suppression hearing).

The plea-bargaining process forces you to give up the last of your bothersome rights, including the right to adequate notice of the charges against you—you'll admit to whatever's in that vague police report (pages 221–22)—the right to confront witnesses against you, the right to hold the prosecutor to his burden of proof, the right not to be forced to incriminate yourself, and the right to have a jury decide whether the cop beat a confession out of you. All are gone. In their place is you standing before the judge admitting that it was your dope, with the prosecutor standing behind you holding a Dirty Harry hand cannon known as a mandatory minimum.

There's Been a Regime Change, Lawbreakers

Mandatory Minimums

Judges have been given Drug War battlefield demotions, essentially reducing them to spectators when the time comes to bring the pain. In the old days, a judge might listen to a story like R. P. Day's (page 46) and decide that five years at hard labor is pretty rough treatment for growing some baby pot plants (likely to soothe his frayed nerves from living with that woman). To prevent arbitrary leniency like that, legislators across the country and in Congress started passing mandatory minimums ("M&M's"), ensuring that no matter what kind of sob story you offer up for mercy, you will be punished and punished good.

The prosecutors have the all power now because they decide what to charge you with, essentially dictating your sentence after you're convicted. Get a look at the prosecutor's arsenal and you'll forget all about that stinking trial and start begging for mercy if you know what's good for you.

$88.30 for Your Life: Fayetteville, Kentucky, man Paul Lewis Hayes passed a bad check for $88.30, and lived to regret it. At his arraignment, the prosecutor offered him five years and told him if he didn't take it he would slam him with a life sentence because Hayes had two prior felonies (one when he was seventeen). But Hayes insisted on wasting everyone's time and asserted his Sixth Amendment right to a jury trial. He went to trial. He lost. He got life in prison. And the Supreme Court decided that Hayes was not unconstitutionally "punished" for exercising his right to a jury trail. *No, I didn't make that up.*

You don't have to have a couple of prior felonies like Mr. Hayes did to make risking a trial suicidal. Say you get nabbed in a Tally Me Bananas situation (page 16). The prosecutor is going to charge you with a separate offense for each drug and also for any paraphernalia that you were busted with. Suddenly you're facing a couple of years, even with no priors.

Enter the new-jack sheriff.

"Listen up, kid. Go to trial and you're facing five years . . . no wait, you were within five hundred feet of that public pool . . . you're facing ten years. Plead guilty right now and I'll charge you with attempted possession of the Ecstasy and the most time you're facing is three months. Tomorrow it's three years. Considering that three years in the joint will blow the butt hole clean off a sweet boy like you, you have to ask yourself one question:

" 'Do I feel lucky?' "

"Well. Do you . . . punk?"

Of course not. There's no decision to make. You plead guilty, no matter what kind of charges you're facing, because there are M&M's for every occasion. Significant weight, distribution, distributing to a minor, and prior busts all point toward M&M's. Even in a first-time misdemeanor bust, the DA is going to have plenty of gun to force you to plead guilty. Flip through "The Dope Law Index." Notice how wide the sentences range for the same crime. The high ends of the sentencing spectrums are reserved for the live chickens.

Jackbooted M&M's: The lethal combination of jackbooted cops and M&M's can compel innocent people to plead guilty. Such was the case with Miguel Hernandez and Joseph Jones, both of whom were set up by rogue LAPD cops during the Rampart era. Facing a life sentence under California's "three strikes" law, Jones pled guilty to selling drugs he hadn't sold and took eight years rather than risking trial and getting buried. Hernandez took sixteen months for possessing a gun he didn't possess rather than risking the four years he would have gotten after trial. (Like most victims of corrupt cops, Hernandez and Jones had priors.)

Your attorney will also be pressuring you to cop out, not only because you will be risking such an outrageous sentence, but because guilty pleas are a defense attorney's bread and butter. In a typical low-level drug bust, your attorney will charge a flat fee to handle your case; the less time that he spends on your case, the more money he makes. A public defender is no more anxious to go trial, since he's got six thousand other clients to deal with and there is no way that your measly little drug case is going to occupy the next year of his life.

DOPE NOTE: *A RECENT SUPREME COURT DECISION HAS FOUND ASPECTS OF THE FEDERAL SENTENCING GUIDELINES UNCONSTITUTIONAL, BUT IN GENERAL M&M'S STILL GET A 👍.*

Dealing with the Devil

Negotiating The Plea Agreement

Most people busted on drug charges have not spent their professional lives negotiating high-stakes contracts; they don't assume that any promise is bullshit if it isn't in writing, and they tend to believe whatever the attorneys tell them, listening only to the bottom line: How much time? But the bottom line is sometimes murky, and all the DA is committed to is right there in black and white.

No more. No less.

Once you sign on the dotted line, the DA owns your ass; you will not be able to withdraw from the deal. It will not matter if you didn't negotiate a good deal or you thought you were getting a better deal. There's no lemon law in the Drug War.

DA Sells Shit Sandwich for $600!: When Hawaiian Joy Modafferi signed her plea agreement she wasn't told that because she had traded an undercover cop seven grams of blow for his Glock 9, she was going to get hit with a "gun bump," exposing her to an extra fourteen months in prison. In the plea agreement she signed, the prosecutor agreed only to waive the $600 in fines she was facing and promised to recommend a sentence "within the sentencing guidelines." Since she was not fined and the gun bump is technically "within the guidelines," the judge told Joy that a deal's a deal; it did not matter that she thought she was getting a better deal. Thus, in exchange for surrendering most of her rights and an extra year in the can, Joy saved $600.

Take a lesson from Joy's "deal"; assume that the DA will do anything that he can do to screw you without technically violating the terms of the plea agreement, and keep the following in mind.

Before You Sign . . .
Be involved in the decision-making process and remember that nothing matters but what's written down. Some things to look for:

1. Maximum Time The prosecutor is only making a "recommendation" to the judge. It does not have to be accepted; you can always be sentenced to the max. Your attorney should be able to accurately predict the worst-case scenario, but even judges have trouble deciphering the federal sentencing guidelines, and defense attorneys regularly miss land mines like the one Joy Modafferi stepped on. (She claimed that her attorney was ineffective in his representation of her, but the court told her to be happy with her shit sandwich.)

Go over the facts of your bust with your attorney. The conduct that you are admitting to in the plea agreement may have factors that could give you a longer sentence than you bargained for. Were you busted near a school or public housing project (see "Schoolhouse Rocks," page 27)? Was there a gun anywhere near the scene? Do you have a prior that has not been discussed? Has your parole ever been revoked? These are all booby traps that can bump your sentence up to hardened-criminal territory.

Make certain you know what the DA's *specific recommendation* is going to be and that the recommendation is *in writing.* Also be aware of the fines you are facing; some states require that you pay for the cops' investigation costs, which can get spendy, and for you meth lab techs, cleaning up the toxic dump will really cut into your profit margin. Finally, note the maximum probation period. A long period of intense probation does not sound bad in the face of prison time, but it can be very onerous. Travel restrictions, drug tests, curfews, and abandonment of Fourth Amendment rights are a few typical examples.

2. Appellate Rights For the prosecutor, the goal of plea bargaining is to lock you up now and forget about your case forever and ever, amen. Your agreement will therefore require that you give up your right to appeal various aspects of your bust. The best you can hope for is a conditional plea, allowing you to challenge the outcome of the suppression hearing. Since the hearing usually dictates the outcome of your case, some jurisdictions do not allow these types of pleas after the hearing, but others do. Ideally, you want the right to appeal the decision, since it will be your last hope.

Otherwise, you want the right to appeal your sentence if you get slammed with more time than the DA agreed to recommend, and the right to argue that you received ineffective assistance of counsel at sentencing. While bad advice like Joy's attorney gave her is considered "merely inaccurate," if your attorney tells you the max is five years and you get hooked up with a twenty-five-year stretch, that's considered "grossly inaccurate" and grounds to vacate the guilty plea.

3. Ask About Collateral Damage Pleading guilty to a drug charge can affect your life in ways you probably did not think possible. As discussed in "Now We Bring the Pain," you can be deported, have your property seized, and lose a professional license, your housing, food stamps, the right to vote, and student aid. But much like "collateral damage" (the death of civilians) in a traditional war, these extra penalties are considered the "collateral consequences" of the Drug War: bad, but not worth dwelling on, and not so important that you have a right to be informed of them before you sign your deal. Nor will your attorney be considered ineffective for failing to clue you in. So you better ask somebody.

Presentence Reports

The Fox News of the Criminal Justice System

Imagine how your ex-boyfriend would describe you. The one who surprised you with that diamond tennis bracelet; the one who moved your sister into her new apartment, scored your dope, painted your toenails, carried your purse in public, let your cat sleep on his head; the one who you introduced as your "friend" to your parents and dumped right after you got a boob job. Now imagine that he's writing a report on your character and recommending an appropriate sentence to your judge after your drug bust.

Welcome to pretrial services. Somebody from this organization will interview you to prepare a presentence report for the judge. Never have I seen a report that failed to depict the defendant as an absolutely antisocial junkie swine. Attempting to charm your interviewer will not be unlike charming that ex-boyfriend, but you must try, and the first thing that you would say to the jilted lover is that you are sorry. Very, very sorry. It was all your fault. You are a loathsome human being, undeserving of sympathy. And tell that stud all about the profound respect you have for the vital role he plays in the criminal justice system. Above all, you must tell no lies or inconsistent stories in an effort to minimize your culpability. False statements can be used to enhance the pain.

DOPE NOTE: *IF YOU DIDN'T MAKE BAIL, THIS INTERVIEW WILL BE CONDUCTED IN YOUR CELL, WHERE IT'S VERY HARD TO MAKE A GOOD IMPRESSION, HARD TO DEMONSTRATE THAT YOU'VE MADE SOME CHANGES IN YOUR LIFE.*

The presentence report will follow you for the rest of your criminal career. Anytime, anywhere you get busted, this document will be forwarded to the new prosecutor, so it must accurately reflect the facts of your bust and your personal history because judges pay attention to the report, particularly if they're interested in seeing you suffer. If you don't object to that slant put on your history or correct false statements, it's carved in stone.

Now it's time for some counterspin. The people who showed up for your bail hearing (see "Defending Your Life," page 241) are the same people you want writing letters to the judge, attesting to your outstanding character, your strong work ethic, and your devotion to God, even if none of that's true. Still employable? Got some "remarkable talent" like, uh, Tim Allen? Put that at the top of anything you submit to the court. Had a shitty childhood? Dad split? Mom a junkie? Put it in there. Suffering from a gnarly disease? Depression? Post-traumatic stress? Put it in there. Does your grandmother still believe in you? Put her in there.

"This is a remarkable talent, don't waste it . . . I expect you to be a very successful comedian."

—THE HONORABLE PATRICK MCCAULEY, JUST BEFORE SENTENCING *HOME IMPROVEMENT'S* TIM ALLEN TO TWENTY-EIGHT MONTHS FOR DEALING COKE. THE JUDGE WAS COMMENTING ON LETTERS ALLEN'S FRIENDS AND FAMILY HAD SENT TO THE JUDGE BEFORE THE COMIC COPPED OUT.

Now that the paperwork is done, it's time to go before the judge, who will listen to you grovel for mercy, accept your plea, and pass out the pain.

Now Say You're Sorry (and Act Like You Mean It, Punk Ass!)

The Allocution

Groveling for mercy and confessing your sins in court is known as the allocution. It is essentially the only moment during the entire criminal justice process where you are required to speak to the judge. If you whack someone, here is where you'll have to tell the judge all the gruesome details about sticking him in the ribs, twisting the blade, and then burning the corpse on the barby. A crime like this can sometimes be a little difficult to cough up. A drug bust is a little more straightforward. *Yes, that was my dope. Yes, I was going to smoke it.*

Nevertheless, the allocution is your last chance to make a good impression, and it can make a difference in the type of punishment meted out. Similar to your interview with Fox News, anything short of total and absolute contrition will not do. Summon tears. Acknowledge all the suffering your dope has caused your loved ones, all the money that could have gone to feed and clothe your children, all the opportunities you snorted up your nose. Curse dope as a scourge upon our society and promise that if given an opportunity to turn your wretched life around, you will never see the inside of a courtroom again. And you've got to do it with feeling, and by now you should be feeling it. As one federal judge put it, "[A]cceptance of responsibility necessitates candor and authentic remorse—not merely a pat recital of the vocabulary of contrition."

Do not attempt to minimize your culpability—that's your attorney's job. Got nabbed at a Hard-core House Party (page 34)? Don't start telling the judge that you were really just sitting around that pile of blow, but felt pressure to plead guilty to get it over with. The DA will immediately start whining that you are not accepting responsibility for your conduct, and the judge will stop listening to your plea for compassion.

"I was young, drunk and stupid. I'm still young, but I'm no longer drunk or stupid, you know. . . . I love partying, you know? I love drugs, you know? . . . So I hope and pray that you give me another chance and everything. Thank you."

—Jose Echeverria's allocution pitch just before being sentenced to the max for a drive-by

Finally, do not blame *anything* on the drugs. As Jose's failed allocution efforts demonstrate, judges hate it when defendants blame their criminal conduct on drugs. While a drive-by shooting is hard to explain away no matter how wasted you happened to have been, the judge will be no more receptive to anything you offer up to explain your drug possession or any additional charges—resisting arrest or inadvertently distributing to a minor, for example.

Accepting Your Plea

After listening your allocution, but before passing final sentencing, the judge is required to inform you of the maximum possible sentence, the length of parole, and possible fines, and to make sure you're not completely out your mind. Anything that doesn't sound like what you bargained for, or anything that might be affecting your decision-making process, and you must speak up *now*. Later is too late. Cleo Hightower of Madison, Wisconsin, for example, thought he was dying of cancer when he copped to a dope charge, but he couldn't take it back when he found out he was going live long enough to serve his entire sentence, because he didn't speak up at sentencing. Stephen Teller of Milwaukee later said he had eleven ludes and a couple of belts of whiskey to mellow him out for his sentencing, but he didn't say so at the time, so he couldn't take his soggy plea back.

Defendants don't speak up at sentencing because they sit in

the courtroom all day listening to the judge pop one McNugget after another into his mouth. The answers to the questions are all the same—a series of yeas and nays that all the McNuggets learn the right answers to. Answer incorrectly, everyone gets irritated and the conveyer belt grinds to halt. *Hold on. Everyone stop. This guy's acting like a live chicken.*

Q. *You are on drugs?*

A. Uh-huh.

Q. *What kind of drugs?*

A. This and that.

Q. *Can you understand what's going on?*

A. You're fucking me, right?

Q. *That's an extra six months. Now what's going on?*

A. I'm pleading guilty to doing dope, Your Honor.

Q. *You understand you're in a court of law?*

A. Uh-huh.

Q. *Answer "yes" or "no"; the court reporter can't take your grunts. Do you understand that you're in a courtroom?*

A. Yes.

Q. *Anyone make any promises or threats?*

A. No.

Q. *Did you do dope?*

A. Yes.

Q. *I find this a knowing and voluntary guilty plea. (Bang gavel.) Next! Bailiff, get me some more sweet-and-sour sauce! That last one tasted funny.*

Each of the yeses and nos is a "solemn declaration," made under oath, and you are bound to all of them for eternity. Anything you claim later influenced your decision while the judge was deciding if you were in your right mind will not matter if you said "yes" when you were supposed to and "no" when you were supposed to.

Pleading at Arraignment

In a small-time misdemeanor dope bust, particularly in a big city, everything in this chapter is often condensed into about a ten-minute hearing at your arraignment, where you'll get your best offer and be under the most pressure to plead. After a night or two in jail, you will never want to go back, and the DA will be promising not to send you back there if you plead *right now*. The following is a checklist to help decide whether to cop out:

1. No Time Taking a plea at arraignment is asserting absolutely none of your rights, so it should be a good deal. Any deal at arraignment should be for "time served," which is generally the time you spent in jail waiting for arraignment. If you've been busted before, look for an opportunity to remove your case to a "drug court," which usually means that you will not serve any time.

2. No Record Ideally, you want a deal in which, after a certain amount of time—anywhere from six months to two or three years—the charges will be dropped. While this is better than having a full-blown conviction on your record, it does not mean that the record will disappear altogether after the charges are dismissed (see "You Want to Pretend This Never Happened?!" page 323).

3. No Collateral Damage Never take a plea if you don't know how it will affect the other areas of your life. As noted in "Now We Bring the Pain" (page 311), a drug bust is often not just a drug bust, particularly if you have a professional license of any sort or got busted transporting drugs in your car.

Lost your suppression hearing? Got a look at the DA's weaponry? Still don't want to cop out? Okay. Let's have a trial.

Your Quick and Painful Jury Trial

Let's see. I had no motive to do that dope? *No, no, that won't work.* I had no opportunity to do that dope? *Mmm, no.* It wasn't me? *Probably not going to fly.* That wasn't dope? *But why was I snorting it then?* The cops planted that dope on me? *But why would they do that? How about* "It wasn't my dope?" *Maybe.* The bitch set me up? *Okay, if we can't think of anything else.*

Traditional defense strategies are simply not available in a run-of-the-mill drug possession case, and jury trials just don't happen. When they do, they're real laughers. Most people go to trial in drug cases because they have nothing to lose. They have so many priors, or so much dope, or both, that no matter what the DA offers, big time is coming, so may as well roll the dice and hope for some jury nullification, maybe a mistrial; some of your more pitiful defendants simply enjoy the spectacle of it all.

Once you have lost the suppression hearing (page 271)—you wouldn't be here if you'd won—you are going to have to explain away the dope at trial. Pounding the table and calling the cops lying bastards is not going to get the job done. Typically, the only defenses available are that the dope wasn't yours, the cops set you up, or yes, it was your dope, but you were not selling it.

When you're "Tipping the Scales of Bullshit" (page 31) prior to trial, you're trying to convince the DA or the judge not to charge you with possession. At trial, it's the jury's decision. The same rules apply, but the stakes are a lot higher. A bitch-set-me-up defense (à la D.C. mayor Marion Barry) works only if you were not inclined to do the dope anyway, and if you're going with entrapment it means that the police put some real effort into busting you and you are in more trouble than *Busted!* is aimed at keeping you out of. Finally, the tips on Keeping Dope Around (page 22) are important prior to trial to discourage the DA from charging you with distributing whatever drugs you were nabbed with. At trial, it's the jury who will be deciding if you can smoke two thousand pounds of bud (see "Devoted Dope Ditty," page 21).

Why Wouldn't an Innocent Person Testify?

To make some hay with any of these so-called defenses, you are going to have to take the stand. Not unreasonably, jurors often wonder why an innocent person would not testify in his own defense. Usually this is because he is guilty. But sometimes it's because the defendant has some prior busts that the judge has decided that the DA can grill him about if he testifies. You run into the boy-who-cried-not-my-dope problem. It may be that it wasn't yours this time, but, really, whom would you believe? Or you might not have any priors, but you just look like a bad motherfucker. Your defense attorney was scared shitless of you when he was left alone in your holding cell and knows that the jury will feel the same way; or he may have had a violent negative reaction to you for no particular reason and knows he won't be alone in that chewing-on-tinfoil feeling. Think you would believe a word of anything Linda Tripp had to say, even if you knew nothing about her? As her attorney, I might be inclined to have her sit this one out and try hard to look pathetic and scared.

Word to the Deeply Dysfunctional Families: Dad, Mom, and the kids can always testify against you, and your spouse can bury you as well. Spousal privilege—the right not to be forced to testify against your mate—is not your right; it's your spouse's right. He or she can bring the pain if he or she has finally had enough of you lying around the house smoking bud in your bathrobe.

Fundamentally, if you find yourself sitting on the wrong side of the defense table and they're starting to pick the jury, that knot in the stomach is going to last. DAs hate to go to trial. If you make them, they will convict you. Then they will punish you for exercising your stinking constitutional right to a jury trial by slamming you with everything they've got for wasting their time.

All right. Now that we've gotten your conviction out of the way, it's time for you to start getting religion.

Time to Get Religion, Baby

Time to Appeal

Your appeal is absolutely hopeless. The interest of "finality" has been used to uphold death sentences on appeal where there were questions about the guilt or innocence of the condemned man. But you will believe in your shitty little appeal like a holy warrior waging jihad. You will march into battle, clinging to faith and willing to fight until the day you prove that you got *screwed! The cop lied, man! I'm innocent, motherfucker!* Whether that's true or not, nobody will even be thinking about your appeal for at least a year, maybe six months if you've got some drug money left over.

So it's time to start adjusting to prison life. Get to know

the VIPDs (very important pimp daddies), and try to avoid owing these dudes a carton of smokes. Your ass is currency. Spend it wisely.

Now is the beginning of your life as a letter writer; most of these will be to nag your appellate attorney, or they will take the form of the *pro se* lawsuits mentioned a couple of times; perhaps you'll whip off a few futile motions for a new trial to the same judge who convicted you; these will be dismissed before the ink on the toilet paper is dry. You will also become an expert on constitutional law, known as "technicalities" on appeal. You will write to your appellate attorney about your stinking Fourth Amendment rights with the fervor and devotion befitting any holy warrior.

And you will pray. Pray for the sun to shine on your ass: a reversal.

These blessed rays of sunlight are the Halley's comet of the criminal justice system. Everyone stands around the public defender's office ooohing and aaahing at them, blinking in the unfamiliar light. And then they go back to work and continue losing the rest of their cases that year, and probably the year after that. Plenty of those cases should have been won. Grossly unfair trials are routinely given the ol' 👍. Mostly this is because the rubber stamp said so, you were guilty, the evidence was overwhelming, and/or we're not overturning a jury verdict. We don't care that the DA called you a rotten little cockroach, bottom feeding in a ghetto cesspool of crack cocaine. You did have the crack, *didn't you*?

That's right, I said it. Crack. *Crack! Crack rocks! Crack ho! Crack slinger! Crack head! Crack baby! Cracked out! Crack house!*

Crack vial! Craaaaaaaack! Say the word and everyone in the criminal justice system goes hog wild. It's the Drug War N word. People who smoke crack smoke it because they're hopelessly addicted and/or because it's what's available to get sufficiently oblivious to get through a mostly miserable existence. But to a judge, and most of the rest of society, the only pitiable explanation for smoking crack is being forced to at gunpoint. Whatever drove you to it, say the C word a few thousand times in an appellate brief, as the DA surely will, and the judges stop listening to all the whining about your rights. (Another reason why "Limbaugh Lesson #1" [page 254] is so important: *Lorcet* just doesn't scream "Keep that junkie off the streets" like a *crack rock!* does.)

But no matter what your dope choice, and even if you had it beaten out of you and the judges are willing to entertain your appeal, anytime a conviction is thrown out you will have spent the entire time your appeal is pending in jail. As pointed out in many of the Dope Ditties that were ultimately overturned, this will take time. Lots and lots of time. The glacial pace of the criminal justice system works in your favor only while you are out on bail (see "Limbaugh Lesson # 7," page 266).

It bites behind bars.

And even if your conviction is ultimately overturned, nobody's coming to your cell with your clothes neatly folded and a sheepish grin. No long, slow, emotive walk down the chain-linked corridor, tears streaming down your face, fellow cons applauding wistfully, hootchie mama waiting for you in a Corvette. No, it will be a letter from your appellate attorney—probably it will have some exclamation points—informing you that you got a new trial! An outright dismissal of the charges is like Halley's comet landing in your cell. It never happens.

But getting a new trial is special news indeed; it will for sure be your best day in jail, but your last day in jail is probably not in your immediate future. What will likely happen is that you'll get a second chance to beg for mercy for a much better deal. Otherwise, we'll do it all over again. Choose to go to trial and you will become some DA's personal mission. Not good.

Okay. Suppression hearing lost? Check. Trial lost? Check. Appeal lost? Naturally. Now We Bring the Pain.

Now We Bring the Pain

Busted! is the bible of not getting busted, and if you do anyway, it's here to keep things from getting out of hand, although there are plenty of judges and DAs that feel the way Chief Gates does. Break Commandment One (deal), Two (to kids), Three (carry weight), or Seven (get busted a second time), and the Drug War gets medieval on your ass. The pain chapter is fair warning for failing to heed the Good Word. Since there's not much you can do about being poor and/or of color, the class warfare and racism

> **"The casual drug user ought to be taken out and shot."**
>
> —L.A. POLICE CHIEF DARYL GATES

inherent in the way punishment is meted out, Drug War style, is simply pointed out.

If punishment in our criminal justice system is intended to fit the crime, then drug dealers, particularly black drug dealers, are this country's most vile criminals—more dangerous than stickup punks, more loathsome than pedophiles, and more menacing than rapists, all of whom get less time than dope dealers (crack dealers get 59 percent more time than rapists). And while black people don't like doing dope any more or any less than everyone else in this country, they are almost three times as likely to get busted as white people, and they're twice as likely to do time. Black women receive prison sentences over eight times longer than white women. (It was these types of numbers that prompted Rush's call for busting more white folks.)

"The history of narcotics legislation in this county reveals the determination of Congress to turn the screw of the criminal machinery—detection, prosecution and punishment—tighter and tighter."

—Supreme Court Chief Justice William Rehnquist (not complaining)

Unlike murder, where if you're extremely pissed off when you did it you get less time, penalties for drug offenses do not take into account the circumstances that drove you to commit the crime. "Three strike" laws—life sentences after a third conviction of any kind—drop the hammer without regard to personal circumstances, and mandatory minimums pass out arbitrary sentences, usually based strictly on drug weight (other varieties of M&M's are complained about on page 288). Before Reagan stripped the softhearted federal judges of their sentencing discretion, the average time for a drug offense was almost two years; now it's seven years.

> **"America has the longest prison sentences in the West, yet the only condition long sentences demonstrably cure is heterosexuality."**
>
> —Professor Bruce Jackson, SUNY Buffalo

Virtually every state has M&M's as well. Before they were recently reformed, New York's notorious Rockefeller drug laws, for example, mandated a prison term of *fifteen years to life* for anyone convicted of selling two ounces of dope. (Now you get "only" eight to twenty years.) The Rockefeller laws, by the way, immediately provided all the boys and girls in the South Bronx an alternative to working at Mickey D's. They could sell crack. Because the law was so draconian, dealers put the shorties on the street because they were not usually subject to The Rock.

At least not the first time.

The Consequences of a Drug Conviction That Go Far Deeper Than Your Cavity Search

Even after you've done your time, you could be taking shrapnel from your Drug War battle for years. Your property can be seized; you can be denied student aid, and lose your right to vote and a professional license; and you can be deported. None of this punishment is considered "punishment" within the meaning of the stinking Constitution, so don't even start with that double-jeopardy nonsense.

Gettin' Jacked by the Police

Civil Forfeitures

The Drug War does not survive on tax dollars alone, and the government does not like to admit how much money it's spending on this interminable war. The answer? Cooking the books is an old favorite, but civil forfeitures are preferred, since there's no fuzzy math and no lobbying bureaucrats in Washington; they just take that shit. The goal of the civil forfeiture system is to create a self-sustaining Drug War, with dope buyers spending the money, drug dealers making the money, DEA agents seizing the money, and cops spending the money to bust more drug dealers. Round and round it goes. Former attorney general Dick Thornburgh summed up the circle of logic nicely: "[I]t is truly satisfying to think that it's now possible for a drug dealer to serve time in a forfeiture-financed prison after being arrested by agents driving a forfeiture-provided automobile while working in a forfeiture-funded sting operation."

The cops, in other words, get to eat what they kill, and their hunger can cloud their judgment.

Deadly Dope Ditty: Donald Scott of Malibu, California, used to live on a fat $5 million ranch that the cops had been admiring for some time. Mr. Scott had always despised dope, but another one of those "known informants" told the police that he had some pot growing on his property. Based on the informant's bogus information, a warrant was obtained, and on the morning of October 2, 1992, thirty-five cops in full jackboot gear—masks, flak jackets, and assault rifles—broke down the door with a battering ram and raided the Scotts' house. An astonished Mrs. Scott started screaming at the masked men; and when Mr. Scott picked up his pistol, apparently to come to her aid, the cops blew him away. The district attorney later conceded that the raid was motivated at least in part to cash in on the proceeds from the seizure and auction of the Scotts' Malibu ranch.

The tragic story of Donald Scott aside, simply keeping dope in your house is not going to result in the house's seizure, but start selling out of the crib, or setting up Nazi labs (for making meth), or growing pot, and DEA agents are going to be playing mixed doubles on your tennis court.

Anything that moves is easier to seize because the dope can go from point A to point B, and transporting drugs is plenty of connection to justify a jacking. Your car, your boat, your double-wide hurricane catcher, and your Gulfstream V are all vulnerable when there are drugs on board. All that is required to seize property is to show that there was a "substantial connection" between that property and the dope. Roughly translated: You use it, you lose it.

But, but . . . Wait! It's Not My Dope!

Up until 2000, there was no "innocent owner" defense. Property was either connected to the crime or it wasn't; it didn't matter if the owner had no idea that someone was using the property illegally. During these salad days of civil forfeiture, the U.S. Coast Guard seized a $2.5 million yacht when agents discovered about a bowl's worth of bud on board, although the owner had rented out the boat to the lawbreaker and had no idea he'd planned a crime spree. (They gave it back years later, after the incident stirred the first cries for forfeiture reform.) Also during this period the Supreme Court gave a 👍 to the seizure of a wife's car that was seized when her husband was busted screwing a prostitute in it, although it was apparent that the wife hadn't given her husband the 👍 to bang hookers in her car. (And nobody gave her back her car.)

The cops still seize first and ask questions later, and your property can still be seized regardless of whether you knew your tenant was growing pot or spinning the Evil Beats. But these days you will have a long shot at proving that you were totally oblivious of what was happening on or in your property, depending on your ability to tip the Scales of Bullshit (page 31). If you are aware of drug crimes being committed on your property, or it will be hard to deny, it's time to get uptight. Discover Mom's little script-fraud ring and you'll have to wrest mama from the menthols and off the couch, and tell her to hit the pavement. It is no defense to simply not be involved in illegal drug activity on your property. You must put a stop to it if you want to keep your crib off the PBA auction block.

Poor in the Drug War

Being poor in the Drug War is never easy. You're suspicious just standing around your own neighborhood (page 89), your house can be searched without a warrant (page 108), it's easier to be charged with possessing the community dope (page 115), you're more likely to be subjected to a Bullshit Stop (page 143), you're less likely to get released on bail (page 244), and even your mail is less respected (page 120).

These are a few of the many ways noted throughout *Busted!* that make it easier to get busted if you're living in poverty. And it's much harder to fight your drug bust. Note how many of the Limbaugh Lessons can truly be utilized by the poor. One. Abandoning Principle. Not so useful if you're at the bottom of the food chain.

While it's easier to get busted, and harder to fight it, the "collateral damage" poor people suffer as a result of a drug conviction is the knockout blow. In twenty-four states, any drug conviction makes you *permanently* ineligible for food stamps and temporary assistance to needy families. Education grants, federal loans, and job training can also be denied for a first-time misdemeanor drug bust. Last, but most medieval, entire families can be evicted from federal public housing for drug use—not sale—of any kind, by any of the occupants, even if no drugs are ever done in the apartment.

It happens. It happened to Pearly Rucker, and it happened to Willie Lee.

Disgraceful Dope Ditties: Sixty-three-year-old Pearly lived in Oakland, California, public housing for over fifteen years with her mentally disabled daughter, her two grandchildren, and a great-grandchild. Pearly's daughter was caught possessing coke three blocks from her apartment one afternoon in the late nineties.

Seventy-one-year-old Willie lived in the public housing project for over twenty-five years. While his grandsons were living with him, they got busted smoking pot in the parking lot of the housing complex.

Following the busts, the Department of Housing and Urban Development sought to evict everyone living in both apartments, including Pearly and Willie, under HUD's "One Strike" policy. The judges of California's top federal court thought that it was outrageous to evict innocent tenants who could not control the behavior of other family members, particularly outside of the apartment. But in 2002 the Supreme Court evicted Pearly and Willie, the disabled daughter, the pot-smoking grandchildren, and everyone else.

So if you're poor, the Drug War is out to get you. As an attorney, I can't advise you to steal this book, but I can tell you that a shoplifting bust is *always* better than a drug bust.

The Ripe Smell of Hypocrisy: The same year that Congress passed the Welfare Reform Act, which banned drug bustees from receiving food stamps, Congress rejected a proposal to ban its members from losing their pensions should they get convicted of a felony. Nice work for the homeboys. (And no drug tests either!)

Now These Dopers Want to Go to School?

Dope smoking has been shaping the minds of our nation's college kids for a couple of generations now. But these days a pot bust, no matter when it occurred, can cost you your opportunity to use the ol' "Yeah, I did some dope, but I was in college" line (page 121), because you will be denied student aid and won't be in college doing your dope. Convictions for crimes like, oh, say, rape and/or murder, however, will not disqualify you. The result of the ironically titled Higher Education Act has been the rejection of over one hundred thousand financial aid applications because of a prior drug bust, and the number is likely much higher if you consider potential applicants who didn't bother applying because they'd been busted before.

DOPE NOTE: *THE APPLICANTS WHO WERE REJECTED EITHER HONESTLY CHECKED THE JUST-*

DENY-MY-AID-NOW BOX OR SKIPPED THE QUESTION. THE FEDS HAVE NO WAY TO INDEPENDENTLY VERIFY WHETHER YOU HAVE BEEN BUSTED; THEY CLAIM TO DO SPOT CHECKS WITH LOCAL LAW ENFORCEMENT OFFICIALS. THE CHOICE IS YOURS. BEWARE, THOUGH; LYING ON THE APPLICATION IS A CRIME.

And They Want to Vote Too?

Nothing like a drug bust to politicize your view of the Drug War, and get you to the polls to vote that bastard who sent you upstate for smoking a fatty out of office. *Not so fast, lawbreaker!*

While no other democracy on the face of the planet disenfranchises convicts after they've served their time, here in the States almost 4 million people cannot vote as a result of a conviction, and 1.4 million of them have completed their sentence and are not on any sort of parole. As a result, *13 percent* of the black people in this country have been disenfranchised. One study of the great state of Florida's contribution to Bush Jr.'s rousing victory in 2000 concluded that Big Al would have squashed Dubya if the ex-felons in that state had been permitted to vote, even accounting for low voter turnout, and the study went so far as to throw some votes Dubya's way. And if you'd like to get your voting rights restored in Florida you'll have to fill out a sixteen-page application, to be personally approved by . . . Governor Jeb Bush. (Listen to the evil laughter.)

Next They'll Want Jobs

Nothing like a cushy government-issued desk to throw your feet up on for twenty years and ease into retirement without having endured a lot of stress over the years. But seven states—Alabama (not a good state in which to party), Indiana (also bad), Arkansas, Iowa, Nevada, Ohio, and South Carolina—deny ex-cons this job opportunity, barring them from any state job (*yes, even the lowly dope smokers*), and nineteen states have some restriction on hiring ex-cons, at least those with felony convictions.

In the private sector, a drug bust can make professional licenses hard to qualify for. While you may have anticipated that with lawyers and doctors and pharmacists, billiard room employees, septic tank cleaners, barbers, embalmers, health care workers, real estate agents, and contractors are all licensed professionals.

And then there is the dreaded background check, required in the banking, health care, and airline industries, but common down at Mickey D's too. Most job applications include a "character component," where you'll have to decide whether to cough it up or not. Check "You Want to Pretend This Never Happened?" (page 323) for some tips on expunging your record, and deciding whether or not to check the just-fire-me-now box. But it gets easier for an employer to do background checks every day. Arrest records are available online in twenty-eight states, and private companies can get at them in any state if the price is right.

Let's Just Deport 'Em

Passed into law in 1996, the Anti-Terrorism and Effective Death Penalty Act (*catchy, eh?*) raised the stakes for all noncitizens living here in the States who like their dope. No matter how long you have legally lived in this country, if you're convicted of an "aggravated felony" or a crime involving "moral turpitude," you can be deported, *after* you've served your sentence. And if you've already served your sentence, the INS can come knock on your door years later, arrest you, and put you in jail with all the rapists and stickup punks while you wait to be deported to a country you may not have been to since you were born. Deportees sometimes sit in jail for months, even years, waiting for deportation.

Aggravated felons and moral-turpitude types sound like just the kind of scumbags we'd want to get rid of, but one man's dope is another man's mortal sin. Drug offenses are high on the list of deportable crimes. *Any* drug conviction, including misdemeanors, aside from *one* bust for *thirty grams* or less of *marijuana* for *"personal use,"* will get you deported. Two misdemeanor busts equals one aggravated felony, which means see . . . you . . . later.

Perhaps Something with a Little More Sex Appeal? Public Humiliation

A judge interested in humiliating you publicly will have either a personal thing for whatever type of crime you have committed—usually a DUI—or a sense of humor, like the judge who ordered a purse snatcher to wear tap shoes whenever he was in public; or she will have a good feel for what would give her constituents a warm feeling come election time, like the judge who ordered Wall Street brokers to clean up the streets of Hoboken, New Jersey, after getting nabbed pissing in public (see "Act Normal, Dude, It's a Cop," pages 74–75).

"My record plus two six-packs equal four years."

—T-SHIRT A PROBATIONER IN CALIFORNIA WAS ORDERED TO WEAR EVERY TIME HE LEFT HIS HOUSE

You are generally given an option between public humiliation and jail, but you will choose whatever humiliation the judge has in mind after spending a night or two in the can. Drunks have been ordered to put stickers on their cars announcing their DUI bust and to wear neon bracelets reading "DUI Convict," and they have been forced to publish moving apologies, along with their mug shots, in their local rag. Judges have ordered grandmothers to whip their grandchildren accused of possessing coke. And a judge in Tennessee personally whipped juvenile offenders.

DOPE NOTE: *JUSTICE SCALIA BELIEVES THAT CANING (PUBLICLY WHACKING YOU ON THE ASS WITH A WET STICK) IS PERFECTLY CONSTITUTIONAL, AND NO COURT HAS FOUND OTHERWISE.*

You Want to Pretend This Never Happened?!

Expunging Your Arrest Record

Twenty-five percent of the citizens of this country live all or most of their life with a criminal record. By reading this far you should be at least dimly aware of all the bad things that flow from an arrest record. It's like a having a long piece of grimy toilet paper stuck to the heel of your shoe. No matter how snappily you dress, you're always going to be hard to take too seriously. Pulling the offending tissue off is not easy; and it remains even if you were only arrested, but never actually charged with a crime. It remains long after the charges were dropped, and it remains after you were acquitted at trial.

Since, as noted in "Carving Your Drug Bust in Stone"

(page 231), arrest records are public documents and are available online in a variety of subscription services, it is in your best interest to do everything in your power to be able to pretend that your little youthful indiscretion never happened. Only an expungement or a sealed record will do that. Nobody "forgets" about his drug bust; it's one of life's defining moments, remember?

But expunging your record does not mean that someone goes and gets the file and throws it in the fires of absolution. It will *always* be there. Harder to rid yourself of than AOL. Not only will it crop up during your Senate confirmation hearing, but it will be front and center the next time you get busted and the judge is deciding on the amount of bail or how much pain to mete out at sentencing. Judges tend to view acquittals or dismissed charges as evidence that you got lucky (you probably did), not that you didn't commit the crime. It is perfectly legal for you to be given higher bail or a harsher sentence because you were once arrested, even if was an obviously bogus bust.

If you haven't broken the First, Second, Third, or Seventh Commandments (pages 327–328), you will have a shot at expunging your record, depending on what state you're in. Every state is different, but arrests that did not result in a conviction are eligible in forty states. But of those forty states first-time, small-time drug possession convictions are eligible for expungement in only sixteen. In those states, after a certain amount of time has passed, usually a few years, you can apply to a judge for expungement, and if it's granted, you can pretend it never happened, depending on how the question is asked and who's asking.

States Where You Can Pretend Your Arrest Never Happened

Some of your more suspicious employers will ask whether you have any sealed or expunged arrest records. In the following states you can deny the bust only if asked whether you have ever been arrested, not if you're asked about expunged cases (or convictions): Alaska, Arkansas, California, Colorado, Connecticut, Delaware, Florida, Hawaii, Illinois, Kansas, Kentucky, Louisiana, Massachusetts, Maryland, Mississippi, Missouri, New Hampshire, New Jersey, Nevada, New York, North Carolina, Ohio, Oklahoma, Oregon, Pennsylvania, Rhode Island, Utah, Virginia, and West Virginia.

States Where You Can Pretend Your Conviction Never Happened

In Arizona, California, Indiana, Kentucky, Massachusetts, Michigan, Mississippi, New Hampshire, New Jersey, Nevada, Ohio, Oklahoma, Oregon, Rhode Island, Utah, and Washington. But in Arizona, California, and Indiana, you have to reveal your conviction if asked about sealed records.

States with Permanent Tattoos

In the following states, the bust never goes away: Iowa, Maine, Montana, (both) Dakotas, Nebraska, New Mexico, Vermont, and Why-oh-why-did-I-get-busted-in-Wyoming.

So Who Wants to Know?

In a private employment setting, if your record has been expunged and you are asked about your arrest record you will have to decide how honest you are going to be. The chance that a private employer has the means or desire to conduct a search sufficiently thorough to discover a sealed arrest record is fairly remote, but your new boss will be able to fire you on the spot if the record ever sees the light of day. Your call. But check the "Dubious Dope Ditty" (page 58). If you're going into law or law enforcement or applying for virtually any type of professional license, you've usually gotta cough it up, no matter where you live or what ultimately happened with the bust. And if the arrest is already part of a state agency's record (the state's real estate board, for example), expungement will not change the records once it's in there.

DOPE NOTE: *LOCAL ATTORNEYS USUALLY CHARGE A FLAT FEE TO HANDLE AN APPLICATION/PETITION FOR EXPUNGEMENT. BROKE? CALL THE LOCAL PUBLIC DEFENDER'S OFFICE AND THEY'LL HAVE SOME FORMS TO DO IT YOUR DAMN SELF.*

THE *BUSTED!* TEN COMMANDMENTS

1 – Thou Shall Not Deal.

Like any other war, in the Drug War there are the grunts (you) and there are the field generals (the dealers). The grunts take far more casualties because there are so many more of them, but the field generals suffer much more when they get hit.

2 – Thou Shall Not Do Dope with Kiddies. If Thou Art a Kiddy, Thou Shall Not Do Dope.

Much like the dealers, kids get special treatment in the Drug War. Anyone over eighteen passes the pipe to anyone under eighteen and the gloves are off. Any time kids are mixed up in your bust, everything is more painful and harder on your karma.

3 – Thou Shall Not Covet More Than a Misdemeanor Buzz.

Misdemeanors are painful and humiliating. Felonies leave scars and speech impediments. Keep your drug weight down and observe the First, Second and Seventh Commandments. Break these and possible pain starts at a year in the joint and runs all the way to life.

4 – Thou Shall Not Piss Away Thy Rights.

Never consent to a search. Always remain silent. Never get wasted in public. Always ask to speak to an attorney. Never sign a plea bargain you don't understand.

5 – Thou Shall Be Calm.

Panic is deadly in the Drug War; it can lead to breaking the Fourth Commandment, and it will make the police suspicious and/or nervous themselves, calmed by several blows with the nightstick. Panic can also lead to additional charges for attempting to destroy evidence and will ensure that you are charged with possessing any drugs in the vicinity. Nervous types should honor the Eighth Amendment at any expense.

6 – Thou Shall Not Piss Off the Police.

Forget the lawmakers in Congress, forget the DAs, and forget the judges; the police have all the power in the Drug War. An angry cop has the power to bring you down no matter what the circumstances may be. Once a cop decides to bust you, you begin your slide down the black hole of the criminal justice system, and it's very, very hard to stop the slide until you're shat out the other end.

7 – Ye Get Busted, Ye Shall Never Get Busted Again.

Now it's not a "mistake." Now it's a "drug problem." Now it is clear that you didn't learn your lesson. Now we bring the pain.

8 – Thou Shall Leave Thy Dope at Home.

The only true right to privacy you have is in your home. Once you take your dope on the road, all the rules change. At the airport and in your car, you're just Drug War cannon fodder.

9 – Know Thy Friends; Mistrust Thy Enemies.

A fellow citizen is almost as powerful a Drug Warrior as a cop. A tip from a fed-up neighbor can lead to a house search. A fellow motorist can have you pulled over. Your roommate can consent to a search of your bedroom. Someone you hooked up can have you busted. An ex-girlfriend can get you drug-tested. So be damn sure whom you're discussing and/or doing dope with. And never give a reporter or blogger any kind of Drug War quote you can't live with; it will end up online and in eternity.

10 – Thou Shall Check Thy Look in the Mirror.

Marching out onto the Drug War battlefield means taking stock of yourself, your faculties. Make an honest assessment of your state of mind, your goals for the night on the razz, and your personal style. If it were your job to bust people for possessing drugs, would you be interested in seeing what's in your pockets? Tattoos, piercings, wacky hair, funky smells, sporting the freshly fucked-up look, political T-shirts and/or bumper stickers, are all suspicious. If you're a suspicious type, heed the Eighth Commandment.

So That's The Drug War. Let's Be Careful Out There.

The Dope Law Index

The Bad News on Marijuana, Cocaine, Ecstacy, and Methamphetamine—from Alabama to Wyoming and D.C. Too

A cross-country drug trip is a roller coaster of criminal liability. A gram of coke in Utah goes for five years, so push hard for Vegas, baby, where it's a year (four if they're feeling nasty). Since nearly all drug possession cases are tried in state court—the feds bust people with cancer smoking pot, campers in our nation's national parks, and dealers—you better keep a copy of *Busted!* on board, hidden in the trunk, in someone else's luggage, of a car you're not driving that has no code violations and no inflammatory bumper stickers, and that never cracks sixty-five miles per hour, and it would be good if you're unmistakably white and elderly. (See "Packing for Your Drug Trip," page 148.)

Always remember the First, Second, Third, and Seventh Commandments. Break any of these commandments and everything gets more painful. In those states where *any* amount of *any* drug other than pot is a felony, the DAs are much more likely to give you a chance to get the charges dismissed after a period of not getting busted again if you keep those commandments in mind. But nothing's guaranteed, which is why we also must keep "Limbaugh Lesson #1" (page 254) in mind at all times.

DOPE NOTE: THIS WAS CURRENT LAW AT THE TIME OF WRITING, BASED ON STATE STATUTE. WHEN THE STAKES ARE JAIL TIME, YOU ARE ALWAYS GOING TO WANT TO DOUBLE CHECK, AND INDIVIDUAL CITIES OFTEN HAVE GUIDELINES FOR POSSESSION BUSTS THAT DIFFER FROM STATE LAW.

Marijuana

The following states have probation eligibility for first offenses: Arizona (first and second with drug treatment and testing), Georgia, Illinois, Iowa, Kansas, Kentucky, Massachusetts, Mississippi, Montana, Nebraska, Nevada, North Carolina, Pennsylvania, and Virginia.

STATE	AMOUNT	FINE	TIME
Alabama	Keep it under 2.2 pounds	\$2,000	1 year
Alaska	Keep it under 8 ounces	\$1,000	90 days
Arizona	Keep it under 2 pounds	\$750–\$150,000	6 months–1.5 years
Arkansas	Keep it under 1 ounce	\$1,000	1 year
California	Keep it under 28.5 grams	\$100	none
	Anything over 28.5 grams	\$500	6 months
Colorado	Keep it under 1 ounce	\$100	none
Connecticut	Keep it under 4 ounces	\$1,000	1 year
Delaware	Any	\$1,150	6 months
Florida	Keep it under 20 grams	\$1,000	1 year

STATE	AMOUNT	FINE	TIME
Georgia	Keep it under 1 ounce	$1,000	1 year
Hawaii	Keep it under 1 ounce	$1,000	30 days
	Keep it under 1 pound	$2,000	1 year
Idaho	Keep it under 3 ounces	$1,000	1 year
Illinois	Keep it under 2.5 grams	$1,500	30 days
	Under 10 grams	$1,500	6 months
	Under 30 grams	$2,500	1 year
Indiana	Keep it under 30 grams	$5,000	1 year
Iowa	Any	$1,500	1 year
	Any (second offense)	$500–$5,000	2 years
Kansas*	Any	$100,000	10–42 months
Kentucky*	Keep it under 8 ounces	$500	1 year
Louisiana	Any	$500	6 months
	Any (subsequent offenses)	$2,000	5 years
Maine	Keep it under 1.25 ounces	$200–$400	civil violation
Maryland	Any	$1,000	1 year
Massachusetts	Any	$500	6 months
Michigan	Any	$2,000	1 year
Minnesota	Keep it under 42.5 grams	$300	drug education
Mississippi*	Keep it under 30 grams	$100–$250	none
Missouri	Keep it under 35 grams	$1,000	1 year
Montana*	Keep it under 60 grams	$100–$500	6 months
Nebraska	Keep it under 1 ounce	$100	citation/none
	Second offense	$200	5 days
	Subsequent offenses	$300	7 days
	Under 1 pound	$500	7 days
Nevada	Any	$600	none
	Second offense	$1,000	drug treatment
	Subsequent offenses	$2,000	1 year
New Hampshire	Any	$2,000	1 year
New Jersey	Keep it under 50 grams	$1,000	6 months
New Mexico	Keep it under 1 ounce	$100	15 days
	Subsequent offenses	$1,000	1 year
	Under 8 ounces	$100–$1,000	1 year
	Under 18 ounces	$5,000	18 months
New York	Keep it under 15 grams	$100	citation/none

STATE	AMOUNT	FINE	TIME
	Second offense	$200	citation/none
	Subsequent offenses	$250	15 days
	Under 2 ounces	$500	3 months
	Under 8 ounces	$1,000	1 year
North Carolina	Keep it under 0.5 ounce	none	30 days
	Under 1.5 ounces	none	1–120 days
Ohio	Keep it under 100 grams	$100	citation
	Under 200 grams	varies	none
	Under 1000 grams	varies	6 months–1 year
Oklahoma	Any (first offense)	none	1 year
	Any (subsequent offenses)	none	2–10 years
Oregon	Keep it under 1 ounce	$500–$1,000	none
Pennsylvania*	Keep it under 30 grams	$500	30 days
	Anything over 30 grams	$5,000	1 year
Rhode Island	Keep it under 1000 grams	$200–$500	1 year
South Carolina	Keep it under 1 ounce	$100–$200	30 days
	Subsequent offenses	$200–$1,000	1 year
South Dakota	Keep it under 2 ounces	$1,000	1 year
Tennessee	Keep it under 0.5 ounce	$2,500	1 year
Texas	Keep it under 2 ounces	$2,000	6 months
	Under 4 ounces	$4,000	1 year
	Under 1 pound	$10,000	6 months–2 years
Utah	Keep it under 1 ounce	$1,000	6 months
	Under 1 pound	$2,500	1 year
Vermont*	Keep it under 2 ounces	$500	6 months
Virginia	Any (first offense)	$500	30 days
	Subsequent offenses	$2,500	1 year
Washington*	Keep it under 40 grams	$1,000	90 days
West Virginia	Keep it under 15 grams	automatic conditional discharge	
	Over 15 grams	$1,000	90 days–6 months
Wisconsin*	Any	$1,000	6 months
Wyoming*	Keep it under 3 ounces	$1,000	90 days
Washington, D.C.	Any	$1,000	6 months

* Subsequent convictions can double penalties or qualify as felonies.

COCAINE

STATE	AMOUNT	FINE	TIME
Alabama	Keep it under 28 grams	$5,000	1–10 years
Alaska	Any	$50,000	5 years
Arizona	Any	$2,000–$150,000	2.5 years
Arkansas	Any	$10,000	3–10 years
California	Any	$20,000	1.5–3 years
Colorado	Keep it under 25 grams	$2,000–$500,000	2–6 years
Connecticut	Any	$50,000	7 years
Delaware	Any	$1,000	2 years
Florida	Keep it under 28 grams	$5,000	5 years
Georgia	Keep it under 28 grams	none	2–15 years
Hawaii	Keep it under 3.54 grams	$10,000	5 years
Idaho	Keep it under 28 grams	$15,000	7 years
Illinois	Keep it under 15 grams	$25,000	1–3 years
Indiana	Keep it under 3 grams	$10,000	1.5 years
Iowa	Any (first offense)	$250–$1,500	1 year
	Any (second offense)	$5,000	2 years

STATE	AMOUNT	FINE	TIME
Iowa	Any (third and subsequent offenses)	felony	
Kansas	Any	$2,500	1 year
Kentucky	Any (first offense)	$500	1 year
	Any (subsequent offense)	$1,000–$10,000	1–5 years
Louisiana	Keep it under 28 grams	$5,000	5 years
Maine	Keep it under 14 grams	$2,000	1 year
Maryland	Keep it under 28 grams	$25,000	4 years
Massachusetts	Any (first offense)	$1,000	1 year
Michigan	Keep it under 25 grams	$25,000	4 years
Minnesota	Keep it under 3 grams	$10,000	5 years
Mississippi	Keep it under 0.1 gram	$1,000	1 year
Missouri	Keep it under 150 grams	$5,000	7 years
Montana	Any	$50,000	5 years
Nebraska	Any	$10,000	5 years
Nevada	Keep it under 4 grams	$5,000	1–4 years
New Hampshire	Any	$25,000	7 years
New Jersey	Any	$35,000	3–5 years
New Mexico	Any	$5,000	1.5 years
New York	Keep it under 500 milligrams	$1,000	1 year
North Carolina	Keep it under 28 grams	none	4–6 months
North Dakota	Keep it under 500 grams	$5,000	5 years
Ohio	Keep it under 25 grams	$5,000	6 months–1.5 years
Oklahoma	Any	none	2–10 years
Oregon	Any	$100,000	5 years
Pennsylvania	Any	$5,000	1 year
Rhode Island	Keep it under 28.35 grams	$500–$5,000	3 years
South Carolina	Keep it under 10 grams	$5,000	2 years (misdemeanor)
South Dakota	Any	$10,000	10 years
Tennessee	Any (first two offenses)	$750–$2,500	1 year

STATE	AMOUNT	FINE	TIME
Texas	Keep it under 1 gram	$10,000	6 months–2 years
Utah	Any	$5,000	5 years
Vermont	Keep it under 2.5 grams	$2,000	1 year
Virginia	Any	$2,500	1–10 years
Washington	Any	$10,000	5 years
West Virginia	Any	$1,000	6 months–1 year
Wisconsin	Any (first offense)	$5,000	1 year
Wyoming	Keep it under 3 grams powder	$1,000	1 year
	0.5 gram crack (first two offenses)	$1,000	1 year
Washington, D.C.	Any	$1,000	6 months

ECSTASY

STATE	AMOUNT	FINE	TIME
Alabama	Any	felony, not specified	felony, not specified
Alaska	Any	$50,000	5 years
Arizona	Any	$1,000–$150,000	2.5 years
Arkansas	Any	$10,000	3–10 years
California	Any	$1,000	1 year
Colorado	Keep it under 25 grams	$3,000–$750,000	4–12 years
Connecticut	Any (first offense)	$1,000	1 year
	Any (subsequent offenses)	$2,000	5 years
Delaware	Any	$1,150	6 months
Florida	Keep it under 10 grams	$5,000	5 years
Georgia	Any	none	2–15 years
Hawaii	Keep it under 7.09 grams	$10,000	5 years
Idaho	Any	$1,000	1 year
Illinois	Any	$25,000	1–3 years
Indiana	Any	$10,000	1.5 years
Iowa	Any (first offense)	$250–$1,500	1 year

STATE	AMOUNT	FINE	TIME
Iowa	Any (second offense)	$500–$5,000	2 years not specified
	Any (third offense and beyond)	felony, not specified	felony, not specified
Kansas	Any	$2,500	1 year
Kentucky	Any (first offense)	$1,000	1 year
Louisiana	Any	$5,000	10 years
Maine	Any	$2,000	1 year
Maryland	Any	$25,000	4 years (misdemeanor)
Massachusetts	Any (first offense)	$1,000	1 year
Michigan	Any	felony, not specified	felony, not specified
Minnesota	Any	felony, not specified	felony, not specified
Mississippi	Keep it under 0.1 gram/1 dose	$1,000	1 year
Missouri	Any	$5,000	7 years
Montana	Any	$50,000	5 years
Nebraska	Any	$10,000	5 years
Nevada	Keep it under 4 grams	$5,000	1–4 years
New Hampshire	Any	felony, not specified	felony, not specified
New Jersey	Any	$35,000	3–5 years
New Mexico	Any	$500–$1,000	1 year
New York	Keep it under 25 milligrams	$1,000	1 year
North Carolina	Keep it under 28 grams	none	4–6 months
North Dakota	Any	$5,000	5 years
Ohio	Keep it under 30 grams	$2,500	6 months–1 year
Oklahoma	Any	felony, not specified	felony, not specified
Oregon	Any	$200,000	10 years
Pennsylvania	Any	$5,000	1 year
Rhode Island	Any	$500–$5,000	3 years
South Carolina	Keep it under 15 doses	$1,000	6 months

STATE	AMOUNT	FINE	TIME
South Dakota	Any	$10,000	10 years
Tennessee	Any (first two offenses)	$750–$2,500	1 year
Texas	Keep it under 1 gram	$10,000	6 months–2 years
Utah	Any	$5,000	5 years
Vermont	Keep it under 2 grams	$2,000	1 year
Virginia	Any	$2,500	1–10 years
Washington	Any	$10,000	5 years
West Virginia	Any	$1,000	6 months–1 year
Wisconsin	Any	felony, not specified	felony, not specified
Wyoming	Keep it under 3 grams (first two offenses)	$1,000	1 year
Washington, D.C.	Any	$1,000	6 months

METHAMPHETAMINE

STATE	AMOUNT	FINE	TIME
Alabama	Any	$10,000	2–20 years
Alaska	Any	none	10 years
Arizona	Any	$1,000–$150,000	2.5 years
Arkansas	Any	$10,000	3–10 years
California	Any	$1,000	1 year
Colorado	Any	$2,000–$500,000	2–6 years
Delaware	Any	$1,000	2 years (misdemeanor)
Florida	Any	$5,000	5 years
Georgia	Any	none	2–15 years
Hawaii	Any	$10,000	10 months–5 years
Idaho	Any	$15,000	7 years
Illinois	Any	$25,000	1–3 years
Indiana	Any	$10,000	1.5 years
Iowa	Any (first offense)	$1,500	1 year

STATE	AMOUNT	FINE	TIME
	Any (second offense)	$5,000	2 years (misdemeanor)
	Any (subsequent offenses)	felony	not specified
Kansas	Any	$2,500	1 year
Kentucky	Any (first offense)	$500	1 year
	Any (subsequent offenses)	$1,000–$10,000	1–5 years
Louisiana	Any	$5,000	5 years
Maine	Any	$5,000	5 years
Maryland	Any	$25,000	4 years
Massachusetts	Any (first offense)	$1,000	1 year
Michigan	Any	$2,000	2 years
Minnesota	Any	$5,000–$1 million	30 years
Mississippi	Keep it under 0.1gram/1 dose	$1,000	1 year
Missouri	Any	$5,000	7 years
Montana	Any	$50,000	5 years
Nebraska	Any	$10,000	5 years
Nevada	Any	$5,000	1–4 years
New Hampshire	Any	$25,000	7 years
New Jersey	Any	$35,000	3–5 years
New Mexico	Any	$5,000	1.5 years
New York	Keep it under 14.18 grams	$1,000	1 year
North Carolina	Keep it under 28 grams	none	4–6 months
North Dakota	Any	$5,000	5 years
Ohio	Keep it under 3 grams	$2,500	6 months–1 year
Oklahoma	Any	none	2–10 years
Oregon	Any	$100,000	5 years
Pennsylvania	Any	$5,000	1 year
Rhode Island	Any	$500–$1,000	3 years
South Carolina	Any	$5,000	2 years
South Dakota	Any	$10,000	10 years
Tennessee	Any (first two offenses)	$750–$2,500	1 year
Texas	Any	$10,000	6 months–2 years

STATE	AMOUNT	FINE	TIME
Utah	Any	$5,000	5 years
Vermont	Keep it under 2.5 grams	$2,000	1 year
Virginia	Any	$2,500	1–10 years
Washington	Any	$10,000	5 years
West Virginia	Any	$5,000	6 months–1 year
Wisconsin	Any	$5,000	1 year
Wyoming	Keep it under 3 grams	$1,000	1 year
Washington, D.C.	Any	$1,000	6 months

Notes

Much of the advice and commentary in this book is based upon my own experience as a criminal defense attorney, but I also benefited from the research of others. In these notes I have tried to credit the many people whose writing and research benefited mine. Richard Davenport-Hines's *The Pursuit of Oblivion: A Global History of Narcotics* (New York: W.W. Norton, 2002) offers an outstanding and comprehensive history of narcotics and a particularly insightful history of the Drug War in this country. *Illegal Drugs: A Complete Guide to Their History, Chemistry, Use, and Abuse,* by Paul Gahlinger, M.D., Ph.D. (New York: Plume Books, 2004), covers all 178 illegal drugs in this country and is absolutely stuffed with interesting facts. *Drug Abuse and the Law,* by Gerald F. Uelmen and Victor G. Haddox (New York: Clark Boardman, 1983), which I was first introduced to in Professor Eric Sirulnik and Professor Peter Meyers's class on drug law at GW, provided much of the basis of my initial research and, like all law school textbooks, poses many provocative questions. Push and Mireille Silcott's *The Book of E* (London: Omnibus Press, 2000) is a must-read for anyone interested in the evolution of the dance/rave scene and the accompanying world-wide explosion of Ecstasy.

Note: Some literary license has been taken with the facts of all the "dope ditties." I don't, for example, know what the police or the defendants were thinking.

Getting Wasted in the Drug War

$65 billion on illegal drugs (p. 1): This is a conservative estimate based on the Department of Justice's estimate for the year 1998—it was $67 billion that year, so the figure is probably much higher because everyone is still doing plenty of dope. The stats are available at http://www.usdoj.gov/dea/demand/speakout/05so.htm.

$75 billion on booze (p. 1): The estimated amounts Americans spend on booze every year vary widely from source to source; this figure is from the National Institute on Drug Abuse, available at http://www.drugabuse.gov/EconomicCosts/Chapter2.html.

$3 billion on good-time pills (p. 1): This figure is based on the Office of National Drug Control Policy's estimated number of "abusers" of prescription meds—6.3 million in this country—assuming each spends about $500 a year getting high. One black market pill of OxyContin can go for as much as $40, so $500 a year is a conservative estimate. The stats for pill abusers are available at http://www.whitehousedrugpolicy.gov/pda/102504.html.

$1 billion on bongs (p. 1): This is the Department of Justice's figure for all drug paraphernalia. Available at http://www.usdoj.gov/opa/pr/2003/February/03_crm_106.htm.

Part 1. How (Not) to Possess Drugs

The following law review articles were the foundation of my research on the general principles of drug possession law: *Offense of Aiding and Abetting Illegal Possession of Drug or Narcotics,* by J. A. Bryant, Jr., J.D., LL.M., 47 A.L.R.3d 1239 (2004); *Drug Abuse: What Constitutes Illegal Constructive Possession Under 21 U.S.C.A. § 841(A)(1), 87* by Martin J. McMahon, J.D., 87 A.L.R. Fed 309 (2004); *Under What Circumstances Should Total Weight of Mixture or Substance in Which Detectable Amount of Controlled Substance Is Incorporated Be Used in Assessing Sentence Under United States Sentencing Guideline § 2D1.1* by Richard Belfiore, J.D., 113 A.L.R. Fed. 91 (2004); *Minimum Quantity of Drug Required to Support Claim That Defendant Is Guilty of Criminal "Possession" of Drug Under State Law* by Danny R. Veilleux, J.D., 4 A.L.R. 5th 1 (2004); *Validity, Construction, and Application of State Statutes Prohibiting Sale or Possession of Controlled Substances Within Specified Distance of Schools* by Tracy A. Bateman, J.D., 27 A.L.R. 5th 593 (2004).

Everything You Need to Know About Drug and Drug Paraphernalia Possession

A "very thin film of dust, comparable to one or two grains of salt" (p. 8): *Scott v. State,* 825 S.W.2d 521 (Tex. Crim. App. 1992).

My *Precious*

But I Was Just Passing the Pipe, Officer (p. 14): *State v. McCluskey,* 514 N.W.2d 423 (Wis. Ct. App. 1993).

Diddly Dope Ditty (p. 14): *State v. Hironaka,* 53 P.3d 806 (Haw. 2002).

That's My Houseboy's Dope! (p. 17): Oscar Dixon, "Lawyer: Anthony Marijuana Charge May Be Dropped," *USA Today,* Oct. 22, 2004.

The Circumstantial Dope Ditty (p. 19): *U.S. v. Garza,* 531 F.2d 309 (5th Cir. 1976).

Devoted Dope Ditty (p. 21): *United States v. Rush,* 738 F.2d 497 (5th Cir. 1984).

Catherine Berkland's Crib (p. 21): *People v. Shaw,* 258 Cal. Rptr. 693 (Cal. Ct. App. 1989).

Robert "the Chief" Parish (p. 24): Available, among other places, at NORML's website http://www.norml.org/index.cfm?Group_ID=4439&wtm_format=print.

The Kiddy Corner

Dad's Dope Ditty (p. 26): *State v. Cartee,* 577 N.W.2d 649 (Iowa 1998).

High school students buying dope (p. 27): The study is from the National Center on Addiction and Substance Abuse, available at www.cbsnews.com.

The Community Dope

Hip-hop superstar 50 Cent (p. 30): www.thesmokinggun.com, available at http://www.thesmokinggun.com/archive/50cent1.html.

Jeff Carter's Dope Ditty (p. 34): *State v. Carter,* 582 N.W.2d 164 (Iowa 1998).

Snoop Dogg's Dope Ditty (p. 39): www.thesmokinggun.com, available at http://www.thesmokinggun.com/archive/snooppot1.html.

Paraphernalia: From Coke Cans to Crack Pipes

Up in Smoke Ditty (p. 44): Steven Mikulan, "Chong Family Values," *LA Weekly,* Dec. 5, 2003.

Growing the Felony Forest

America's number one cash crop, $32 billion (p. 45): Gahlanger, *Illegal Drugs,* p. 322; Paul Tolme, "High Time," *Newsweek,* Oct. 28, 2002.

Growing Dope Ditty (p. 46): *State v. Day,* 838 So.2d 74 (La. App. 2003).

Bloomberg's "You bet I did" quote (p. 46): From NORML.com, available at, among other places http://www.norml.org/index.cfm?Group_ID=5229.

Priest turned in by parishioner (p. 46): Phil Trexler, "Summit Jury Indicts Priest in Drug Raid," *Akron Beacon Journal,* Feb. 5, 2004.

Medical Marijuana

Medical marijuana studies (p. 49): Mary Curtius and Bettina Boxall, "Pot Has Uses as Medicine," *Los Angeles Times,* March 18, 1999.

Free Dope Ditty (p. 50): Christopher Largen, "A History of Medical Marijuana," *Nashville Scene,* Dec. 12, 2001, available at http://www.alternet.org/drugreporter/12068/.

"Ask Ed" Ditty (p. 51): Rona Marech, "Medical Patients Flock to 'Oaksterdam,'" *San Francisco Chronicle,* Aug. 10, 2003; Bob Egelko, "U.S. Appeals Court Reviews First Medical Pot Conviction," *San Francisco Chronicle,* June 17, 2004.

Hookin' a Brother Up

Raymond Washington's cross-examination (p. 54): *United States v. Washington,* 41 F.3d 917 (4th Cir. 1994).

Driving buddy to the dealer (p. 57): *U.S. v. Bailey,* 2003 West Law 1949583 (6th Cir. 2003).

Dubious Dope Ditty (p. 58): In re *Application of VMF to the Florida Bar,* 491 So.2d 1104 (Fla. 1986).

"Bloody Bad Ass" nickname (p. 61): *People v. Caver,* 302 A.D.2d 604 (2nd Dept. 2003).

The Death and Dismemberment Section

Irma Perez (p. 63): Tim Hay, "Man Receives Five Years in Ecstasy Case," *San Mateo Daily Journal,* Oct. 27, 2004; Dana Yates, "Girl Still

Jailed for Ecstasy Death," *San Mateo Daily Journal,* May 31, 2004; Matt Elliser and Josh Wein, "School Remembers Irma," *San Francisco Examiner,* April 30, 2004.

Belushi's Deadly Dope Ditty (p. 65): Bob Woodward, *Wired: The Short Life and Fast Times of John Belushi* (New York: Simon and Schuster, 1984); Crimelibrary.com, "Famous Cases," available at http://www.crimelibrary.com/criminal_mind/forensics/time/6.html?sect=21.

The lesson Michael Harrison learned (p. 67): "Trip to Emergency Room Leads to Meth Bust," Sherburne County, Minnesota, Sheriff Press Release, Nov. 13, 2002.

Part 2. Search and Seizure

My research on Fourth Amendment/search and seizure law was aided greatly by the following law review articles and treatises: *Validity of Warrantless Search of Motor Vehicle Occupant Based on Odor of Marijuana—Federal Cases* by Richard P. Shafer, J.D., 192 A.L.R. Fed. 391 (2004); *Searches and Seizures, Arrests and Confessions, Execution of the Warrant* by William E. Ringel, (2004); *The Fourth Amendment: Dormitory Room Searches in Public Universities* by Joseph M. Smith, M.S., and John L. Strope Jr., Ph.D., J.D., 97 Ed. Law Rep. 985 (May 1995); *Drug Testing Law, Technology and Practice* by David G. Evans, West Group Cummulative Supplement (2004); *Employee Privacy Law* by L. Camille Hebert, West Group Cummulative Supplement (June 2004); *Propriety of Search Involving Removal of Natural Substance or Foreign Object from Body by Actual or Threatened Force* by Michelle Migdal Gee, J.D., 66 A.L.R. Fed. 119 (2004); *Validity of Search of Computer, Computer Disk, or Computer Peripheral Equipment* by Robin Cheryl Miller, J.D., 84 A.L.R, 5th 1 (2004); *Targeting Ecstasy Use at Raves* by Michael H. Dore, 88 VA. L. Rev. 1583 (November 2002).

The Incredible Shrinking Fourth Amendment

$50 billion more spent on dope than fighting the Drug War (p. 72): This figure is based on the Department of Justice's claim that the entire budget for fighting the Drug War in 2002 was $18.8 billion, $3 billion of which was spent on drug treatment. The Justice Department also estimates that Americans spent $67 billion on illegal drugs that same year (although that wasn't really their point). The figures are available at http://www.usdoj.gov/dea/demand/speakout/05so.htm.

Alabama housewife Loretta Nall (p. 72): James Diffee, "Cannabis Campaign: Alabama Native Takes Drug Reform Battle National," *Auburn Plains Dealer,* Feb. 14, 2004; Alternet.org, "Red Dirt Justice," February 13, 2004.

Seven hundred thousand busts (p. 72): This is an approximate number of drug busts a year. According to NORML, there are almost six hundred thousand simple pot possession busts every year. The number of total drug busts is likely higher. NORML's figures are available at http://www.norml.org/index.cfm?Group_ID=5799.

Consensual Dope Ditty (p. 76): *Howe v. State*, 916 P.2d 153 (Nev. 1996).

Consent by handcuffed suspects and Spanish speakers (p. 77): *U.S. v. Mendoza*, 250 F.3d 626; *U.S. v. Cepulonis*, 127 F.2d 238 (1st Cir. 1976); *U.S. v. Phillips*, 664 F.2d 971 (5th Cir. 1981).

Street Busts

James McMurty's Dropsy Ditty (p. 86): *People v. McMurty*, 314 N.Y.S.2d 194 (N.Y. 1970).

The "One Hell of a Fight" Dope Ditty (p. 87): *State v. Tapp*, 353 So.2d 265 (La. 1977).

Lloyd Desmond knockout blow quote (p. 89): *State v. Desmond*, 593 So.2d 965 (La. App. 1992).

"Hmmm . . . that must be, wait, wait . . ." Ditty (p. 93): *People v. Custer*, 640 N.W.2d 576 (Mich. Ct. App. 2001).

Rocks Is Rocks (p. 94): *Minnesota v. Dickerson*, 598 U.S. 366 (1993).

Fraidy Cops (p. 94): *U.S. v. Brown*, 88 F.3d 860 (7th Cir. 1999) (butt of gun); *State v. Evans*, 618 N.E.2d 162 (Ohio Supreme Ct. 1993) (cash); *State v. Yuresko,* 493 P.2d 536 (Div. 1, Ct. of Appeals, Ariz. 1972) (cash).

"Where there are drugs . . ." quote (p. 94): *U.S. v. Stanfield*, 109 F.3d 976 (4th Cir. 1997).

Maria Gonzalez's Dope Ditty (p. 96): Reggie Sheffield, "Strip Search Policy Was 'understood,'" *Standard Times,* available at www.southcoast today.com/daily/06-96/06-12-96/a011o044.htm.

Repulsive Dope Ditty (p. 98): *U.S. ex rel. Guy v. McCauley,* 385 F.Supp. 193 (D.C. Wis. 1974).

Rough Texas Dope Ditty (p. 99): *Lewis v. State*, 56 S.W.3d 617 (Tex. Crim. App. 2001).

Home Searches

Matthew McConaughey's Dope Ditty (p. 102): www.thesmokinggun.com, available at http://www.thesmokinggun.com/archive/mcconaughey 1.html.

"Rediscovering" dope after illegal search (p. 103): *U.S. v. Leon*, 1468 U.S. 897, 104 S.Ct. 3405 (1984).

Rebecca Cardenas won the liberty lottery (p. 104): *State v. Cardenas*, 980 P.2d 594 (Kan. App. 1999).

Dangling Dope Ditties (p. 106): *State v. Ruiz*, 360 So.2d 1320 (Fla. Dist. Ct. App. 1978).

Carl Overdahl's Bust (p. 107): *Washington v. Chrisman,* 455 U.S. 1 (1982).

Oooh that smell and busting down the door (p. 111): *State v. Decker*, 580 P.2d 333 (Ariz. 1978); *Mendez v. People*, 986 P.2d 275 (Colo. 1999); *Haggard v. Commonwealth*, 2003 WL 1948881 (Ky. Ct. App. April 25, 2003); *Wisconsin v. Hughes*, 607 N.W.2d 621 (Wis. 2000).

Whitey Pig Dope Ditty (p. 116): *U.S. v. Penn,* 647 F.2d 876 (9th Cir. 1980).

The Student Handbook

Old-school dorm quote (p. 122): *People v. Cohen*, 292 N.Y.S.2d 706 (N.Y. Crim. Ct. 1968).

McNeese State search warrant (p. 124): *State v. Boudreaux*, 304 So.2d 343 (La. 1974).

Dartmouth drug policy (p. 125): *State v. Newser*, 807 A.2d 1289 (N.H. 2002).

Random drug testing for high school students (p. 126): *Brd. of Ed. v. Earls*, 122 S.Ct. 2559 (2002).

The Party Section

A Don't-Do-This-at-Home Dope Ditty (p. 132): *Waugh v. Texas*, 51 S.W.3d 714 (Tex. Ct. Appeals, 2001).

Peter Jennings quote (p. 135): "Ecstasy Rising: Federal Campaign to Curb Club Drug's Use Hasn't Dimmed Its Popularity," ABC News, April 1, 2004.

Racine rave (p. 136): www.aclu.org, available at http://www.aclu.org/DrugPolicy/DrugPolicy.cfm?ID=11628&c=185.

The history of NYC's cabaret laws (p. 136): Tricia Romano, "A Crash Course in Cabarets," *Village Voice,* Nov. 27, 2002.

Nixon quote (p. 137): Davenport-Hines, *The Pursuit of Oblivion*, p. 421.

The UK's antirave statute (p. 138): Push and Silcott, *The Book of E*, p. 132.

The Sound Factory Goes Boom (p. 138): Ben McGrath, "Man Blames Dog," Talk of the Town, *New Yorker,* March 22, 2004; Greg Gittrich, "Hot Spot Raided as a Drug Depot," *New York Daily News,* March 8, 2004; DEA news release, March 7, 2004, available at http://www.usdoj.gov/dea/pubs/states/newsrel/nyc030704.html; Patricia O'Shaughnessy, "Drug-Fueled Dens Back in Business," *New York Daily News,* March 30, 2003.

NORML benefit shutdown (p. 140): Bryan O'Connor, "Eagles Get Drug Law Clarification," *Billings Gazette*, June 26, 2003; available at http://www.alternet.org/drugreporter/16134/.

Drug War Driving Lessons

Justice O'Connor's H-bomb quote (p. 142): *Atwater v. Lago Vista*, 121 S.Ct. 1536 (2001).

Gail Atwater's seat belt (p. 142): *Ibid.*

Legendary front man George Clinton (p. 143): Judy Keller, "George Clinton's in a Funk over His Recent Drug Arrest," *E Online*, Dec. 12, 2003, available at http://www.eonline.com/News/Items/0,1,13095,00.html.

The Long and Winding Dope Ditty (p. 144): *U.S. v. Padron,* 657 F.Supp. 840 (D.Del. 1987).

Griswold family quote (p. 146): *State v. Zavala*, 5 P.3d 993 (Idaho Ct. App. 2000).

Racial Profiling Dope Ditty (p. 146): *State v. Brumfield*, 42 P.3d 706 (Idaho Ct. App. 2001).

Phony roadblocks (p. 155): *Indianapolis v. Edmond*, 531 U.S. 32 (2000); *U.S. v. Flynn,* 309 F.3d 736 (10th Cir. 2002); *People v. Roth,* 85 P.3d 571 (Colo. Ct. App. 2004).

Driving While Wasted

A million and a half DUI busts a year (p. 157): "Test Questions: In Fight to Stop Drunk Driving, Police Draw Blood," *Wall Street Journal,* March 23, 2004.

Choke hold quote (p. 162): *People v. Sanders,* 268 Cal.App.2d 802, 74 Cal.Rptr. 350 (Cal. Ct. App. 1969).

San Diego judge describing taking blood (p. 162): *Carleton v. Superior Court*, 216 Cal.Rptr. 890 (Cal. App. 4th 1985).

Nick Nolte's drugged-driving bust (p. 164): E! *True Hollywood Story*, available at, among many other places, http://www.eonline.com/On/Holly/Shows/Nolte/facts2.html.

Dumb Ass Dope Ditty (p. 166): *State v. Ryun,* 939 P.2d 1174 (Or. Ct. App. 1997).

Airport and Border Busts

Orlando airport searches (p. 168): www.aclu.org, available at http://archive.aclu.org/news/2002/n031502b.html.

Ion track technology (p. 168): Anthony Ramirez, "Stop! And Be Sniffed," *New York Times*, Aug. 30, 2004, available at http://www.geindustrial.com/cwc/products.

Woody's Dodgy Dope Ditty (p. 170): Interview with "Woody the Surfer," Ko Phan Nang, Thailand, Feb. 26, 2004.

Damon Stoudamire's Ditty (p. 171): Sara Thorson, "Portland's Stoudamire Arrested on Drug Charges at Tucson Airport," Associated Press, July 7, 2003.

"Excessive calmness" is suspicious (p. 172): *U.S. v. Himmelwright*, 406 F.Supp 889 (D.Ct. Fla. 1975).

Eighty-eight Red Balloons (p. 173): *U.S. v. Montoya de Hernandez,* 731 F.2d 1369 (9th Cir. 1984) ("heroic efforts"); *U.S. v. Montoya de Hernandez*, 473 U.S. 531 (1985) (Supreme Court decision).

Raymond Lindell of Word to the Pill Heads (p. 174): Charisse Jones and Valerie Alvord, "Search for Prescription Bargains Can Lead to Jail," *USA Today,* international edition, Aug. 20, 2004.

The New Millennium Drug War

DEA's Internet paraphernalia crackdown (p. 179): "Up in Smoke: Online Privacy Becomes the Latest Casualty in the War on Drugs," *American Journal of Trial Advocacy* 27, p. 169. (Summer 2003, Student Note).

Limbaugh E-mail (p. 181): Tracy Connor, "Rush Limbaugh in Pill Probe," *New York Daily News,* Oct. 2, 2003.

PATRIOT Act/seizing work computer (p. 182): Debbie A. Mukamal and Paul N. Samuels, "Statutory Limits on Civil Rights of People with Criminal Records," *Fordham Urban Law Journal* (July 2003).

Muzzling Your Hard Drive (p. 185): Tu Tran, "Computer Forensics and Your Rights," available at http://www.cpsr.org/essays/2002/2pcl7.html.

CIA's involvement in drug trafficking (p. 187): Davenport-Hines, *The Pursuit of Oblivion*, p. 423.

8 percent of international trade (p. 187): Ibid., p. 431.

39 percent of gross domestic product (p. 188): "Harper's Index," *Harper's*, Jan. 2004.

Drug Test?

Justice Marshall's "Drag net" quote (p. 191): *Skinner v. Railway Labor Executives' Ass'n*, 489 U.S. 602 (1989).

Clinton Drug War spending (p. 192): Davenport-Hines, *The Pursuit of Oblivion*, p. 425.

Extent of drug testing statistics (p. 192): Camille Hebert, "Extent of Drug Testing in Employment," *Employee Privacy Law* § 2:3, June 2004; Dana Hawkins, "Tests on Trial," *U.S. News & World Report*, Aug. 12, 2002.

Drug-testing politicians (p. 193): *Chandler v. Miller*, 520 U.S. 305 (1997).

Dope In, Dope Out Ditty (p. 194): *Pernell v. Montgomery County Board of Com'rs*, 1996 West Law 665008 (Ohio Ct. App. 1996).

Tommy Everett's drug test (p. 195): *Everett v. Napper*, 833 F.2d 1507 (11th Cir. 1987).

Daryel Garrison's drug test (p. 195): *Garrison v. Dept. of Justice*, 72 F.3d 1566 (Ca. Fed. 1995).

Curtis Moore's drug test (p. 195): *Wrightsell v. City of Chicago*, 678 F.Supp. 727 (N.D.Ill. 1998).

Georgia's Board of Lights and Water (p. 195): *Allen v. Board of Lights and Water*, 693 F.Supp. 1122 (N.D.Ga. 1987).

But I Can Explain (p. 200): *Hinkley v. Texas State Bd. of Medical Examiners*, 140 S.W.3d 737 (Tex. Ct. App. 2004)(cooked on stove); *Guitard v. U.S. Secretary of Navy*, 967 F.2d 737 (2nd Cir. 1992)(brownies); *Adams v. Pennington*, 2001 West Law 1512570 (E.D.La. Nov. 26, 2001)(hemp oil); *Quintanilla v. K-Bin, Inc. Graney*, 8 F.Supp.2d 928 (S.D.Tex. 1998)(cocaine tea); *People v. Wiegant*, 2003 WL 1958880 (Cal. Ct. App. 3 Dist., April 28, 2003)(meth lab); *Anderson v. Exxon Coal U.S.A., Inc.*, 1997 West Law 157378 (10th Cir.[Wyo.] April 4, 1997)(mother's mix); Ed Graney, "Friends Baffled by Russell's Plight," *San Diego Union-Tribune*, June 19, 2002 (Russell's three tests).

Bulldog Lab Ditty (p. 204): Diana Baldwin, "Drug-Testing Lab Workers Face Charges," *Oklahoma City (OK) Daily Oklahoman*, Feb. 23, 2002.

Sean Salisbury quote (p. 207): ESPN *SportsCenter*, July 29, 2004.

Ricky Williams masking agent (p. 207): Dan Le Batard, "Marijuana Plays Key Role in Williams' Retirement," Night-Ridder News Service, July 30, 2004.

Notifying employer of bust (p. 209): Drug-Free Workplace Act of 1988, 41 U.S.C. § 701 (employer must be receiving at least $25,000 in federal funds).

Part 3. Busted!

Busted!

Dry Heaving Dope Ditty (p. 221): In re *Peter G.*, 110 Cal.App.3d 576 (Cal. Ct. App. 1980).

Ms. Albert's punch quote (p. 224): *Alberts v. City of New York*, 548 F.Supp. 227 (S.D.N.Y. 1987).

So swore Arthur Lockett (p. 225): *Lockett v. Donnellon*, 2002 West Law 1363479 (6th Cir. 2002).

Doper credibility quote (p. 226): *Coates v. United States*, 558 A.2d 1148 (D.C. 1989)

The He Said, She Said, You Must Be High Dope Ditty (p. 227): *Jones v. Buchanan*, 164 F.Supp.2d 734 (W.D.N.C. 2001) (trial court decision); *Jones v. Buchanan*, 325 F.3d 520 (4th Cir. 2003) (appellate court decision).

Perp walk quote (p. 231): *Caldarola v. County of Westchester*, 343 F.3d 570 (2nd Cir. 2003).

Justice Marshall's description of jailhouse search (p. 236): *Bell v. Wolfish*, 99 S.Ct. 1861 (1979).

"Ah want mah beer" quote (p. 238): *Inmates of Suffolk County Jail v. Eisenstadt, et al.*, 360 F.Supp. 676 (D. Mass. 1971).

10 percent mentally ill (p. 238): Caroline Harlow Wolf, "Profile of Jail Inmates 1996," U.S. Dept. of Justice, Bureau of Justice Statistics Special Report.

Cigarette butt quote (p. 239): Ibid.

Sheriff Joe Arpaio's Ditty (p. 239): "'Big Brother' Behind Bars," *Cincinnati Post*, July 27, 2001; "ACLU Joins Lawsuit over Conditions at Jail Run by Infamous Arizona Sheriff," ACLU Press Release, Dec. 4, 2003, available at http://www.aclu.org/Prisons/Prisons.cfm?ID=14510&c=121.

Gangster swagger quote (p. 241): *People v. Brown*, 82 Cal.App.4th 736 (Cal. Ct. App. 2000).

Poor bustees denied bail in Boston (p. 242): Denise Lavoie, "Defendants' Rights Being Violated by Lawyer Shortage, Pay Dispute," *Boston Herald*, July 2, 2004.

Only 17 percent making bail go back to jail (p. 245): *United States v. Joyeros*, 204 F.Supp.2d. 412 (E.D.N.Y. 2002) (citing study).

Hartford, Connecticut, man John Bailey (p. 247): *Jackson v. Bailey*, 605 A.2d 1350 (Supreme Ct. Conn. 1992).

Part 4. Fighting Your Drug Bust

Fighting Your Drug Bust

Bush Sr., carrying Rush's bags (p. 253): Tom Zucco, "Rush's Drug Use Has Palm Beach in Tizzy," *St. Petersburg Times Online*, Dec. 14, 2003, available at http://www.sptimes.com/2003/12/14/state/Rush_s_drug_use_has_p.shtml.

Bush Jr., Rush is a "great American" (p. 253): www.drudgereport.com, available at http://www.drudgereport.com/mattrn.htm.

"Personal choice" quote (p. 254): Billy Cox, "Double Standards Rush to Forefront," *Florida Today*, Oct. 23, 2003.

Privacy quote (p. 257): Rush Limbaugh, *The Way Things Ought to Be* (New York: Pocket Books, 1992).

Resealing of records (p. 257): "Judge Reseals Limbaugh Records," AP/CBS, available at http://www.cbsnews.com/stories/2004/01/05/entertainment/main591362.shtml.

"Too many whites . . ." quote (p. 258): available at, among other places, http://www.takebackthemedia.com/gophotwrush.html.

Twelve thousand pills (p. 258): Tracy Connor, "Rush Limbaugh in Pill Probe," *New York Daily News*, Oct. 2, 2003; Hendrick Hertzberg, "Rush in Rehab," *New Yorker*, Oct. 6, 2003.

"I refuse to let anyone think I am doing something great here" (p. 259): Salon.com, "Rush Limbaugh Tells His Listeners That He's Taking a Leave of Absence, and Entering a Treatment Facility," Oct. 10, 2003, available at http://archive.salon.com/opinion/feature/2003/10/10/rush_transcript/index_np.html.

In-court drug-test quote (p. 259): *Harvey v. State*, 751 N.E.2d 254 (Ind. Ct. App. 2001).

Roy Black's Salvador Magluta trial (p. 260): Larry Lebowitz, "Jurors Plead Guilty to Fixing Trial," *Miami Herald*, Sept. 20, 2003.

Tim Allen's bust (p. 265): "No Hope for Parole: 650 Lifer Law," *60 Minutes II*, Dan Rather, transcript available at 1999 West Law 18104135; "And Then There's . . ." *Newark Star Ledger (New Jersey)*; March 19, 1999.

Rush's plea offer (p. 268): Jill Barton, "Rush's Plea Offer Rejected," *Tallahassee Democrat,* Jan. 24, 2004.

Part 5. Trial?

The following law review articles were instrumental to my research on police perjury and corruption, prosecutorial misconduct, and the enabling role judges play: *Testilying: Police Perjury and What to Do About It* by Christopher Slobogin, *U. Colo. L. Rev.* (Fall 1995); *Proving the Lie: Litigating Police Perjury* by David N. Dorfman, *Am. J. Crim. Law* (Summer 1999); *Police, Plus Perjury, Equals Polygraphy* by Donald A. Dripps, *J. Crim. Law & Criminology* (Spring 1996); *"Just the Facts, Ma'am": Lying and the Omission of Exculpatory Evidence in Police Reports* by Stanley Z. Fisher, New Eng. Law Rev. (Fall 1993); *Warrants and Fourth Amendment Remedies* by William J. Stuntz, Va. L. Rev. (August 1991).

The Suppression Hearing

Mollen Commission report (p. 273): City of New York, Commission to

Investigate Allegations of Police Corruption and Anti-Corruption Procedures of the Police Department, Commission Report, 36.

Tulia, Texas (p. 274): Thomas Adcock, "A New York Lawyer Who Made a Name for Herself in Texas," *New York Law Journal,* June 11, 2004; Paul Duggan, "Massive Drug Sweep Divides Texas Town," *Washington Post,* Jan. 22, 2001; PBS *Frontline,* www.pbs.org, available at http://www.pbs.org/now/society/tuliatimeline.html; "38 Cases Thrown into Question," CBS News, available at http://www.cbsnews.com/stories/2003/04/03/eveningnews/main547479.shtml.

Philadelphia scandal (pp. 274–75): Ruben Castaneda, "Police Officer Perjury Not Rare, Observers Say," *Washington Post,* Feb. 17, 1999.

Rampart scandal (p. 275): PBS *Frontline,* available at http://www.pbs.org/wgbh/pages/frontline/shows/lapd/scandal/.

Kansas City and San Jose police chief quote (pp. 275–76): Joseph D. McNamara, "Has the Drug War Created an Officer Liars' Club?" *Los Angeles Times,* Feb. 11, 1996.

80 Percent Rise Study (p. 276): *People v. McMurty*, supra, 314 N.Y.S.2d 194 (citing study).

Utah pot smell rule (p. 277): *State v. Maycock*, 947 P.2d 695 (Utah Ct. App. 1997).

Two-inch glass vial (p. 277): *People v. Heath*, 214 A.D.2d 519 (2nd Dept. 1995).

The Sound of Falling Grass (p. 278): *U.S. v. Thomas,* 211 F.3d 1186 (9th Cir. 2000).

Judge J. Skelly Wright's quote (p. 281): *Veney v. United States*, 344 F.2d 542 (C.A.D.C. 1965).

Judge Harold Baer's two opinions (pp. 282–83): *United States v. Bayless (I)*, 913 F.Supp. 232 (S.D.N.Y. 1996); *United States v. Bayless (II)*, 921 F.Supp. 211 (S.D.N.Y. 1996).

Beg for Mercy, Punk

The constitutionality of plea-bargaining process (p. 287): PBS.org, "Interview with Professor Stephen Bright," June 17, 2004 (comparing criminal justice system to fast-food restaurants and commenting generally on the inherent unconstitutionality of the plea-bargaining system), available at http://www.pbs.org/wgbh/pages/frontline/shows/plea/interviews/bright.html.

95 percent guilty pleas (p. 287): *United States v. Joyeros*, 204 F.Supp.2d. 412 (E.D.N.Y. 2002) (citing study).

$88.30 for Your Life (p. 289): *Bordenkircher v. Hayes*, 434 U.S. 357 (1978).

Jackbooted M&M's (p. 290): Ted Rohrlich, "Scandal Shows Why Innocent Plead Guilty," *Los Angeles Times*, Dec. 31, 1999.

DA Sells Shit Sandwich for $600! (p. 291): *United States v. Modafferi*, 112 F.Supp.2d 1192 (D. Haw. 2000).

Tim Allen's sentencing quote (p. 296): Newark (NJ) *Star Ledger* "And Then There's . . . ," March 19, 1999.

Authentic remorse quote (p. 297): *U.S. v. Royer*, 895 F.2d 28 (1st Cir. 1990).

Jose Echeverria's quote (p. 298): In re *Personal Restraint of Echeverria*, 6 P.3d 573 (Wash. 2000).

Cleo Hightower of Madison, Wisconsin (p. 298): *United States v. Ivory*, 11 F.3d 1411 (7th Cir. 1993).

Stephen Teller of Milwaukee (p. 298): *United States v. Teller*, 762 F.2d 569 (7th Cir. 1985).

Now We Bring the Pain

The following law review articles formed the basis of my research on the "collateral consequences" of drug convictions and on "alternative sanctions": *Unequal Protection: Comparing Former Felons' Challenges to Disenfranchisement and Employment Discrimination* by Elena Saxonhouse, Stan. L. Rev. (May 2004); *Re-Evaluating America's Drug Control Laws: A Legal, Philosophical and Economic Proposal* by Roy Whitehead, J.D., LLM, Katherine Wingfield, and Dr. Walter Block, Okla. City U.L. Rev. (Spring 2003); *Restoring Civility—the Civil Asset Forfeiture Reform Act of 2000: Baby Steps Towards a More Civilized Civil Forfeiture System* by Barclay Thomas Johnson, Ind. L. Rev. (2002); *What Do Alternative Sanctions Mean?* by Dan M. Kahan, U. Chi. L. Rev. (Spring 1996).

Darryl Gates quote (p. 311): Davenport-Hines, *The Pursuit of Oblivion*, 447.

Sentencing disparity stats (p. 312): Ibid., 442–43.

Justice Rehnquist quote (p. 312): *Albernaz v. United States*, 450 U.S. 333 (1981).

Average federal sentence stat (p. 312): Gahlinger, *Illegal Drugs*, 67.

Prof. Bruce Jackson quote (p. 313): www.Bartleby.com, citing *New York Times*, Sept. 12, 1968.

Rockefeller drug laws putting kids to work selling crack (p. 313): Terry Williams, *The Cocaine Kids: The Inside Story of a Teenage Drug Ring* (New York: Perseus Books, 1989).

Dick Thornburgh quote (p. 314): Evan Williford, *The Basics of Forfeiture: Testing the Limits of Constitutionality*, 14-WTR Crim. Just. 26 (Winter 2000) (citing the *Washington Times*, Sept. 28, 1989).

Deadly Dope Ditty (p. 314): This case is retold in the *Oklahoma City University Law Review*, cited above.

$2.5 million yacht (p. 315): Davenport-Hines, *The Pursuit of Oblivion*, 445.

Seizure of wife's car (p. 315): *Bennis v. Michigan*, 516 U.S. 442 (1996).

Disgraceful Dope Ditties (p. 317): *Dep't of Hous. & Urban Dev. v. Rucker*, 122 S.Ct. 1230 (2002)(Supreme Court decision); 237 F.3d 1113 (9th Cir. 2001)(California federal court decision).

Denial-of-student-aid discussion (p. 318): Michael Kranish, "Truth and Its Consequences If You . . . 1. Get Caught with Drugs . . . and . . . 2. Admit It on Federal Student Aid Application," *Boston Globe,* Sept. 9, 2001; Mary Leonard, "Student Drug Offender Law Knocked," *Boston Globe,* May 22, 2002; "Members of Congress, Students and Educators to Host Forum Highlighting Negative Impact of Student Drug Provision," U.S. News Wire, April 3, 2003.

13 percent of black people disenfranchised (p. 319): This statistic is cited in the *Stanford Law Review* article cited above.

Disenfranchised ex-con impact on Bush's 2000 election (p. 319): Ibid.

Personal approval by Governor Jeb Bush (p. 319): Abby Goodnough, "Disenfranchised Florida Felons Struggle to Regain Their Rights," *New York Times*, March 28, 2004.

Arrest records available online in twenty-eight states (p. 320): Debbie A. Mukamal and Paul N. Samuels, "Statutory Limits on Civil Rights of People with Criminal Records," *Fordham Urban Law Journal* (July 2003).

AEDPA deportation discussion (p. 321): Franco Capriotti, Linda Ramirez Friedman, Nori Leslie Kay, and Rachel Unger, "Small-Time Crime, Big-Time Trouble: The New Immigration Law," *Criminal Justice* (Summer 1998); Nora V. Demleitner, "Collateral Damage: No Re-Entry for Drug Offenders," *Villanova Law Review* (2002).

Public humiliation cases (p. 321): *United States v. Gementera*, 2004 West Law 1770101 (9th Cir.[Cal.], August 9, 2004 citing additional cases).

"My record plus two six-packs" quote (p. 322): Ibid.

Justice Scalia's view on caning (p. 322): Scalia's thoughts are discussed in the *University of Chicago Law Review* article cited above.

States Where You Can Pretend It Never Happened (p. 325): The various state laws on expungement are from Debbie A. Mukamal and Paul N. Samuels's article, "The Statutory Limits on Civil Rights of People with Criminal Records," *Fordham Urban Law Journal* (July 2003).

The Dope Law Index

As noted in Part 6, "Beg for Mercy, Punk," sentencing for drug crimes in this country is largely left to prosecutorial discretion. The Dope Law Index has been compiled through the actual state statutes, NORML's Web site, and *Illicit Drug Policies: Selected Laws from 50 States,* available at http://www.andrews.edu/BHSC/impacteen-illicitdrugteam. The information in the index is the best available, but its accuracy cannot be guaranteed, as the statutes are often vague. (The only way to truly find out is to get busted and see what the DA has in mind for you.)

Acknowledgments

For their unconditional support: Mom (the writer), Dad (the lawyer), Joan, the Lesters, and the McKays.

For their support, inspiration, and/or free beer (none of these people should be considered suspicious): Will Bensussen, Camilla Borthwick, Fred Burt, Claudio Campuzano, Annie Carlson, Ari Ellis, Daniel Eichner, Carolyn Newman, Amelia Pan, Natalie Slocum, Emmanuella Souffrant, Ann Volkwein, Gabriele Wilson, and my anonymous dope-despising agent.

Special thanks to my fearless editor Josh Behar and his assistant Will Hinton; to Lauren Cusick for her first-rate research assistance; to Jenny Roberts, whose insight on the criminal justice system was invaluable to my research; to Ron Brown of the NYU Law Library for his vital assistance; to Barbara Lerner for everything; and to my wife, Tonya Lester, who patiently and mercilessly edited every word of the manuscript.

And cheers to the gang at Ara for all the support and good vibe.